D0205496

RALPH WALDO EMERSON

RALPH WALDO EMERSON

A Collection of Critical Essays

Edited by
Lawrence Buell

Prentice Hall, Englewood Cliffs, New Jersey 07632

Library of Congress Cataloging-in-Publication Data

Ralph Waldo Emerson : a collection of critical essays / edited by
Lawrence Buell.
   p. cm.—(New century views)
   Includes bibliographical references.
   ISBN 0-13-276783-X
   1. Emerson, Ralph Waldo, 1803–1882—Criticism and interpretation.
I. Buell, Lawrence. II. Series.
PS1638.R29 1993
814'.3–dc20   92–17658
                                     CIP

Acquisitions editor: Phil Miller
Editorial assistant: Heidi Moore
Editorial/production supervision and interior design: Joan Powers
Copy editor: Liz Pauw
Cover design: Karen Salzbach
Prepress buyer: Herb Klein
Manufacturing buyer: Patrice Fraccio/Robert Anderson

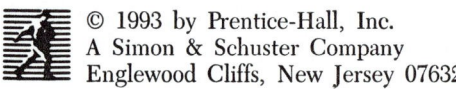 © 1993 by Prentice-Hall, Inc.
A Simon & Schuster Company
Englewood Cliffs, New Jersey 07632

Printed in the United States of America
10 9 8 7 6 5 4 3 2 1

ISBN 0-13-276783-X

Prentice-Hall International (UK) Limited, *London*
Prentice-Hall of Australia Pty. Limited, *Sydney*
Prentice-Hall Canada Inc., *Toronto*
Prentice-Hall Hispanoamericana, S.A., *Mexico*
Prentice-Hall of India Private Limited, *New Delhi*
Prentice-Hall of Japan, Inc., *Tokyo*
Simon & Schuster Asia Pte. Ltd., *Singapore*
Editora Prentice-Hall do Brasil, Ltda., *Rio de Janeiro*

Contents

A Note on Documentation

Footnotes and citations of secondary sources in this volume are those of the individual authors, except where square brackets appear to mark editorial insertions. Citations of Emerson's works have been reformatted to refer to the following standard editions, which are cited throughout the text in the abbreviated form indicated here.

CW   *The Collected Works of Ralph Waldo Emerson*. Ed. Alfred R. Ferguson et al. Cambridge: Harvard University Press, 1971– , 4 vols. to date. (Supersedes W.)

EL   *The Early Lectures of Ralph Waldo Emerson*. Ed. Robert E. Spiller et al. Cambridge: Harvard University Press, 1966–72, 3 vols.

J   *The Journals of Ralph Waldo Emerson*. Ed. Edward Waldo Emerson and Waldo Emerson Forbes. Boston: Houghton, 1909–14, 10 vols.

JMN *The Journals and Miscellaneous Notebooks of Ralph Waldo Emerson*. Ed. William H. Gilman et al. Cambridge: Harvard University Press, 1960–82, 16 vols. (Supersedes *J*.)

L   *The Letters of Ralph Waldo Emerson*. Ed. Ralph Leslie Rusk. New York: Columbia University Press, 1939, 6 vols.

W   *The Complete Works of Ralph Waldo Emerson*. Ed. Edward Waldo Emerson. Boston: Houghton, 1903–4, 12 vols.

Introduction

Lawrence Buell

Ralph Waldo Emerson profoundly influenced American literature, religion, philosophy, and social thought. In the unending series of modern attempts to define the nature of American distinctiveness, no creative writer has been more often held up as a key reference point. If a volume of profiles of American culture's dozen most "Representative Men" were written in imitation of Emerson's book of that same title, he would surely be included among them.

I

Emerson's master principle of Self-Reliance ("the infinitude of the private man," he once defined it), which was also the main theme of the American Transcendentalist movement that he helped inspire, is now considered one of the classic formulations of American individualism. The essays and poems in which Emerson ramified his vision both augured and nurtured the growth of an American literature worthy of comparison to the major literatures of Europe and Asia. So did the practical example of Emerson's success as lecturer and writer. None of our other "classic" writers of the so-called American literary Renaissance (including Hawthorne, Poe, Thoreau, Melville, Whitman, Dickinson, and Stowe) was more seriously listened to—and quarreled with—by his or her contemporaries. That American literature has been markedly didactic, visionary, and experimental in form, that American writers have repeatedly assumed the stance of prophets speaking from society's margins, whatever their actual class or level of affluence—all this owes much to Emerson.

This brief formulation also begins to suggest why one of Emerson's legacies as a writer is the legacy of the writer as nonspecialist, and why Emerson should have made his mark upon fields other than literature alone. American religion, for one. Emerson's first ambition was to be a soul-stirring preacher in the Unitarian church, the Boston-centered liberal wing of New England Congregationalism. Although he resigned his pastorate at the age of 30, his imagination remained strongly religiocentric. He liked to describe his essays as "lay sermons," and with reason. His concept of Self-Reliance is built upon the paradox of reverence for individual personhood as inherently divine. This doctrine, and Emerson's style of advocacy (as a self-unfrocked minister believing in the superiority of unsystematic eloquence over reasoned theologizing) eventually made him a hero of the nineteenth century liberal Protestantism that at first found him threatening and scandalous. Emerson helped accelerate the secularization of piety and the erosion of structures of religious authority at every level for the sake of what came to be widely regarded as a more appropriately democratic faith.

Religious and philosophical inquiry were closely intertwined in premodern America, especially New England, where philosophical rigor chiefly manifested itself in theological discourse. So it is not surprising that Emerson also influenced the history of American philosophy, although he was wilfully unsystematic in his methods of presentation. The concept of Self-Reliance, for example, rests on an epistemological claim about the ground of that reliance; Emerson's first three books take the form of informal inquiries into the meaning of great abstractions (nature, history, intellect, experience, character). Emerson's pursuit of these topics is governed by the view that formal argument counts for less than experience, and by the good Unitarian principle that beliefs are to be tested by their life-results. Emerson is therefore rightly seen as a harbinger of America's most distinctive philosophical tradition, pragmatism, several of whose major figures have claimed him as forefather: for example, William James and John Dewey. Others have claimed an important place for Emerson in post-Kantian thought as a precursor to Nietzsche and modern continental philosophy. Today there is still no agreement as to whether Emerson ought to be reckoned a legitimate philosopher, but the question is discussed as vigorously as ever.

Emersonian Self-Reliance has to do not merely with the realm of abstruse intellection but with the social arena as well. It is a way of defining the individual's participation in—and against—the body politic. Self-Reliance sanctions an anarchistic secession of the individual from social constraints, justifying it on the ground of an indwelling God-principle or moral sense that all individuals share, thereby reinjecting a kind of social contract at a more abstract level. This ambivalent vision Emerson pursued not only as cloistered speculation but also with reference to major nineteenth-century crises, especially the Antislavery Movement, and from the standpoint of a potential actor, not just as a witness. His writing provides a memorable commentary on issues basic to liberal democratic theory and practice, such as the right, duty, and possibility of individual dissent; and his career as a citizen strikingly exemplifies the ambiguous position of the American intellectual drawn both to privatism and to public action.

II

Since Emerson has become a cultural property appropriated for disparate uses, it is impossible to select a dozen critical discussions that will span his entire achievement. Yet some basic points are clear enough. One is that Emerson's place in an imaginary volume of representative Americans—alongside the likes of Abraham Lincoln, Frederick Douglass, P. T. Barnum, and Andrew Carnegie—would most likely be as "the writer" or "the man of letters." For although Emerson is known to have made a deep impression on philosopher William James, business tycoon Henry Ford, architect Louis Sullivan, and composer Charles Ives (who also found Emerson inspirational when concocting advertising copy), his influence has been consistently strongest among creative writers and critics. It is partly but only partly arbitrary that students encounter Emerson chiefly in English courses and that those who write about him are chiefly professors of American Literature. Emerson called himself a "scholar"—by which he meant an intellectual generalist—but after a brief ministerial career, his professional life consisted of public lecturing and the publication of essays and poems. This collection therefore concentrates more on Emerson the literary figure than on any other dimension of his achievement.

All of the contents except the first and the fourth essays were written after the publication of this book's predecessor, *Emerson: A Collection of Critical Essays*, edited by Milton R. Konvitz and Stephen E. Whicher, "the first selection of Emerson criticism ever made."[1] Since its appearance in 1962 the study of Emerson has become a much larger, more confident, and more heteroglot enterprise. In 1962, someone who wanted to master the best that had been thought and said about Emerson could easily cover the essential ground in a month or so by reading the two biographies, the half-dozen first-rate books that treated Emerson in whole or part, and a score of miscellaneous essays, a number of which were conveniently reprinted in the Konvitz–Whicher collection.[2] Today, so much is annually written about Emerson that only dyed-in-the-wool Emersonians read as much as half of it, and what is written is apt to be more specialized (as the weight of scholarship accumulates) and also less judgmental, less anxious to weigh the question of whether Emerson was truly great than to define his status as an American institution more precisely. These trends partially explain each other (as a subject gets more established as unshakably *there*, its importance is taken more for granted), but there is a good deal more to the explanation as well.

In the early 1960s, Emerson was already an historical landmark, but recovering from a temporary decline in his reputation between the two world wars. First he had been criticized for facile optimism by debunkers of the late Victorian genteel traditionists, who idealized him. Beyond that, he had been recurringly criticized as standing for timid theory as against resolute practice, as well as for the supposed incoherence of his writings, the

---

[1]Stephen E. Whicher, "Preface" to *Emerson: A Collection of Critical Essays*, ed. Konvitz and Whicher (Englewood Cliffs, N.J.: Prentice-Hall, 1962), v.

[2]For additional reflections on the expansion of Emerson studies since the 1960s, see Lawrence Buell, "The Emerson Industry in the 1980s: A Survey of Trends and Achievements," *ESQ* 30 (1984), 117–36; and Michael Lopez, "De-Transcendentalizing Emerson," *ESQ* 34 (1988); 77–139.

latter deemed a great handicap from the standpoint of the "new critical" formalist standards of literary excellence that strongly influenced American criticism from the 1940s through the 1960s. Today, by contrast, Emerson's abstractness seems an asset in the climate of much greater interest in theory throughout the human sciences; his "formlessness" seems excusable if not positively advantageous to a literary criticism more interested in rhetoric than in form; his hesitancy to enter the political arena and take fixed positions seem less reprehensible than in the post-McCarthy and Vietnam Eras; even his most questionable aspects, such as the cosmic optimism of his later years, seem less like depravities than interesting symptoms of the national ideology that he played a major role in shaping. These are gross generalizations, to which many exceptions can be found; but the truth is that Emerson is proving to be a more fascinating figure in the 1980s and 1990s than ever before.

<h2 style="text-align:center">III</h2>

The contents of this volume begin to illustrate Emerson's range of achievement. The first two essays, by Perry Miller and William Hedges, place Emerson in the context of two different but interrelated strands of American and more specifically Yankee culture. The precedents of Jonathan Edwards and Benjamin Franklin, the two giants of colonial intellectual history, are important not as direct influences on Emerson (neither, in fact, were heroes or even major interests of his) so much as symbols of two complementary— and sometimes warring—sides of Emerson, whom a fellow poet once described as "A Plotinus-Montaigne, where the Egyptian's gold mist / And the Gascon's shrewd wit cheek-by-jowl coexist."[3] For Perry Miller, American Transcendentalism was "most accurately defined as a religious demonstration" that had its roots deep in the pietistic strain of New England Puritanism. Miller diagnosed "Emerson as an Edwards in whom the concept of original sin has evaporated." "From Edwards to Emerson" (1940) works this diagnosis out.[4] Miller's astringent thinkpiece, perhaps the single most influential article-length treatment of Emerson ever written, remains potent to this day, owing to the popularity of the "Puritan legacy" theory of American cultural distinctiveness (a theory that Miller's influence was instrumental in making central to American studies), despite the fact that the essay raises as many questions as it answers. What exactly happened between Edwards and Emerson? Does

[3]James Russell Lowell, *A Fable for Critics* (1848), *Poetical Works* (Boston: Houghton, 1885), 128.
[4]Perry Miller, Introduction to *The Transcendentalists: An Anthology* (Cambridge: Harvard University Press, 1950), 8; Introduction to "From Edwards to Emerson" (1940), in *Errand into the Wilderness* (Cambridge: Harvard University Press, 1956), 185.

not the liberal Unitarian culture of Emerson's boyhood explain more about him than do his more remote Puritan ancestors? Is Miller not too condescending toward Emerson, whom he calls "Waldo" and seems to regard as a watered-down Edwards? Is a religious history explanation really sufficient to explain Emerson's genius? These are the most obvious questions Miller's article raises.

Some of them are dealt with by William Hedges, whose "From Franklin to Emerson" (1976) is a direct response to Miller. "What Franklin represents for Emerson," Hedges argues, "is the practical side of Puritanism" (page 41). Hedges sees Franklin and Emerson as kindred spirits in their sagelike detachment, their interest in the practical conduct of life as well as abstract values, their experimentation with different moods and roles. Miller's Edwardsian Emerson is the Romantic prophet afire with his vision; Hedges' Franklinian Emerson is the empiricist tinkerer, "trying to learn from an experience which has its endless complications" (page 47). The difference in critical styles reflects their differing positions: Miller's vehemence and sweeping generalization making him look like the critic as prophet, Hedges pursuing a measured, circumspect, detached observer's tone. Against Miller's polarized vision of early American history as a battleground of pietist ideologues versus rationalist temporizers, Hedges imagines a scenario in which apparent opposites are reconciled.

Both portraits have validity. Neither is complete. For one thing, neither reckons with Emerson's status as an assimilator of European, not to mention Asian, influences. It made sense for Miller, one half-century ago, to focus on Emerson's colonial antecedents, because American literary studies was young and American influences had been relatively uncharted, compared with the European. But by the time Hedges answered Miller in the mid-1970s the tendency for Americanists to concentrate on the inner coherence of our literary history had caused many of us to lose sight of the fact that no precursor had a more formative influence on Emerson's thinking than the English Romantic Samuel Taylor Coleridge, from whom he derived the liberating distinction between Reason (which intuitively apprehends Truth) and Understanding (the faculty of empirical induction and rational calculation traditionally called "reason"). The American-genesis approach to understanding Emerson may also keep us from appreciating that he fits almost as well among the Victorian sages, such as Carlyle and Ruskin, as among the writers of the so called American literary renaissance he helped instigate. But if one wishes to place Emerson in the American grain, one can hardly do better than start with Miller and Hedges. My own essay, "Emerson in His Cultural Context" (1992), tries to supplement theirs by emphasizing the two dimensions of Emerson's intellectual context that their accounts necessarily foreshorten—his immediate local roots and his cosmopolitan international learning—and to show how these different dimensions imply each other despite any appearance of antithesis.

The following three essays survey from different perspectives the central "problematic" of Emerson's life and thought, the individual-society relation. Stephen Whicher's "The Dream of Greatness" (1953), taken from the book on Emerson that has had greater influence upon modern Emerson studies than any other, undertakes to map Emerson's psyche. Appraising Emerson's personal struggles, Whicher shows him to have been an insecure but intensely ambitious individual who sought to transform his private struggles into a memorable public identity and message as the spokesperson for the ideal of the private man. With Mary Kupiec Cayton's "The Making of an American Prophet" (1987), we move from a biographer's to a social historian's perspective. Examining Emerson's career in the American lyceum, his preferred medium for meeting the public, Cayton identifies the paradoxical consequence that resulted from his success in that forum: how Emerson's gospel of self-reliance became a middle-class institution. Emerson appears here not as personality but as historical catalyst. Sacvan Bercovitch's "Emerson, Individualism, and the Ambiguities of Dissent" (1990) concentrates on the structure, movement, and vacillation of Emerson's thinking about the place of the individual within or against the socio-political order as a case study in the symbiosis between dissent and consensus in American ideology. Whereas for Whicher Emerson is the aspiring mind and for Cayton the public icon, for Bercovitch he is the exemplary American thinker.

Whicher is especially interested in how Emerson was energized by his discovery of "the God within" and the heady prospect this seemed to offer for the "transfer of the world into the consciousness" (pages 61–62). Whicher's Emerson is driven by the ideal of greatness almost to the point of narcissism but held in check by an ideal of public service, derived from both regional and classical sources, that directed his attention toward the social arena and ensured that his image of greatness would be the "soldier of virtue" (page 74), not the Napoleonic or Nietzchean man of force and will. We find from the remainder of *Freedom and Fate* that Whicher believes Emerson's assertiveness gave way quite soon, after the sudden death of his son (1842), to a resigned acquiescence to the forces of nature and history. For Whicher, the really great—although also problematic—Emerson was the radical Transcendentalist of *Nature*, the Divinity School Address, and "Self-Reliance"; and the Emerson of the mid-1840s and thereafter was a spectacle of tragic decline. This declensionary vision of Emerson's career, promoted by Whicher through an influential anthology of Emerson's selected writings, remains powerful today, even if it no longer seems so inevitable as it once did. (Whicher was responsible for making central to the Emerson canon the only work by which most nonspecialists know his later writing, the exceptionally grim essay on "Fate").[5] The essays by Kupiec and Bercovitch both draw upon and modify

[5]Stephen E. Whicher, ed., *Selections from Ralph Waldo Emerson: An Organic Anthology* (Boston: Houghton, 1957).

Whicher's analysis, making much of the later Emerson's rapprochement with mainstream thinking, but resisting Whicher's diagnosis of this late work as a decline. Indeed from Cayton's essay one might gain the sense of an accelerating momentum as Emerson's words became a cultural force. Cayton and Bercovitch certainly share Whicher's sense of the irony of Emerson's retreat from his earlier radicalism, but they evaluate it differently, for its cultural rather than its intrinsic results, and thus not as a self-betrayal so much as a predictable effect of the emerging democratic ideology in nineteenth-century America. The difference is not simply a difference in methodology, but a difference in critical climate: humanistic scholars today are much more likely than their predecessors to minimize the power of independent individual agency. Such a climate is less likely to deplore Emerson's "fall" as a personal tragedy or moral betrayal than to see it as confirmation of the normal workings of institutional processes.

For Cayton, the starting point is not a map of Emerson's mind but the cultural marketplace, wherein Emerson appears as as a commodity procured, consumed, interpreted, misinterpreted, and enshrined by audiences who "had come to a sense of group identity long before his arrival" (page 83). Audiences thus tended to create a normalized version of Emerson in their own image; in this forum devoted to self-culture Emerson's gospel of Self-Reliance was felt to be a mechanism by which collective standards of morality could be defined and maintained. This helps explain why American businessmen came to see Emersonianism as congenial. Cayton further argues that Emerson as lyceum entrepreneur "adapted his philosophy to the needs of the popular audience" by ceasing to use "the languages of philosophy or religion to make his points" (page 89).

Bercovitch's discussion of the oscillations within Emerson's own thinking complements Cayton's analysis of the paradox of the intellectual radical absorbed by "bourgeois mercantile audiences" (page 83). Bercovitch is as aware as Cayton of how Emerson's thought was modulated by the decorum of his age. For Cayton, Emerson's career exemplifies how "an intellectual may be 'made' by the interpretative stance of a public community" (page 100); for Bercovitch, Emerson exemplifies how the individual constructs his ideas from the repertoire of available public discourses. Emerson wished to espouse an intellectual position centered "first and last on the independent self" (pages 105–106); but his thinking about the individual was inevitably colored by two powerful ideologies of his day, by which he felt both drawn and repelled: the valuation of "individuality" by socialists and other groups opposed to bourgeois liberalism and the "individualism" of the laissez-faire liberalism that was becoming the civil religion of Jacksonian America. Bercovitch charts the drift of Emerson's thought, as he became increasingly hard on socialism and receptive to liberal individualism, though always with reservations. Emerson emerges here as a co-fashioner of American ideology more fastidious and self-divided than in Cayton's portrait but still a consenting party: the inventor of a mode of individualistic dissent that cannot be seen merely as co-optation but that remained part of the American consensus even in its will to stand radically apart, because individualism was already part of that consensus.

Cayton and Bercovitch are unshakably convinced of Emerson's historical importance, whereas Whicher, writing more than thirty years earlier, had to be more wary. (His biography ends with the embattled plea, "To reject Emerson utterly is to reject mankind."[6]) Even as Whicher wrote, however, what has come to be called "the Emerson revival" was starting to take place. We see its trajectory from the next group of selections, which focus on Emerson the writer and his impact on literary history. *Emerson on the Soul* (1964), by Whicher's younger Cornell colleague Jonathan Bishop, was the first and in many ways the most profound of a series of contemporary book-length reappraisals centering on Emerson's literary achievement that culminated around the time of the centennial of Emerson's death (1982) in important monographs by David Porter, Barbara Packer, Julie Ellison, and others.[7] Richard Poirier's *A World Elsewhere* (1966), an interpretation of "The Place of Style in American Literature," from which this volume's selection of Poirier's work is taken, accords Emerson a position of greater centrality to American literary history than had any other major "thesis book" on the American imagination, from D. H. Lawrence's *Studies of Classic American Literature* (1921) to Leo Marx's *The Machine in the Garden* (1964). For Poirier, "Emerson in many respects *is* American literature" (page 134), given that "the most interesting American books are an image of the creation of America itself, of the effort, in the words of Emerson's Orphic poet, to 'Build therefore your own world.' "[8] This reading of Emerson as paradigmatic in his role as verbal nation-builder underlies the thinking of the more recent contributions to this volume by Harold Bloom and Stanley Cavell.

The essays following Bishop's and Poirier's show a development of tone and perspective analogous to the shift from Whicher to Cayton and Bercovitch. For example, Poirier is inclined to see Emersonian discourse as more circumscribed by its status as *textual* edifice than it seems to Harold Bloom in "Emerson: Power at the Crossing" (1984). In Poirier's judgment, Emerson's "opposition to conventional systems prevents his appealing for support to any realities constituted outside his own language" (page 133), and it is rendered doubly problematic by his inability to maintain this posture of detachment. Bloom is struck rather by the force than by the delicacy of Emerson's project, and Emerson's language hardly seems a constraint. Emerson for Bloom looms up as the great American shaman: no mere exemplar but positively the inventor of the American poetic tradition and the inventor of American

---

[6]Stephen E. Whicher, *Freedom and Fate: The Inner Life of Ralph Waldo Emerson* (Philadelphia: University of Pennsylvania Press, 1953), 173.

[7]See Suggestions for Further Reading (pages 213–215).

[8]Richard Poirier, *A World Elsewhere* (New York: Oxford University Press, 1966), 3.

political radicalism besides, both the left and the right. The difference of occasion undoubtedly accentuates the contrast between cautious discrimination and bold assertion, Poirier's discussion being written for a scholarly book, Bloom's originally for the *New York Review of Books*. But the deeper contrast is between the underlying visions: an Emerson dominating over, indeed positively constructing, the mind of America versus an Emerson as typifying the American imagination rather by hovering on the margins, fashioning a verbal counter-construct.[9] Indeed Bloom makes larger claims for Emerson's importance than any other contributor to this anthology. He shares Cayton's and Bercovitch's late twentieth-century predilection for approaching Emerson as a cultural force rather than as an independent craftsman, but Bloom is more the individualist in his understanding of how great individuals make history.

The difference between Bloom's and Poirier's readings of Emerson's centrality to American culture is partially mirrored by our two essays on Emerson's rhetoric. Jonathan Bishop and Julie Ellison envision almost antithetical Emersonian personae. In Jonathan Bishop's chapter on "Tone" from his *Emerson on the Soul* (1964), the salient point is Emerson's ability to maintain a critical distance and at the same time to stake a position, resulting in the effect of one voice seeming to lurk within or behind another and a disorienting mobility of tonal range. Emerson's integrity consists of "a certain hovering evaluation" (page 139) that offsets the temptation to overstatement. "It is an experimental rather than an inevitable self that he throws 'bodily' into his books" (page 137). Ellison's "Aggressive Allegory" (1983) is equally mindful of the strategized quality of the Emersonian persona, but the strategy is not reserve but power. For Ellison, the salient point is Emerson's will to dominate over reader and subject by a form of stylized exaggeration that she describes as functioning with the schematic intensity of allegory. Whereas for Bishop, as for Poirier, Emerson at his best is a consummate verbal craftsman—an image compatible with the then-dominant aesthetics of new critical formalism although neither Bishop nor Poirier are bound by a formalist theology—for Ellison, Emerson belongs in a great tradition of assertive theoretical discourse from Romantics like Schiller and Coleridge to Harold Bloom, one of the hallmarks of which has been "the relationship between critical theory and perceived aggression" (page 168).

We must not be too tidy. In some crucial respects, Bishop is more like Bloom than like Poirier. Bishop and Bloom are each, in their own ways, "religiocentric" critics. Bloom's "power" and Bishop's "soul" are kindred terms. Bishop differs from Bloom stylistically rather than structurally in seeing literary dexterity as a vehicle for visionary expression, uttered in order

---

[9]Richard Poirier has elaborated and refined his position on Emerson and his legacy in *The Renewal of Literature: Emersonian Reflections* (New York: Random House, 1987), especially 67–94.

to make an impact upon others, and identifying the spiritual-ethical domain beyond language as that which language seeks to make present. But Bishop's Emerson, like Poirier's and like Whicher's, is a figure who must be presented with a certain cautious reserve: a writer who achieved surpassing excellence only in fits and starts, a figure concerning whose prestige and authority in the reader's eyes one does not assume too much. For Ellison and Bloom, Emerson is self-evidently the American patriarch. What needs to be explained is not whether he remains potent but where that potency comes from.

Earlier, I ventured some reasons for this change, the currents within American culture and within the discipline of literary studies. These forces include individual personalities. Because Whicher, Bishop, and Poirier wrote as they did, it was easier for Emersonians of the 1970s like Bloom to assume Emerson's centrality and to transmit this vision to younger scholars like Ellison, who was originally Bloom's student. Another factor has been the rise of modern bibliographical textual work on Emerson. Emerson was the first of the major American Renaissance authors whose letters were published in a scholarly edition (1939); among the many current longterm scholarly editions-in-progress of works by classic American authors, the Emerson project was one of the first to begin (1960) and has so far produced the most impressive results: a sixteen-volume edition of his *Journals and Miscellaneous Notebooks*, four volumes of his collected essays, three of lectures, four of sermons, two of previously uncollected notebooks. These editions have consolidated Emerson's position further by their very existence, by the scholarship on which they rest and to which they are giving rise. One such example is Glen Johnson's "Emerson's Craft of Revision" (1980), a genetic study of how Emerson reworked his texts at different stages as he followed his demanding regimen of weaving journal entries into lectures and reshaping lectures into essays. Johnson's study of the composition of *Essays, First Series* could not have been written a generation earlier with the authority that the new editions permit. Findings like his should put decisively to rest the old myth of Emerson as a careless assembler. Johnson's Emerson "seems to have been incapable of simply copying his earlier changes verbatim" (page 181); his printed discourses lacked reassuringly conventional structures, and transitions resulted from a series of conscious decisions to make his prose more elliptical. Johnson's analysis confirms the old formalist charge that Emerson's discourses are broken, discontinuous structures but renders it impotent. In the process it also confirms, at least up to a point, the apparently disparate arguments of Poirier, Bishop, Ellison, and Bloom.

The first of the two final essays in this volume, Stanley Cavell's "Thinking of Emerson" (1981), provides another glimpse of Emerson's modern reputation in flux. It begins by recording the start of a quasi-conversion experience from a Thoreauvian's initial hostility toward Emerson to the intimation that Emerson might in fact occupy a significant place in American and modern continental philosophy from Kant to Heidegger, might even offer guidance as to what it means to do philosophy. These are themes that Cavell has since vigorously pursued. "Thinking of Emerson" thus gives a sense of how Emerson's fitful, puzzling, and disruptive impact on American philosophy continues, an impact that is likely not only to persist but to grow more complicated with the revival of interest in pragmatism and the Nietzchean mode of aphoristic philosophy. Cavell's essay makes a companion to Merton Sealts's "Emerson as Teacher" (1982), which reflects more straightforwardly upon the range of responses that Emerson has provoked in individual hearers and readers. Both of the final essays personalize the author-audience relation that Cayton describes in the aggregate. Cavell gives a deliberately idiosyncratic personal witness; Sealts provides a synoptic, analytical account, animated by a generous array of examples, of how Emerson's message has charmed and repelled the famous and the obscure. From this evidence Sealts seeks to define what the *practice* of scholarship meant for Emerson and the lesson it teaches the teacher. For Sealts, that lesson is that one is "no teacher unless, like Emerson, he truly creates independence." This is quite similar to the lesson of "onwardness" Cavell infers from him (page 192). Emerson leaves us, as Cavell says elsewhere, almost disconcertingly "at liberty to discover whether he belongs to us and we to him."[10]

IV

Cavell and Sealts rightly suggest that the proper conclusion to any study of Emerson is that there is no conclusion. No one will ever say the final word about him, and any attempt to represent the work of several decades is bound to be incomplete. One conspicuous omission, for example, is the large number of critical readings of individual Emerson works—*Nature*, "The American Scholar," the Divinity School Address, "Self-Reliance," and "Experience"—having been discussed with special frequency and keenness during the past thirty years. Nor have I included any case studies of Emerson's influence on particular individuals or movements. Perhaps the most questionable limitation of this anthology, however, is its failure to give voice to substantial doubts that might be expressed about Emerson's centrality as an American icon, a point worth amplifying here.

The contents of the Konvitz–Whicher volume, in keeping with its historical moment, presented a more guarded estimate of Emerson's historical importance than this volume does, including for example one essay debunking Emerson's claims to be a thinker of any importance.[11] I have already explained

[10]Stanley Cavell, "An Emerson Mood." In *The Senses of Walden*, rev. ed. (San Francisco: North Point Press, 1981), 160.

[11]Henry B. Parkes, "Emerson." In *Emerson: A Collection of Critical Essays*, ed. Konvitz and Whicher (Englewood Cliffs, N.J.: Prentice Hall, 1962), 121–135; essay originally published in 1941.

why a collection of representative Emerson criticism from the later twentieth century might be expected to sound more confidently affirmative; yet this phase of Emerson studies may in time produce a counter-claim that Emersonians after the 1960s anaesthetized themselves by ritual affirmations of Emerson's centrality. Already we see some signs of this. For example, David Simpson's *The Politics of American English* (1986) argues that a text like James Fenimore Cooper's novel *The Pioneers*, with its spectacle of the frontier village as a site of diverse unassimilated ethnic cultures in collision, makes a more productive starting point for understanding American literary culture than the urbane "monoglossic" voice of the Transcendentalist essay.[12] Although Simpson overstates his case, he is right that to posit Emerson as the period's pivotal figure is to risk committing oneself to a Yankee Protestant-centered vision which looks increasingly obsolete as an explanation of what America is about. Recent feminist revisionary work on Emerson's misunderstanding of fellow Transcendentalist Margaret Fuller makes this point from a nearer angle.[13]

Future Emerson studies, then, will need to reckon more soul-searchingly with the fact that Emerson's status as a Yankee ethnic and Victorian patriarch who thought in terms of racial and gender hierarchies needs closer scrutiny both in itself and in light of the restrictedness of standard notions of cultural representativeness. But even though Emerson will thus be exposed as less the paradigmatic American thinker and as more the product of an elite oligarchy than we might wish to think, it will continue to be found, as Miller and Bercovitch in their different ways suggest, that Emerson helped to decenter that oligarchy by making his work a memorable dramatization of the battle between establishment and insurgent in thought, text, and history. Meanwhile, readers of this volume are cordially invited after savoring its contents to decenter *its* center by turning to the bibliography of extra readings, which lists a number of excellent additional studies on various concerns that perforce have been marginalized here.

[12]Simpson, *The Politics of American English, 1776–1850* (New York: Oxford University Press, 1986), especially Chapters 5 and 7.

[13]See, for example, Dorothy Berkson, " 'Born and Bred in Different Nations': Margaret Fuller and Ralph Waldo Emerson," in *Patrons and Protegees: Gender, Friendship, and Writing in Nineteenth-Century America*, ed. Shirley Marchalonia (New Brunswick, N.J.: Rutgers University Press, 1988), 3–30. For two important extended studies of Emerson as a hegemonic figure, see the works by Jehlen and Thurin noted in the Suggestions for Further Reading (page 215).

Part 1
BACKGROUNDS

From Edwards to Emerson

Perry Miller

Ralph Waldo Emerson believed that every man has an inward and immediate access to that Being for whom he found the word "God" inadequate and whom he preferred to designate as the "Over-Soul." He believed that this Over-Soul, this dread universal essence, which is beauty, love, wisdom, and power all in one, is present in Nature and throughout Nature. Consequently Emerson, and the young transcendentalists of New England with him, could look with complacence upon certain prospects which our less transcendental generation beholds with misgiving:

> If the red slayer thinks he slays,
>   Or if the slain think he is slain,
> They know not well the subtle ways
>   I keep, and pass, and turn again.
>   (W 9:195)

Life was exciting in Massachusetts of the 1830's and '40's; abolitionists were mobbed, and for a time Mr. Emerson was a dangerous radical; Dr. Webster committed an ingenious murder; but by and large, young men were not called upon to confront possible slaughter unless they elected to travel the Oregon Trail, and the only scholar who did that was definitely not a transcendentalist. Thus it seems today that Emerson ran no great risk in asserting that should he ever be bayoneted he would fall by his own hand disguised in another uniform, that because all men participate in the Over-Soul those who shoot and those who are shot prove to be identical, that in the realm of the transcendental there is nothing to choose between eating and being eaten.
It is hardly surprising that the present generation, those who are called upon to serve not merely as doubters and the doubt but also as slayers and slain, greet the serene pronouncements of Brahma with cries of dissent.

Originally published in *The New England Quarterly*, 13 (1940), 589–617, under the title "Jonathan Edwards to Emerson." Reprinted by permission of the publishers from *Errand into the Wilderness* by Perry Miller, Cambridge, Mass.: The Belknap Press of Harvard University Press, Copyright © 1956, 1984 by the President and Fellows of Harvard College. (Footnotes occur in the 1940 version only.)

Professors somewhat nervously explain to unsympathetic undergraduates that of course these theories are not the real Emerson, much less the real Thoreau. They were importations, not native American growths. They came from Germany, through Coleridge; they were extracted from imperfect translations of the Hindu scriptures, misunderstood and extravagantly embraced by Yankees who ought to have known better—and who fortunately in some moments did know better, for whenever Emerson and Parker and Thoreau looked upon the mill towns or the conflict of classes they could perceive a few realities through the haze of their transcendentalism. They were but transcendental north-north-west; when the wind was southerly they knew the difference between Beacon Hill and South Boston. I suppose that many who now read Emerson, and surely all who endeavor to read Bronson Alcott, are put off by the "philosophy." The doctrines of the Over-Soul, correspondence, and compensation seem nowadays to add up to shallow optimism and insufferable smugness. Contemporary criticism reflects this distaste, and would lead us to prize these men, if at all, for their incidental remarks, their shrewd observations upon society, art, manners, or the weather, while we put aside their premises and their conclusions, the ideas to which they devoted their principal energies, as notions too utterly fantastic to be any longer taken seriously.

Fortunately, no one is compelled to take them seriously. We are not required to persuade ourselves the next time we venture into the woods that we may become, as Emerson said we might, transparent eyeballs, and that thereupon all disagreeable appearances—"swine, spiders, snakes, pests, madhouses, prisons, enemies"—shall vanish and be no more seen (W 1: 10, 76). These afflictions have not proved temporary or illusory to many, or the compensations always obvious. But whether such ideas are or are not intelligible to us, there remains the question of whence they came. Where did Emerson, Alcott, Thoreau, and Margaret Fuller find this pantheism which they preached in varying degrees, which the Harvard faculty and most Boston businessmen found both disconcerting and contemptible? Was New England's transcendentalism wholly Germanic or Hindu in origin? Is there any sense, even though a loose one, in which we can say that this particular blossom in the flowering of New England had its roots in the soil? Was it foolishly transplanted from some desert where it had better been left to blush unseen? Emerson becomes most vivid to us when he is inscribing his pungent remarks upon the depression of 1837, and Thoreau in his grim comments upon the American blitzkrieg against Mexico. But our age has a tendency, when dealing with figures of the past, to amputate whatever we find irrelevant from what the past itself considered the body of its teaching. Certain fragments may be kept alive in the critical test tubes of the Great Tradition, while the rest is shoveled off to potter's field. The question of how much in the transcendental philosophy emerged out of the American background, of how much of it was not appropriated from foreign sources, is a question that concerns the entire American tradition, with which and in which we still must work. Although the metaphysic of the Over-Soul, of self-reliance, and of compensation is not one to which we can easily subscribe, yet if the particular formulations achieved by Emerson and Thoreau, Parker and Ripley, were restatements of a native disposition rather than amateur versions of *The Critique of Pure Reason*, then we who must also reformulate our traditions may find their philosophy meaningful, if not for what it held, at least for whence they got it.

Among the tenets of transcendentalism is one which today excites the minimum of our sympathy, which declared truth to be forever and everywhere one and the same, and all ideas to be one idea, all religions the same religion, all poets singers of the same music of the same spheres, chanting eternally the recurrent theme. We have become certain, on the contrary, that ideas are born in time and place, that they spring from specific environments, that they express the force of societies and classes, that they are generated by power relations. We are impatient with an undiscriminating eclecticism which merges the Bhagavad-Gita, Robert Herrick, Saadi, Swedenborg, Plotinus, and Confucius into one monotonous iteration. Emerson found a positive pleasure—which he called "the most modern joy"—in extracting all *time* from the verses of Chaucer, Marvell, and Dryden, and so concluded that one nature wrote all the good books and one nature could read them. The bad books, one infers, were written by fragmentary individuals temporarily out of touch with the Over-Soul, and are bad because they do partake of their age and nation. "There is such equality and identity both of judgment and point of view in the narrative that it is plainly the work of one all-seeing, all-hearing gentleman" (W 3: 232). We have labored to restore the historical time to Chaucer and Dryden; we do not find it at all plain that they were mouthpieces of one all-seeing agency, and we are sure that if there is any such universal agent he certainly is not a gentleman. We are exasperated with Emerson's tedious habit of seeing everything *sub specie aeternitatis*. When we find him writing in 1872, just before his mind and memory began that retreat into the Over-Soul which makes his last years so pathetic, that while in our day we have witnessed great revolutions in religion we do not therefore lose faith "in the eternal pillars which we so differently name, but cannot choose but see their identity in all healthy souls," we are ready to agree heartily with Walt Whitman, who growled that Emerson showed no signs of adapting himself to new times, but had "about the same attitude as twenty-five or thirty years ago," and that he himself was "utterly tired of these scholarly things" (L 6: 192–93). We may become even more tired of scholarly things when we find that from the very beginning Emerson conceived the movement which we call transcendentalism as one more expression of the benign gentleman who previously had spoken in the persons of Socrates and Zoroaster, Mohammed and Buddha, Shakespeare and St. Paul. He does not assist our quest for native origins, indeed for any origins which we are prepared to credit, when he says in 1842, in the Boston Masonic Temple, that transcendentalism is a "Saturnalia of Faith," an age-old way of thinking which, falling upon Roman times, made Stoic philosophers; falling on despotic times, made Catos and Brutuses; on Popish times, made Protestants; "on prelatical times, made Puritans and Quakers; and falling on Unitarian and commercial times, makes the peculiar shades of Idealism which we know" (W 1: 339). Were we to take him at his word, and agree that he himself was a Stoic revisiting the glimpses of the moon, and that Henry Thoreau was Cato redivivus, we might then decide that both of them could fetch the shades of their idealism from ancient Rome or, if they wished, from Timbuktu, and that they would bear at best only an incidental relation to the American scene. We might conclude with the luckless San Francisco journalist, assigned the task of reporting an Emerson lecture, who wrote, "All left the church feeling that an elegant tribute had been paid to the Creative genius of the First Cause," but we should not perceive that any compliments had been paid to the intellectual history of New England.

Still, to take Emerson literally is often hazardous. We many allow him his Stoics, his Catos and Brutuses, for rhetorical embellishment. He is coming closer home, however, when he comes to Puritans and Quakers, to Unitarian and commercial times. Whether he intended it or not, this particular sequence constitutes in little an intellectual and social history of New England: first Puritans and Quakers, then Unitarians and commercial times, and now transcendentalists! Emerson contended that when poets spoke out of the transcendental Reason, which knows the eternal correspondence of things, rather than out of the shortsighted Understanding—which dwells slavishly in the present, the expedient, and the customary, and thinks in terms of history, economics, and institutions—they builded better than they knew. When they were ravished by the imagination, which makes every dull fact an emblem of the spirit, and were not held earthbound by the fancy, which knows only the surfaces of things, they brought their creations from no vain or shallow thought. Yet he did not intend ever to dispense with the understanding and the fancy, to forget the customary and the institutional—as witness his constant concern with "manners." He would not raise the siege of his hencoop to march away to a pretended siege of Babylon; though he was not conspicuously successful with a shovel in his garden, he was never, like Elizabeth Peabody, so entirely subjective as to walk straight into a tree because "I saw it, but I did not realize it." Could it be, therefore, that while his reason was dreaming among the Upanishads, and his imagination reveling with Swedenborg, his understanding perceived that on the plain of material causation the transcendentalism of New England had some connection with New England experience, and that his fancy, which remained at home with the customary and with history, guided this choice of words? Did these lower faculties contrive, by that cunning which distinguishes them from reason and imagination in the very moment when transcendentalism was being proclaimed a saturnalia of faith, that there should appear a cryptic suggestion that it betokened less an Oriental ecstasy and more a natural reaction of some descendants of Puritans and Quakers to Unitarian and commercial times?

I have called Emerson mystical and pantheistical. These are difficult adjectives; we might conveniently begin with Webster's dictionary, which declares mysticism to be the doctrine that the ultimate nature of reality or of the divine essence may be known by an immediate insight. The connotations of pantheism are infinite, but in general a pantheist holds that the universe itself is God, or that God is the combined forces and laws manifested in the existing universe, that God is, in short, both the slayer and the slain. Emerson and the others might qualify their doctrine, but when Professor Andrews Norton read that in the woods "I become a transparent eyeball; I am nothing, I see all; the currents of the Universal Being circulate through me; I am part or particle of God" (W 1: 10), in his forthright fashion he could not help perceiving that this was both mysticism and pantheism, and so attacking it as "the latest form of infidelity."[1]

Could we go back to the Puritans whom Emerson adduced as his predecessors, and ask the Emersons and Ripleys, not to mention the Winthrops, Cottons, and Mathers, of the seventeenth century whether the eyeball passage was infidelity, there would be no doubt about the answer. They too might call it the "latest" form of infidelity, for in the first years of New England Winthrop and Cotton had very bitter experience with a similar doctrine. Our wonder is that they did not have more. To our minds, no longer at home in the fine distinctions of theology, it might seem that from the Calvinist doctrine of regeneration, from the theory that a regenerate soul receives an influx of divine spirit, and is joined to God by a direct infusion of His grace, we might deduce the possibility of receiving all instruction immediately from the indwelling spirit, through an inward communication which is essentially mystical. Such was exactly the deduction of Mistress Anne Hutchinson, for which she was expelled into Rhode Island. It was exactly the conclusion of the Quakers, who added that every man was naturally susceptible to this inward communication, that he did not need a special and supernatural dispensation. Quakers also were cast into Rhode Island or, if they refused to stay there, hanged on Boston Common. Emerson, descendant of Puritans, found the descendants of Quakers "a sublime class of speculators," and wrote in 1835 that they had been the most explicit teachers "of the highest article to which human faith soars[,] the strict union of the willing soul to God & so the soul's access at all times to a verdict upon every question which the opinion of all mankind cannot shake & which the opinion of all mankind cannot confirm" (L 1: 433). But his ancestors had held that while the soul does indeed have an access to God, it receives from the spirit no verdict upon any question, only a dutiful disposition to accept the verdict confirmed

---

[1]Andrews Norton, *A Discourse on the Latest Form of Infidelity* (1839), rpt. (abridged). In *The Transcendentalists: an Anthology*, ed. Perry Miller (Cambridge, Mass., 1950), pp. 210–214. —ED.

by Scripture, by authority, and by logic. As Roger Clap remarked, both Anne Hutchinson and the Quakers "would talk of the Spirit, and of revelations by the Spirit without the Word, . . . of the Light within them, rejecting the holy Scripture";[2] and the Puritan minister declared that the errors of the Antinomians, "like strong wine, make men's judgments reel and stagger, who are drunken therwith."[3] The more one studies the history of Puritan New England, the more astonished he becomes at the amount of reeling and staggering there was in it.

These seventeenth-century "infidels" were more interested in enlarging the soul's access to God from within than in exploring the possibilities of an access from without, from nature. But if we, in our interrogation of the shades of Puritans, were to ask them whether there exists a spirit that rolls through all things and propels all things, whose dwelling is the light of setting suns, and the round ocean, and the mind of man, a spirit from whom we should learn to be disturbed by the joy of elevated thoughts, the Puritans would feel at once that we needed looking after. They would concede that the visible universe is the handiwork of God, that He governs it and is present in the flight of every sparrow, the fall of every stone, the rising and setting of suns, in the tempests of the round ocean. "Who set those candles, those torches of heaven, on the table? Who hung out those lanterns in heaven to enlighten a dark world?" asked the preacher, informing his flock that although we do not see God in nature, yet in it His finger is constantly evident.[4] The textbook of theology used at Harvard told New England students that every creature would return into nothing if God did not uphold it—"the very cessation of Divine conservation, would without any other operation presently reduce every Creature into nothing."[5] In regard of His essence, said Thomas Hooker, God is in all places alike, He is in all creatures and beyond them, "hee is excluded *out* of no place, included *in* no place."[6] But it did not follow that the universe, though created by God and sustained by His continuous presence, was God Himself. We were not to go to nature and, by surrendering to the stream of natural forces, derive from it our elevated thoughts. We were not to become nothing and let the currents of Universal Being circulate through us. Whatever difficulties were involved in explaining that the universe is the work of God but that we do not meet God face to face in the universe, Puritan theologians knew that the distinction must be maintained, lest excitable Yankees reel and stagger with another error which they would pretend was an elevated thought. The difficulties of explanation were so great that the preachers often avoided the issue, declaring, "this is but a curious question: therefore I will leave it," or remarking that the Lord fills both heaven and

[2]Alexander Young, *Chronicles of the First Planters* (Boston, 1846), p. 360.
[3]Thomas Shepard, *Works*, ed. John A. Albro (Boston, 1853), 3: 194.
[4]*Ibid.*, 1: 10.
[5]William Ames, *The Marrow of Sacred Divinity* (London, 1643), p. 42.
[6]Thomas Hooker, *Heavens Treasure Opened* (London, 1645), pp. 20–21.

earth, yet He is not in the world as the soul is in the body, "but in an incomprehensible manner, which we cannot expresse to you."[7] Thomas Shepard in Cambridge tried to be more explicit: the Godhead, he said, is common to everything and every man, even to the most wicked man, "nay, to the vilest creature in the world." The same power that made a blade of grass made also the angels, but grass and angels are not the same substance, and so the spirit of God which is in the setting sun and the round ocean is not the same manifestation which He puts forth as a special and "supernatural" grace in the regenerate soul. "There comes another spirit upon us, which common men have not."[8] This other spirit teaches us, not elevated thoughts, but how to submit our corrupt thoughts to the rule of Scripture, to the law and the gospel as expounded at Harvard College and by Harvard graduates.

The reason for Puritan opposition to these ideas is not far to seek. The Renaissance mind—which was still a medieval mind—remembered that for fifteen hundred years Christian thinkers had striven to conceive of the relation of God to the world in such a fashion that the transcendence of God should not be called in question, that while God was presented as the creator and governor of the world, He would always be something other than the world itself. Both mysticism and pantheism, in whatever form, identified Him with nature, made Him over in the image of man, interpreted Him in the terms either of human intuitions or of human perceptions, made Him one with the forces of psychology or of matter. The Renaissance produced a number of eccentrics who broached these dangerous ideas—Giordano Bruno, for instance, who was burned at the stake by a sentence which Catholics and Calvinists alike found just. The Puritans carried to New England the historic convictions of Christian orthodoxy, and in America found an added incentive for maintaining them intact. Puritanism was not merely a religious creed and a theology, it was also a program for society. We go to New England, said John Winthrop, to establish a due form of government, both civil and ecclesiastical, under the rule of law and Scripture.[9] It was to be a medieval society of status, with every man in his place and a place for every man; it was to be no utopia of rugged individualists and transcendental freethinkers. But if Anne Hutchinson was correct, and if men could hear the voice of God within themselves, or if they could go into the woods and feel the currents of Universal Being circulate through them—in either event they would pay little heed to governors and ministers. The New England tradition commenced with a clear understanding that both mysticism and pantheism were heretical, and also with a frank admission that such ideas were dangerous to society, that men who imbibed noxious errors from an inner voice or from the presence of God in the natural landscape would reel and stagger through the streets of Boston and disturb the civil peace.

[7]John Preston, *Life Eternall* (London, 1631), Part 2, pp. 45, 148.
[8]Shepard, *Works*, 1: 168; 2: 212–213.
[9]*Winthrop Papers*, Massachusetts Historical Society, 3 (1931), 293.

Yet from the works of the most orthodox of Calvinists we can perceive that the Puritans had good cause to be apprehensive lest mystical or pantheistical conclusions arise out of their premises. Anne Hutchinson and the Quakers commenced as Calvinists; from the idea of regeneration they drew, with what seemed to them impeccable logic, the idea that God imparted His teaching directly to the individual spirit. With equal ease others could deduce from the doctrines of divine creation and providence the idea that God was immanent in nature. The point might be put thus: there was in Puritanism a piety, a religious passion, the sense of an inward communication and of the divine symbolism of nature. One side of the Puritan nature hungered for these excitements; certain of its appetites desired these satisfactions and therefore found delight and ecstasy in the doctrines of regeneration and providence. But in Puritanism there was also another side, an ideal of social conformity, of law and order, of regulation and control. At the core of the theology there was an indestructible element which was mystical, and a feeling for the universe which was almost pantheistic; but there was also a social code demanding obedience to external law, a code to which good people voluntarily conformed and to which bad people should be made to conform. It aimed at propriety and decency, the virtues of middle-class respectability, self-control, thrift, and dignity, at a discipline of the emotions. It demanded, as Winthrop informed the citizens of Massachusetts Bay in 1645, that men forbear to exercise the liberty they had by nature, the freedom to do anything they chose, and having entered into society thereafter, devote themselves to doing only that which the authorities defined as intrinsically "good, just and honest."[10] The New England tradition contained a dual heritage, the heritage of the troubled spirit and the heritage of worldly caution and social conservatism. It gave with one hand what it took away with the other: it taught men that God is present to their intuitions and in the beauty and terror of nature, but it disciplined them into subjecting their intuitions to the wisdom of society and their impressions of nature to the standards of decorum.

In the eighteenth century, certain sections of New England, or certain persons, grew wealthy. It can hardly be a coincidence that among those who were acquiring the rewards of industry and commerce there should be progressively developed the second part of the heritage, the tradition of reason and criticism, and that among them the tradition of emotion and ecstasy should dwindle. Even though a few of the clergy, like Jonathan Mayhew and Lemuel Briant, were moving faster than their congregations, yet in Boston and Salem, the centers of shipping and banking, ministers preached rationality rather than dogma, the Newtonian universe and the sensational psychology rather than providence and innate depravity. The back country, the Connecticut Valley, burst into flame with the Great Awakening of the 1740's; but the massive Charles Chauncy, minister at the First Church, the

---

[10]Winthrop, *Journal*, ed. J. K. Hosmer (New York, 1908), 2: 239.

successor of John Cotton, declared that "the passionate discovery" of divine love is not a good evidence of election. "The surest and most substantial Proof is, *Obedience to the Commandments of God,* and the *stronger* the Love, the more uniform, steady and pleasant will be this *Obedience.*" Religion is of the understanding as well as of the affections, and when the emotions are stressed at the expense of reason, "it can't be but People should run into Disorders."[11] In his ponderous way, Chauncy was here indulging in Yankee understatement. During the Awakening the people of the back country ran into more than disorders; they gave the most extravagant exhibition of staggering and reeling that New England had yet beheld. Chauncy was aroused, not merely because he disapproved of displays of emotion, but because the whole society seemed in danger when persons who made a high pretense to religion displayed it in their conduct "as something wild and fanciful." On the contrary, he stoutly insisted, true religion is sober and well-behaved; as it is taught in the Bible, "it approves itself to the Understanding and Conscience, . . . and is in the best Manner calculated to promote the Good of Mankind."[12] The transformation of this segment of Puritanism from a piety to an ethic, from a religious faith to a social code, was here completed, although an explicit break with the formal theology was yet to come.

Charles Chauncy had already split the Puritan heritage. Emerson tells that Chauncy, going into his pulpit for the Thursday lecture (people at that time came all the way from Salem to hear him), was informed that a little boy had fallen into Frog Pond and drowned. Requested to improve the occasion,

> the doctor was much distressed, and in his prayer he hesitated, he tried to make soft approaches, he prayed for Harvard College, he prayed for the schools, he implored the Divine Being "to—to—to bless to them all the boy that was this morning drowned in Frog Pond." (W 8: 127)

But Jonathan Edwards felt an ardency of soul which he knew not how to express, a desire "to lie in the dust, and to be full of Christ alone; to love him with a holy and pure love; to trust in him; to live upon him; to serve and follow him; and to be perfectly sanctified and made pure, with a divine and heavenly purity."[13] To one who conceived the highest function of religion to be the promotion of the good of mankind, Jonathan Edwards stood guilty of fomenting disorders. Chauncy blamed Edwards for inciting the populace, and was pleased when the congregation at Northampton, refusing to measure up to the standards of sanctification demanded by Edwards, banished him into the wilderness of Stockbridge. Edwards, though he was distressed over the disorders of the Awakening, would never grant that a concern for the good of mankind should take precedence over the desire to be perfectly sanctified and made pure. In his exile at Stockbridge he wrote the great tracts which have secured his fame for all time, the magnificent studies of the freedom of the

[11]Charles Chauncy, *Seasonable Thoughts on the State of Religion* (Boston, 1743), pp. 26, 422.
[12]*Ibid.*, p. 406.

will, of the nature of true virtue, of the purpose of God in creating the universe, in which Chauncy and Harvard College were refuted; in which, though still in the language of logic and systematic theology, the other half of the Puritan heritage—the sense of God's overwhelming presence in the soul and in nature—once more found perfect expression.

Though the treatises on the will and on virtue are the more impressive performances, for our purposes the eloquent *Dissertation Concerning the End for which God Created the World* is the more relevant, if only because when he came to this question Edwards was forced to reply specifically to the scientific rationalism toward which Chauncy and Harvard College were tending. He had, therefore, to make even more explicit than did the earlier divines the doctrines which verged upon both mysticism and pantheism, the doctrines of inward communication and of the divine in nature. It was not enough for Edwards to say, as John Cotton had done, that God created the world out of nothing to show His glory; rationalists in Boston could reply that God's glory was manifested in the orderly machine of Newtonian physics, and that a man glorified God in such a world by going about his rational business: real estate, the triangular trade, or the manufacture of rum out of smuggled molasses. God did not create the world, said Edwards, merely to exhibit His glory; He did not create it out of nothing simply to show that He could: He who is Himself the source of all being, the substance of all life, created the world out of Himself by a diffusion of Himself into time and space. He made the world, not by sitting outside and above it, by modeling it as a child models sand, but by an extension of Himself, by taking upon Himself the forms of stones and trees and of man. He created without any ulterior object in view, neither for His glory nor for His power, but for the pure joy of self-expression, as an artist creates beauty for the love of beauty. God does not need a world or the worship of man; He is perfect in Himself. If He bothers to create, it is out of the fullness of His own nature, the overflowing virtue that is in Him. Edwards did not use my simile of the artist; his way of saying it was, "The disposition to communicate himself, or diffuse his own fulness, which we must conceive of as being originally in God as a perfection of his nature, was what moved him to create the world,"[14] but we may still employ the simile because Edwards invested his God with the sublime egotism of a very great artist. God created by the laws of His own nature, with no thought of doing good for anybody or for mankind, with no didactic purpose, for no other reason but the joy of creativeness. "It is a regard to himself that disposes him to diffuse and communicate himself. It is such a delight in his own internal fulness and glory, that disposes him to an abundant effusion and emanation of that glory."[15]

Edwards was much too skilled in the historic problems of theology to lose

[13]Edwards, *Works* (New York, 1844), 1: 25.
[14]*Ibid.*, 2: 206.
[15]*Ibid.*, 2: 215.

sight of the distinction between God and the world or to fuse them into one substance, to blur the all-important doctrine of the divine transcendence. He forced into his system every safeguard against identifying the inward experience of the saint with the Deity Himself, or of God with nature. Nevertheless, assuming, as we have some right to assume, that what subsequent generations find to be a hidden or potential implication in a thought is a part of that thought, we may venture to feel that Edwards was particularly careful to hold in check the mystical and pantheistical tendencies of his teaching because he himself was so apt to become a mystic and a pantheist. The imagery in which a great thinker expresses his sense of things is often more revealing than his explicit contentions, and Edwards betrays the nature of his insight when he uses as the symbol of God's relation to the world the metaphor that has perennially been invoked by mystics, the metaphor of light and of the sun:

> And [it] is fitly compared to an effulgence or emanation of light from a luminary, by which this glory of God is abundantly represented in Scripture. Light is the external expression, exhibition and manifestation of the excellency of the luminary, of the sun for instance: it is the abundant, extensive emanation and communication of the fulness of the sun to innumerable beings that partake of it. It is by this that the sun itself is seen, and his glory beheld, and all other things are discovered; it is by a participation of this communication from the sun, that surrounding objects receive all their lustre, beauty and brightness. It is by this that all nature is quickened and receives life, comfort, and joy.[16]

Here is the respect that makes Edwards great among theologians, and here in fact he strained theology to the breaking point. Holding himself by brute will power within the forms of ancient Calvinism, he filled those forms with a new and throbbing spirit. Beneath the dogmas of the old theology he discovered a different cosmos from that of the seventeenth century, a dynamic world, filled with the presence of God, quickened with divine life, pervaded with joy and ecstasy. With this insight he turned to combat the rationalism of Boston, to argue that man cannot live by Newtonian schemes and mathematical calculations, but only by surrender to the will of God, by reflecting back the beauty of God as a jewel gives back the light of the sun. But another result of Edwards's doctrine, one which he would denounce to the nethermost circle of Hell but which is implicit in the texture, if not in the logic, of his thought, could very easily be what we have called mysticism or pantheism, or both. If God is diffused through nature, and the substance of man is the substance of God, then it may follow that man is divine, that nature is the garment of the Over-Soul, that man must be self-reliant, and that when he goes into the woods the currents of Being will indeed circulate through him. All that prevented this deduction was the orthodox theology, supposedly derived from the Word of God, which taught that God and nature are not one, that man is

[16]*Ibid.*, 2: 254.

corrupt and his self-reliance is reliance on evil. But take away the theology, remove this overlying stone of dogma from the wellsprings of Puritan conviction, and both nature and man become divine.

We know that Edwards failed to revitalize Calvinism. He tried to fill the old bottles with new wine, yet none but himself could savor the vintage. Meanwhile, in the circles where Chauncy had begun to reëducate the New England taste, there developed, by a very gradual process, a rejection of the Westminster Confession, indeed of all theology, and at last emerged the Unitarian churches. Unitarianism was entirely different wine from any that had ever been pressed from the grapes of Calvinism, and in entirely new bottles, which the merchants of Boston found much to their liking. It was a pure, white, dry claret that went well with dinners served by the Harvard Corporation, but it was mild and was guaranteed not to send them home reeling and staggering. As William Ellery Channing declared, to contemplate the horrors of New England's ancestral creed is "a consideration singularly fitted to teach us tolerant views of error, and to enjoin caution and sobriety."[17]

In Unitarianism one half of the New England tradition—that which inculcated caution and sobriety—definitely cast off all allegiance to the other. The ideal of decorum, of law and self-control, was institutionalized. Though Unitarianism was "liberal" in theology, it was generally conservative in its social thinking and in its metaphysics. Even Channing, who strove always to avoid controversy and to appear "mild and amiable," was still more of an enthusiast than those he supplied with ideas, as was proved when almost alone among Unitarian divines he spoke out against slavery. He frequently found himself thwarted by the suavity of Unitarian breeding. In his effort to establish a literary society in Boston, he repaired, as Emerson tells the story, to the home of Dr. John Collins Warren, where

> he found a well-chosen assembly of gentlemen variously distinguished; there was mutual greeting and introduction, and they were chatting agreeably on indifferent matters and drawing gently towards their great expectation, when a side-door opened, the whole company streamed in to an oyster supper, crowned by excellent wines; and so ended the first attempt to establish aesthetic society in Boston. (*W* 10: 340–41)

But if the strain in the New England tradition which flowered so agreeably in the home of Dr. Warren, the quality that made for reason and breeding and good suppers, found itself happily divorced from enthusiasm and perfectly enshrined in the liberal profession of Unitarianism, what of the other strain? What of the mysticism, the hunger of the soul, the sense of divine emanation in man and in nature, which had been so important an element in the Puritan character? Had it died out of New England? Was it to live, if at all, forever caged and confined in the prison house of Calvinism? Could it be asserted only by another Edwards in another treatise on the will and a new dissertation

---

[17]Channing, *Works* (Boston, 1880), p. 5.

on the end for which God created the universe? Andover Seminary was, of course, turning out treatises and dissertations, and there were many New Englanders outside of Boston who were still untouched by Unitarianism. But for those who had been "liberated" by Channing and Norton, who could no longer express their desires in the language of a creed that had been shown to be outworn, Calvinism was dead. Unitarianism rolled away the heavy stone of dogma that had sealed up the mystical springs in the New England character; as far as most Unitarians were concerned, the stone could now be lifted with safety, because to them the code of caution and sobriety, nourished on oyster suppers, would serve quite as well as the old doctrines of original sin and divine transcendence to prevent mankind from reeling and staggering in freedom. But for those in whom the old springs were still living, the removal of the theological stopper might mean a welling up and an overflowing of long suppressed desires. And if these desires could no longer be satisfied in theology, toward what objects would they now be turned? If they could no longer be expressed in the language of supernatural regeneration and divine sovereignty, in what language were they to be described?

The answer was not long forthcoming. If the inherent mysticism, the ingrained pantheism, of certain Yankees could not be stated in the old terms, it could be couched in the new terms of transcendental idealism, of Platonism, of Swedenborg, of "Tintern Abbey" and the Bhagavad-Gita, in the eclectic and polyglot speech of the Over-Soul, in "Brahma," in "Self-Reliance," in *Nature*. The children of Puritans could no longer say that the visible fabric of nature was quickened and made joyful by a diffusion of the fullness of God, but they could recapture the Edwardsean vision by saying, "Nature can only be conceived as existing to a universal and not to a particular end; to a universe of ends, and not to one,—a work of *ecstasy*, to be represented by a circular movement, as intention might be signified by a straight line of definite length" (W 1: 201). But in this case the circular conception enjoyed one great advantage—so it seemed at the time—that it had not possessed for Edwards: the new generation of ecstatics had learned from Channing and Norton, from the prophets of intention and the straight line of definite length, that men did not need to grovel in the dust. They did not have to throw themselves on the ground, as did Edwards, with a sense of their own unworthiness; they could say without trepidation that no concept of the understanding, no utilitarian consideration for the good of mankind, could account for any man's existence, that there was no further reason than "*so it was to be.*" Overtones of the seventeenth century become distinctly audible when Emerson declares, "The *royal* reason, the Grace of God, seems the only description of our multiform but ever identical fact," and the force of his heredity is manifest when he must go on to say, having mentioned the grace of God, "There is the incoming or the receding of God," and as Edwards also would have said, "we can show neither how nor why." In the face of this awful and arbitrary power, the Puritan had been forced to conclude that man was empty and insignificant, and account for its recedings on the hypothesis of innate depravity. Emerson does not deny that such reflections are in order; when we view the fact of the inexplicable recedings "from the platform of action," when we see men left high and dry without the grace of God, we see "Self-accusation, remorse, and the didactic morals of self-denial and strife with sin"; but our enlightenment, our liberation from the sterile dogmas of Calvinism, enables us also to view the fact from "the platform of intellection," and in this view "there is nothing for us but praise and wonder" (W 1: 204). The ecstasy and the vision which Calvinists knew only in the moment of vocation, the passing of which left them agonizingly aware of depravity and sin, could become the permanent joy of those who had put aside the conception of depravity, and the moments between could be filled no longer with self-accusation but with praise and wonder. Unitarianism had stripped off the dogmas, and Emerson was free to celebrate purely and simply the presence of God in the soul and in nature, the pure metaphysical essence of the New England tradition. If he could no longer publish it as orthodoxy, he could speak it fearlessly as the very latest form of infidelity.

At this point there might legitimately be raised a question whether my argument is anything more than obscurantism. Do words like "New England tradition" and "Puritan heritage" mean anything concrete and tangible? Do they "explain" anything? Do habits of thought persist in a society as acquired characteristics, and by what mysterious alchemy are they transmitted in the blood stream? I am as guilty as Emerson himself if I treat ideas as a self-contained rhetoric, forgetting that they are, as we are now discovering, weapons, the weapons of classes and interests, a masquerade of power relations.

Yet Emerson, transcendental though he was, could see in his own ideas a certain relation to society. In his imagination transcendentalism was a saturnalia of faith, but in his fancy it was a reaction against Unitarianism and in his understanding a revulsion against commercialism. We can improve his hint by remarking the obvious connection between the growth of rationalism in New England and the history of eighteenth-century capitalism. Once the Unitarian apologists had renounced the Westminster Confession, they attacked Calvinism not merely as irrational but as a species of pantheism, and in their eyes this charge was sufficient condemnation in itself. Calvinism, said Channing, robs the mind of self-determining force and makes men passive recipients of the universal force:

> It is a striking fact that the philosophy which teaches that matter is an inert substance, and that God is the force which pervades it, has led men to question whether any such thing as matter exists. . . . Without a free power in man, he is nothing. The divine agent within him is every thing, Man acts only in show. He is a phenomenal existence, under which the One Infinite Power is manifested; and is this much better than Pantheism?[18]

18*Ibid.*, p. 4.

One does not have to be too prone to economic interpretation in order to perceive that there was a connection between the Unitarian insistence that matter is substance and not shadow, that men are self-determining agents and not passive recipients of Infinite Power, and the practical interests of the society in which Unitarianism flourished. Pantheism was not a marketable commodity on State Street, and merchants could most succcssfully conduct their business if they were not required to lie in the dust and desire to be full of the divine agent within.

Hence the words "New England tradition" and "Puritan heritage" can be shown to have some concrete meaning when applied to the gradual evolution of Unitarianism out of the seventeenth-century background; there is a continuity both social and intellectual. But what of the young men and young women, many of them born and reared in circles in which, Channing said, "Society is going forward in intelligence and charity," who in their very adolescence instinctively turned their intelligence and even their charity against this liberalism, and sought instead the strange and uncharitable gods of transcendentalism? Why should Emerson and Margaret Fuller, almost from their first reflective moments, have cried out for a philosophy which would reassure them that matter is the shadow and spirit the substance, that man acts by an influx of power—why should they deliberately return to the bondage from which Channing had delivered them? Even before he entered the divinity school Emerson was looking askance at Unitarianism, writing in his twentieth year to his southern friend, John Boynton Hill, that for all the flood of genius and knowledge being poured out from Boston pulpits, the light of Christianity was lost: "An exemplary Christian of today, and even a Minister, is content to be just such a man as was a good Roman in the days of Cicero." Andrews Norton would not have been distressed over this observation, but young Emerson was. "Presbyterianism & Calvinism at the South," he wrote, "at least make Christianity a more real & tangible system and give it some novelties which were worth unfolding to the ignorance of men." Thus much, but no more, he could say for "orthodoxy": "When I have been to Cambridge & studied Divinity, I will tell you whether I can make out for myself any better system than Luther or Calvin, or the *liberal besoms* of modern days" (*L* 1: 128). The "Divinity School Address" was forecast in these youthful lines, and Emerson the man declared what the boy had divined when he ridiculed the "pale negations" of Unitarianism, called it an "icehouse," and spoke of "the corpse-cold Unitarianism of Harvard College and Brattle Street." Margaret Fuller thrilled to the epistle of John read from a Unitarian pulpit: "Every one that loveth is born of God, and knoweth God," but she shuddered as the preacher straightway rose up "to deny mysteries, to deny second birth, to deny influx, and to renounce the sovereign gift of insight, for the sake of what he deemed a 'rational' exercise of will." This Unitarianism, she argued in her journal, has had its place, but the time has now come for reinterpreting old dogmas: "For one I would now preach the Holy Ghost as zealously as they have been preaching Man and faith instead of the understanding, and mysticism instead &c—."[19] And there, characteristically enough, she remarks, "But why go on?"

A complete answer to the question of motives is probably not possible as yet. Why Waldo and Margaret in the 1820's and '30's should instinctively have revolted against a creed that had at last been perfected as the ideology of their own group, of respectable, prosperous, middle-class Boston and Cambridge— why these youngsters, who by all the laws of economic determinism ought to have been the white-headed children of Unitarianism, elected to become transcendental black sheep, cannot be decided until we know more about the period than has been told in *The Flowering of New England* and more about the nature of social change in general. The personal matter is obviously of crucial importance. The characters of the transcendentalists account for their having become transcendental; still two facts of a more historical nature seem to me worth considering in the effort to answer our question.

The emergence of Unitarianism out of Calvinism was a very gradual, almost an imperceptible, process. One can hardly say at what point rationalists in eastern Massachusetts ceased to be Calvinists, for they were forced to organize into a separate church only after the development of their thought was completed. Consequently, although young men and women in Boston might be, like Waldo and Margaret, the children of rationalists, all about them the society still bore the impress of Calvinism: the theological break had come, but not the cultural. In a thousand ways the forms of society were still those determined by the ancient orthodoxy, piously observed by persons who no longer believed in the creed. We do not need to posit some magical transmission of Puritanism from the seventeenth to the nineteenth century in order to account for the fact that these children of Unitarians felt emotionally starved and spiritually undernourished. In 1859 James Cabot sent Emerson *The Life of Trust,* a crude narrative by one George Muller of his personal conversations with the Lord, which Cabot expected Emerson to enjoy as another instance of man's communion with the Over-Soul, which probably seemed to Cabot no more crackbrained than many of the books Emerson admired. Emerson returned the volume, accompanied by a vigorous rebuke to Cabot for occupying himself with such trash:

> I sometimes think that you & your coevals missed much that I & mine found: for Calvinism was still robust & effective on life & character in all the people who surrounded my childhood, & gave a deep religious tinge to manners & conversation. I doubt the race is now extinct, & certainly no sentiment has taken its place on the new generation,—none as pervasive & controlling. But they were a high tragic school, & found much of their own belief in the grander traits of the Greek mythology,—Nemesis, the Fates, & the Eumenides, and, I am sure, would have raised an eyebrow at this pistareen Providence of . . . George Muller. (*L* 5: 145)

[19]*Memoirs of Margaret Fuller Ossoli* (Boston, 1884), 2: 84–85.

At least two members of the high tragic school Emerson knew intimately and has sympathetically described for us—his stepgrandfather, the Reverend Ezra Ripley, and his aunt, Mary Moody Emerson. Miss Emerson put the essence of the Puritan aesthetic into one short sentence: "How insipid is fiction to a mind touched with immortal views!" Speaking as a Calvinist, she anticipated Max Weber's discovery that the Protestant ethic fathered the spirit of capitalism, in the pungent observation, "I respect in a rich man the order of Providence." Emerson said that her journal "marks the precise time when the power of the old creed yielded to the influence of modern science and humanity"; still in her the old creed never so far yielded its power to the influence of modern humanity but that she could declare, with a finality granted only to those who have grasped the doctrine of divine sovereignty, "I was never patient with the faults of the good."[20] When Thomas Cholmondeley once suggested to Emerson that many of his ideas were similar to those of Calvinism, Emerson broke in with irritation, "I see you are speaking of something which had a meaning once, but is now grown obsolete. Those words formerly stood for something, and the world got good from them, but not now." The old creed would no longer serve, but there had been power in it, a power conspicuously absent from the pale negations of Unitarianism. At this distance in time, we forget that Emerson was in a position fully to appreciate what the obsolete words had formerly stood for, and we are betrayed by the novelty of his vocabulary, which seems to have no relation to the jargon of Calvinism, into overlooking a fact of which he was always aware—the great debt owed by his generation "to that old religion which, in the childhood of most of us, still dwelt like a sabbath morning in the country of New England, teaching privation, self-denial and sorrow!" The retarded tempo of the change in New England, extending through the eighteenth into the nineteenth century, makes comprehensible why young Unitarians had enough contact with the past to receive from it a religious standard by which to condemn the pallid and unexciting liberalism of Unitarianism (W 1: 220).

Finally, we do well to remember that what we call the transcendental movement was not an isolated phenomenon in nineteenth-century New England. As Professor Whicher has remarked, "Liberal ideas came slowly to the Connecticut Valley."[21] They came slowly also to Andover Theological Seminary. But slowly they came, and again undermined Calvinist orthodoxies as they had undermined orthodoxy in eighteenth-century Boston; and again they liberated a succession of New Englanders from the Westminster Confession, but they did not convert them into rationalists and Unitarians. Like Emerson, when other New Englanders were brought to ask themselves, "And

[20]W 10: 399, 411; L 2: 395; James Elliott Cabot, *A Memoir of Ralph Waldo Emerson* (Boston, 1887), 1: 37.
[21]George Frisbie Whicher, *This Was a Poet* (New York, 1939), p. 189.

what is to replace for us the piety of that race?" they preferred to bask "in the great morning which rises forever out of the eastern sea" rather than to rest content with mere liberation. "I stand here to say, Let us worship the mighty and transcendent Soul"—but not the good of mankind! (*W* 1: 221). Over and again the rational attack upon Calvinism served only to release energies which then sought for new forms of expression in directions entirely opposite to rationalism. Some, like Sylvester Judd, revolted against the Calvinism of the Connecticut Valley, went into Unitarianism, and then came under the spell of Emerson's transcendentalist tuition. Others, late in the century, sought out new heresies, not those of transcendentalism, but interesting parallels and analogues. Out of Andover came Harriet Beecher Stowe, lovingly but firmly underlining the emotional restrictions of Calvinism in *The Minister's Wooing* and *Oldtown Folks*, while she herself left the grim faith at last for the ritualism of the Church of England. Out of Andover also came Elizabeth Stuart Phelps in feverish revolt against the hard logic of her father and grandfather, preaching instead the emotionalism of *Gates Ajar*. In Connecticut, Horace Bushnell, reacting against the dry intellectualism of Nathaniel Taylor's Calvinism just as Margaret Fuller had reacted a decade earlier against the dry rationalism of Norton's Unitarianism, read Coleridge with an avidity equal to hers and Emerson's, and by 1849 found the answer to his religious quest, as he himself said, "after all his thought and study, not as something reasoned out, but as an inspiration—a revelation from the mind of God himself." He published the revelation in a book, the very title of which tells the whole story, *Nature and the Supernatural Together Constituting One System of God*, wherein was preached anew the immanence of God in nature: "God is the spiritual reality of which nature is the manifestation." With this publication the latest—and yet the oldest—form of New England infidelity stalked in the citadel of orthodoxy, and Calvinism itself was, as it were, transcendentalized. At Amherst, Emily Dickinson's mental climate, in the Gilded Age, was still Emerson's; the break-up of Calvinism came later there than in Boston, but when it had come the poems of Emily Dickinson were filled with "Emersonian echoes," echoes which Professor Whicher wisely declines to point out because, as he says, resemblances in Emerson, Thoreau, Parker, and Emily Dickinson are not evidences of borrowings one from another, but their common response to the spirit of the time, even though the spirit reached Emily Dickinson a little later in time than it did Emerson and Thoreau. "Their work," he says, "was in various ways a fulfillment of the finer energies of a Puritanism that was discarding the husks of dogma."[22] From the time of Edwards to that of Emerson, the husks of Puritanism were being discarded, but the energies of many Puritans were not yet diverted—they could not be diverted—from a passionate search of the soul and of nature, from the quest to which Calvinism had devoted them. These New Englanders—a few here

[22]*Ibid.*, p. 199.

and there—turned aside from the doctrines of sin and predestination, and thereupon sought with renewed fervor for the accents of the Holy Ghost in their own hearts and in woods and mountains. But now that the restraining hand of theology was withdrawn, there was nothing to prevent them, as there had been everything to prevent Edwards, from identifying their intuitions with the voice of God, or from fusing God and nature into the one substance of the transcendental imagination. Mystics were no longer inhibited by dogma. They were free to carry on the ancient New England propensity for reeling and staggering with new opinions. They could give themselves over, unrestrainedly, to becoming transparent eyeballs and debauchees of dew.

From Franklin to Emerson

William L. Hedges

1. Perry Miller and Connections in American Literature

To reread Perry Miller's well-known essay "From Edwards to Emerson" is to enter a half-forgotten world in which reputations, connections, and meanings in American literature were more nebulous than they have become for many scholars and critics since 1940. Miller was surprisingly defensive in regard to Emerson, doubtful in his own mind, quite clearly, of the lasting value of so blithe a sage in an era of depression and world war, and well aware of pragmatic America's limited tolerance for mysticism and pantheism. In his essay, however, he unearthed native "roots" for transcendentalism, and his ironic innuendo managed to suggest a contemporary relevance for Emerson which foreshadowed a somewhat strained significance that students seem increasingly to find in American literature generally or in what is taken to be the dominant literary tradition in America.

The hackneyed metaphor of roots and soil justified itself by being part of a snide reference to Van Wyck Brooks, who had obviously failed in Miller's eyes to account satisfactorily for the "particular blossom" of Emerson "in the flowering of New England." Later in his essay the author of *The New England Mind* grumbled that the popular volume by Brooks, which had appeared four years earlier, although ostensibly a search for a usable American past, was based on insufficient knowledge of Emerson's period and of "the nature of social change in general" (pages 14, 28). It is true that Brooks had done little to dispel the prevalent notion that Emerson was basically an amalgam of Kant, Coleridge, Swedenborg, the *Bhagvad-gita* and other assorted foreign influences. Brooks's explanation of Emerson was probably, for Miller, too close to that of Emerson himself, which Miller described sarcastically as seeing in transcendentalism "one more expression of the benign gentleman who previously had spoken in the persons of Socrates and Zoroaster, Mohammed and Buddha, Shakespeare and St. Paul."[1] Going to William James as an authority on religious experience, Brooks had argued that Emerson's doctrine of self-

From *The Oldest Revolutionary: Essays on Benjamin Franklin*, ed. J. A. Leo Lemay (Philadelphia: University of Pennsylvania Press, 1976), 139–53. Copyright 1976 University of Pennsylvania Press. Reprinted by permission of the publisher.

[1]Perry Miller, "From Edwards to Emerson," this volume (pages 13–31).—ED.

reliance was simply the reiteration of a fundamental idea or attitude implicit in "all the periods of revival, the early Christian age and Luther's age, Rousseau's, Kant's and Goethe's."[2]

Although Emerson identified transcendental idealism with a sequence of antiauthoritarian moments in philosophy and religion reaching back as far as the Stoics, Miller largely scoffed at his antihistoricism: it was part or parcel of transcendentalism's alarming eclecticism, its tendency to lump things together indiscriminately, its declaring "all ideas to be one idea, all religions the same religion, all poets singers of the same music." For Perry Miller in 1940 in the wake of the Nazi *Blitzkreig* it was imperative to be able to distinguish between the slayer and the slain, whatever their ultimate merger in the Over-Soul. So too it was necessary to insist "that ideas are born in time and place, that they spring from specific environments, that they express the force of societies and classes, that they are generated by power relations" (page 15).

And yet ironically Miller's own accounting for Emerson is in one sense not very different from that of Emerson or Brooks. Fundamental for all three is the notion of a periodic revival of religious enthusiasm. The difference is that Miller locates Emerson within the framework of a recurrent New England impulse in the direction of mystical piety, whereas for Emerson and Brooks the framework is much more vast. The two views, however, might well be made to coexist.

The heart of "From Edwards to Emerson" is the outline which Miller offers of the intellectual history of New England from 1630 to 1830. It emphasizes the polarity in Puritan thought, its intense piety and spirituality on the one hand and its diligent attention to the practical world on the other. As he put it, "At the core of the theology there was an indestructible element which was mystical, and a feeling for the universe which was almost pantheistic; but there was also a social code demanding obedience to external law, a code to which good people voluntarily conformed and to which bad people should be made to conform." This contradiction produced or characterized the conflicts between the Antinomians and John Winthrop and John Cotton and between Edwards and Charles Chauncy. In the nineteenth century Miller saw a recurrence of the same tension in the opposition between Emerson and the Unitarians. Passing over the terror in Edwards at the wrath of the Omnipotent, Miller stressed the revivalist's sense of the word as "dynamic . . . , filled with the presence of God, quickened with divine life, pervaded with joy and ecstasy" (page 23). Edwards thus became an incipient transcendentalist, held in check only by the bonds of Calvinist theology. Emerson, Miller noted, was fortunate enough to have had Chauncy and Unitarianism liberate New England (or at least Boston and Cambridge) before the mystical pantheistic urge made its presence felt in himself.

Thus was transcendentalism given native roots, and mysticism and pantheism Americanized. I hope I have made the reader a bit uneasy by my glib use

[2]Van Wyck Brooks, *The Flowering of New England 1815–1865* (n.p.: Dutton, 1936), p. 207.

of "mysticism" and "pantheism." I deliberately echo Miller, who I think is also uneasy with these words but who seems determined to make the reader swallow them as representing the essential Emerson. What is amazing about the essay is that Miller largely rejects a traditional view of Emerson that could easily have been made to mesh with his interpretation of Puritanism. The view goes back at least as far as James Russell Lowell, who laid it out very obviously in his deft caricature of Emerson in "A Fable for Critics." The personality was polarized: "Plotinus-Montaigne," Lowell called him, or "Greek head on right Yankee shoulders." Why did Miller not look at Emerson as himself an embodiment of the tension between the two pronounced tendencies in New England thought, especially in view of Emerson's own fascination with polarities, his sense of experience as oscillation?

The answer is that to concede that Emerson had much of the shrewd Yankee in him would have meant weakening what Miller obviously saw as Emerson's strongest claim for sympathy in 1940. Although he specifically disclaims any interest in having the higher metaphysics of transcendentalism taken "seriously" by his own contemporaries, Miller does stress Emerson's sense of transcendentalism as a reaction against the evils of the "commercial times" of Jacksonian America—as well as against Unitarianism (page 16). In Miller's mind, perhaps more than in Emerson's, the "commercial times" are intimately connected with the social and political conservatism of the worldly-minded commonsensical Unitarians. Miller's depression-sharpened liberalism makes itself clearly felt. Call Emerson a "mystagogue," as Lowell did, if you like, Miller seems to say, but first and last there has been a lot of mystagoguery in America and it has something to do with the dominance in this culture of the State Street mentality and the failures of industrial capitalism.

The trouble is that for many the sharp distinction between Emerson and Yankee industry, frugality, and finance has been hard to maintain. Lowell was quite specific: Emerson's "range" was from the "pole" of "Olympus" to that of "the Exchange." Bliss Perry began his *Emerson Today* in 1931 by noting the "open parable in the very lines of his face. . . . Seen from one side, it was the face of a Yankee of the old school, shrewd, serious, practical; the sort of face that may still be observed in the quiet country churches of New England or at the village store. Seen from the other side, it was the face of a dreamer, a seer, a soul brooding on things to come, things as yet very far away."[3] While Miller in the lead article of the December 1940 issue of *The New England Quarterly* was relating transcendental pantheism to puritan piety, Alexander C. Kern in "Emerson and Economics," the final article, was suggesting that the "influence of Emerson's puritan New England background" on the "crass portion of his thought" was much stronger than had generally been noticed. Emphasizing the conflict in Emerson between materialism and idealism, Kern argued the fundamental domination of the latter but admitted that the Emersonian concern with practical endeavor sometimes amounted to almost overt advo-

[3]Bliss Perry, *Emerson Today* (Princeton: Princeton University Press), p. 1.

cacy of "rugged individualism."[4] The next year Miller's colleague F. O. Matthiessen was to suggest that Emerson's "most balanced" assessment of his own position "was that which placed him between the transcendentalists and Franklin."[5] And Miller himself was later in speaking of Emerson to praise his "levelheadedness" as "his most precious bequest to a posterity which is understandably exasperated by his unction."[6]

Miller would have been the first to recognize that his own thought, as much as Emerson's, was a product of a particular time and place. It is well, however, for those of us who utilize his ideas to develop an equal awareness. I propose therefore an inquiry into Emerson's relation to Benjamin Franklin to balance Miller's study of Emerson and Edwards. My primary purposes concern the two classic American sages themselves: if, as I believe, they are closer to each other than Miller would have admitted, then we are missing something important in both of them if we ignore the affinity.

True, nothing is more commonplace in Emerson scholarship than recognition of the tension between his practicality and his piety.[7] But "From Edwards to Emerson" has given comfort to those who would rather forget Emerson's pragmatic side. These days Emerson's detractors—of whom there are still a fair number, especially among devotees of Thoreau, Hawthorne, and Melville—are apt to be the ones who make the most of his interest in wealth, power, and success. It is not uncommon to find him at least briefly compared to Franklin, but the Franklin who is invoked in the most detailed and extended comparison that I know of is a one-dimensional figure, a flat abstraction out of Max Weber.[8]

In the back of my mind also is a sense that Miller's widely reprinted essay serves as keystone in an overarching framework of general concepts which for many people greatly affect the ways in which American literature is seen and interpreted.[9] What, one wonders, is the strength of the whole structure if the

[4]Alexander C. Kern, "Emerson and Economics," *New England Quarterly*, 13 (1940), 683, 681.

[5]F. O. Matthiessen, *American Renaissance* (New York: Oxford University Press, 1941), p. 66.

[6]Perry Miller, "Emersonian Genius and the American Democracy," *New England Quarterly*, 26 (1953), 43.

[7]In his *Emerson Handbook* (New York: Hendricks House, 1953) Frederic Ives Carpenter lists "*The Two Sides of the Face*" as the first major problem in Emerson biography and maintains, "There are not only two sides to Emerson's face and philosophy, but also two (or more) interpretations of each side. The best biographies are those which recognize and describe this dualism without falsely simplifying its complexity" (pp. 1, 3).

[8]See Jesse Bier, "Weberism, Franklin, and the Transcendental Style," *New England Quarterly*, 43 (1970), 179–92. Contrasting Emerson unfavorably with Thoreau, Bier reads the opposition of piety and practicality in the older transcendentalist as hypocrisy, self-deception, or confusion. Interestingly he ridicules Kern for having put a more favorable construction on Emerson's "ambivalence," charging him with having written a "simple apologia" (p. 191).

[9]I have made no systematic investigation of the reprinting of "From Edwards to Emerson," but its popularity in books of essays designed to supplement college and university courses in American literature is obvious. It is included in *Interpretations of American Literature*, ed. Charles Feidelson and Paul Brodtkorb (New York: Oxford University Press, 1959); *American Literature: A Critical Survey*, ed. T. D. Young and R. E. Fine (New York: American Book Co., 1968); and *Theories of American Literature*, ed. D. M. Kartiganer and M. A. Griffith (New York: Macmillan, 1972).

keystone is loose or out of line? This is a question I propose only to raise, not answer, except to say generally that I believe there is cause for concern. But let me, before getting on with Franklin and Emerson, briefly explain what I take to be the larger significance of "From Edwards to Emerson."

These days Emerson is much less apologized for than he was in 1940. If Thoreau seems to many to have given a more thoroughly satisfying literary expression to basic Emersonian insights and awareness than the master himself, the seminal power of Emerson in the development of a central tradition in American literature is now not only recognized but much more fully understood. The year after Miller's essay Matthiessen in *American Renaissance* demonstrated the fundamental modernity of the sensibility of Emerson and his illustrious contemporaries Thoreau, Hawthorne, Melville, and Whitman. And once the significance of Emerson's theory of language and poetics was more clearly discerned, the temptation to dismiss transcendentalism as moonshine diminished. Matthiessen paid less attention to the early native roots of the American renaissance than to its affinities with some of the baroque and metaphysical literature which the taste of T. S. Eliot and other moderns had resuscitated. But the net effect was very much the same, especially after Edward Taylor became better known and after Edwards's *Images or Shadows of Divine Things* was published by Miller and the Puritan interest in symbolism came to be more and more fully explored.

Something like what Miller called Puritan "piety, a religious passion, the sense of an inward communication and of the divine symbolism of nature" came to seem the motive being realized most powerfully in a great deal of American literature (page 20). Indeed it may not be too much to say that there gradually emerged out of the conjunction of implications in the works of the two Harvard professors—one focusing primarily on the seventeenth and the other on the nineteenth centuries—a theory or ideology of American literature which has won wide acceptance. It is a theory which sees the main tradition leaping from early Puritanism into the mid-nineteenth century and which tends to ignore much that came between. Miller made the vital connection between Puritan piety and transcendentalism with an enthusiasm and a flair for irony which have a lot to do with his essay's continuing appeal. What he suggests is what has been said over and over again since 1940 in discussions of major tendencies and developments in American literature: in essence that literature is not what we should expect it to be. It is not primarily a body of open straightforward, realistic, practical-minded, commonsensical expression, the embodiment of progressive dreams, but rather something private, cryptic, symbolic, mysterious, sometimes mystic, often nightmarishly fantastic. Obviously the irony implicit in what I am calling the ideology of American literature is congenial to the modern (and postmodern) sensibility and its dionysian distrust of the pragmatic and the merely rational. An inquiry into Franklin and Emerson therefore is to some extent an exercise in distrust of that distrust.

2. Franklin to Emerson

We may begin by noting that in 1962 Miller published an essay on Edwards and Franklin. Perhaps had he lived longer he would himself have completed what I hope to make clear ought to be seen as a natural or logical triangulation. As was to be expected, he found in Franklin the perfect foil of Edwards that so many others have seen and, in the contrast between the two "massively symbolic characters," a made-to-order representation of the split in Puritanism which he had posted two decades earlier. That the split still lived on in the mid-twentieth century he implictly demonstrated by showing his own admiration for Edwardsean piety coupling snugly with an inherent skepticism and irreverence. He responded with gusto to Franklin's independent-mindedness, his shrewd wit, his down-to-earth style and his ribaldry. He saw an understanding of Franklin as an important part of an understanding of America. And finally he saw a crucial connection: underneath the surface Edwards was "Franklin's brother."[10]

Why? Because of what Carl Becker had called Franklin's "disinterestedness." Miller observed that in the "most perceptive sentence yet written about Franklin," Becker had said "that it was no wonder he sought for his ultimate satisfaction in natural science, because only in the physical universe could he find a 'disinterestedness' equal to his own." Going on, Miller wrote that "one learns to appreciate that the actual charm of [Franklin's] writing is his disengagement from all the multifarious activities of his career. He could never have . . . written about them . . . in exactly the quizzical spirit he unfailingly maintains, unless he had somewhere in his intricate constitution an ultimate sense that all . . . local aims were subordinate to a larger one, in relation to which they were indeed trivial." In the end Miller sensed that Franklin the "master worldly-wiseman," like Edwards the "archspiritualist," somehow felt himself a "negligible finite in the face of a glorious incomprehensibility."[11] Thus piety and practicality merge.

Emerson, I shall maintain, felt and responded to this same quality in Franklin which Becker and Miller tried to define as disinterestedness or disengagement. The terminology may not be quite adequate to the elusiveness of the attitude in question. Were it not for the fact that no one shows less indication of having gone through a dark night of the soul than Franklin, Eliot's prayer from "Ash-Wednesday," "Teach us to care and not to care," might serve as appropriate text for the peculiar equilibrium one senses in Franklin. But let us put it this way, that Franklin's empiricism was something more than a commitment to scientific method; it was a receptivity to experience and its complex possibilities that *practically* speaking amounted to reverence—or to

[10]Miller, "Benjamin Franklin, 1706–1790, Jonathan Edwards, 1703–1758," in *Major Writers of America*, gen. ed. Perry Miller (New York: Harcourt, Brace & World, 1962), I, 97, 95.
[11]Ibid., I, 95, 96.

what Emerson might have called absolute trust, the self-reliance that is ultimately reliance on Nature. One thinks of the third paragraph of "Self-Reliance," with its paradoxical movement from the "iron-string" of "Trust thyself" to what seems a contradictory imperative, "Accept the place the divine providence has found for you, the society of your contemporaries, the connection of events. Great men have always done so, and confided themselves childlike to the genius of their age, betraying their perception that the absolutely trustworthy was seated at their heart, working through their hands, predominating in all their being." We shall be reminded of this reference to heart and hands a bit later.

To the author of "Self-Reliance," Franklin was quite clearly a great man. His name appears frequently on the lists of great men which Emerson compiled in his notebooks and journals.[12] And part of the greatness obviously was his capacity for feeling perfectly at home in the world. Emerson comments explicitly on the "extraordinary ease" with which Franklin's mind worked; he was "unconscious of any mental effort in detailing the profoundest solutions of phenomena & therefore [made] no parade" (*JMN* 2: 208). And in 1841 he wrote, "When the great man comes, he will have that social strength which Dr. Kirkland or Dr. Franklin or Robert Burns had & so will engage us to the moment that we shall not suspect his greatness until late afterward[;] in some dull hour we shall say I am enlarged. . . . This man! this man! whence came he?" (*JMN* 8: 126–27).

Franklin's early "Articles of Belief and Acts of Religion" are a clear indication of the coexistence in him of impulses that, for all their connection with the early Enlightenment, suggest Edwards and traditional Puritanism on the one hand and on the other Emerson and transcendentalism. He acknowledges himself as "less than nothing" in the face of the supreme perfection of the "INFINITE." And yet he conceives human happiness and pleasure to be part of the system created by that Infinite Being, who in Himself can have no regard for man. As elsewhere in Franklin, virtue and happiness are conceived of as bound together, though the logic of the relationship is quite unclear. Superficially this may seem to point toward the total secularization and hence vulgarization of the Protestant ethic and the notion that material success is demonstration of moral virtue. Or he may seem simply shallow in equating virtue with happiness rather than suffering. There certainly is a material dimension to the pleasure which this religious confession is so much concerned with: it involves awareness of a world in which "many Things . . . seem purely design'd for the Delight of Man"—though this emphasis, it is worth observing, represents a welcome awakening out of Puritan inhibition. But one suspects a kernel of deep awareness in the assertion that "without Virtue Man can have no Happiness in this World."[13]

[12]*JMN* 1: 193, 250; 2: 227; 3: 200, 357; 4: 36, 50, 315. Franklin's greatness was the subject of a draft of an early composition. (*JMN* 2: 223–24).

[13]*The Papers of Benjamin Franklin*, ed. Leonard W. Labaree et al. (New Haven: Yale University Press, 1959–), I, 102–3.

The absoluteness of the statement is what startles: *"no* happiness" except with virtue. This goes farther than routine neoclassical couplings of happiness and virtue such as the one in the excerpt from Addison's *Cato* which Franklin uses as an inscription to the "Articles of Belief." It suggests the surprising intensity of his personification of virtue a few weeks later in the third of the "Busy-Body" papers—the idealized figure of an American "Cato," a compound of "Innocence and Wisdom" dressed in "plainest Country Garb," whose moral force, apparent in "the Air of his Face" and "every Part of his Behavior," compels "Respect from every Person in the Room." And one thinks ahead also from "without Virtue . . . no Happiness" to Emerson's "All things are moral" and Thoreau's pronouncement from the tranquility of *Walden,* "Our whole life is startlingly moral. There is never an instant's truce between virtue and vice. Goodness is the only investment that never fails."[14] Franklin is obviously active rather than meditative, more interested in *doing* good than in contemplating the nature of goodness. And yet when he talks of the "inward Joy" of "ADORATION," one wonders for an instant who was the incipient transcendentalist, he or Edwards.[15] In any case his "Articles of Belief" represent the man of reason in effect throwing up his hands, confiding himself to the genius of the world, which is ultimately irrational or incomprehensible. This is the larger context of his empiricism.

In some passages Emerson sees Franklin as we would expect a transcendentalist to see him. In the lecture on Milton we hear, "Franklin's man is a frugal, inoffensive, thrifty citizen, but savours of nothing heroic." On another occasion he associates Franklin with the "vulgar Utilitarianism" of the late eighteenth century, content with "Common Sense" and incapable of transcendental "Reason."[16] But on the whole Emerson's response to Franklin is surprisingly positive. While most of his references to him in the journals occur in the 1820s and 1830s—and we may speculate that Franklin came to mean less to him in his later years—the frugal man of common sense also figured earlier as a "moral philosopher" and revolutionary (*JMN* 2: 208) and was clearly involved in the original formulation of some key Emersonian ideas.

To begin with, the American Revolution was a crucial event in Emerson's sense of his heritage. It marked for him an epoch of mental and moral as well as political liberation. In the same entry in which he marveled at Franklin's intellectual brilliance, he declared, "That age abounded in greatness," and he compared it with his own, in which "men . . . do not produce new works but admire old ones" (*JMN* 2: 208). In another early entry he wrote of "the cowed benevolence of" his own "dismal time" (*JMN* 4: 37). His dim view of the

---

14For the "Busy-Body," see *Papers,* I, 119. Emerson's statement occurs in the "Discipline" chapter of *Nature,* which speaks of the "ethical character" penetrating "the bone and marrow of nature." Thoreau's statement is from "Higher Laws" in *Walden.*

15*Papers,* I, 104.

16*EL* 1: 150; 2: 67. Even so, in the latter passage Franklin remains for Emerson "the clearest name" of his period, in contrast to "Rousseau and Voltaire, Diderot and other unclean democrats." For other less flattering references to Franklin, see *JMN* 5: 202; 6: 232; 8: 398.

present, so crucial to *Nature*, "Self-Reliance," and especially "The American Scholar," clearly formed itself against a strong sense of the preceding age as nonretrospective. "Where is the master that could have instructed Franklin or Washington," he wrote in 1832, going on to add, "or Bacon or Newton?" (*JMN* 4: 50). He reiterated the question in "Self-Reliance." He also transcribed in his journal the Latin inscription (by Turgot) from Houdon's bust of Franklin, which in English reads, "He snatched the thunderbolt from heaven, then the scepter from tyrants" (*JMN* 6: 208).

At the same time, one sees that Emerson's conception of the Revolutionary period is intimately tied to his sense of himself as a New Englander. It is not Jefferson or Patrick Henry he looks back to, but James Otis, John Hancock, Samuel Adams, and in that context Franklin, born only a few doors away from the Emerson house in Boston. And the Revolutionary group relate to Bradford, Winthrop, Mather, and Edwards. If there is any division in this heritage for Emerson, it is between the overzealousness of the seventeenth-century Puritans and the comparative moderation of their eighteenth-century descendants—a view, by the way, which Otis and Sam Adams make difficult to substantiate. The earlier period had seen lamentable excesses of bigotry and persecution; it was well that the original Puritan ardor had cooled down into the "*Good Sense*" which he at first thought Franklin, but then realized Gibbon, had called "as rare as genius." All in all Emerson valued his "Puritan stock" for its "vigorous sense, or practical genius" (*JMN* 2: 107, 227). Its piety he seems to have taken for granted. He was at one point, very early, disturbed by Franklin's reputation for skepticism, but before long let himself be persuaded—rather too easily, one is tempted to conclude—that the philosopher who stole the thunderbolt from heaven believed in immortality (*JMN* 2: 108, 208).

Franklin, it may be argued, was for Emerson a model of the American scholar. His life obviously taught the greater importance of "observation of men & things" over books as a source of knowledge. He and, intriguingly, Edwards were the early American writers who Emerson thought showed most clearly the stamp of a native American genius (*JMN* 2: 230, 197). As one would expect, he clearly admired Franklin's delight in proverbial wisdom. In Franklin's style, one suspects, Emerson felt himself in touch with one thing he was looking for in poetry—"the common": the "meal in the firkin; the milk in the pan; the ballad in the street; the news of the boat" (*CW* 1: 67).[17] "In a journal passage which must offend those who see Franklin primarily as the embodiment of smugness, Emerson observed that the "greatest men have been most thoughtful for the humblest. Socrates, . . . Alfred, Franklin, Jesus Christ, & all the Pauls and Fenelons he has made. . . . And, so keep me, heaven, I will love the race in general if I cannot in any particular" (*JMN* 4: 315). So Emerson apparently was not one of the readers put off by the

---

[17]Emerson makes note of aphorisms, epigrams, and fables by Franklin in *JMN* 2: 208, 237, 377; 4: 132; 6: 170.

addition of "Humility," with its attendant exhortation, "Imitate Jesus and Socrates," to Franklin's list of virtues.[18]

At times in talking about Franklin, Emerson balances him against an opposing tendency in a polar relationship, thus seeming to sever practical ingenuity completely from morality or spirituality. "Transcendentalism says, the Man is all," he observes, whereas "Franklin says, the tools. . . ." And in another passage he substitutes for the conventional head/heart dichotomy one between hand and heart, "the hand of Franklin & the heart of Paul." Yet even as he makes the distinctions there is a sense of an ultimate relationship, as is implied in the passage from "Self-Reliance" quoted above that "the absolutely trustworthy" being "seated" at the "heart" and working through the "hands." Both Franklin and Paul are examples of trust in oneself, secure "among gluttons & sycophants." And, "A master *and* tools,—is the lesson I read in every shop and farm and library" (*JMN* 3: 249; 10: 53, 54).

What Franklin represents for Emerson is the practical side of Puritanism, which for the most part he found it impossible to repudiate, however much he may have wanted to, because Nature is real as well as ideal, fact as well as spirit. The soul, at least in this life, is nothing without the body. The body has to be cared for, and taking care of the body or learning to cope with the physical demands of Nature is the beginning of the cultivation of the mind or spirit. Franklin, the journals suggest, belongs as much with the "Discipline" chapter of *Nature* as with "Commodity." As early as 1830 Emerson associates him with the phrase "the conduct of life" and calls him one of the "astonishing instances" of it. And the very next entry in the journal deals with the subject of virtue in a way strongly reminiscent of Franklin (*JMN* 3: 200).[19]

First comes an insistence on virtue as action, *doing* good, not just talking about it. The problem, as in Franklin, is method, how to produce virtue. And the answer is surprisingly similar to Franklin's. It is astounding to discover that Emerson may have taken seriously just that part of Franklin which most tempts the modern reader's laughter or derision, that "bold and arduous Project of arriving at moral Perfection."[20] Instead of talking about all the virtues being "comprehended" in "self-trust" he specifies individual virtues that are worth acquiring, starting with "Early Spartan rising," then "Temperance" and "fasting," after which he calls for "attention to . . . personal habits."[21] The habits that Emerson is most concerned to cultivate tend, it is true, to reveal his predilection for contemplation over action. If he has Franklin's list of virtues in mind, he seems to get stalled on "Silence," as he

---

[18]*The Autobiography of Benjamin Franklin*, ed. Leonard W. Labaree et al. (New Haven: Yale University Press, 1964), p. 150. Emerson elsewhere links Franklin and Socrates for their humility (*JMN* 10: 298) and also speaks of the latter's "Franklin-like wisdom" ("Plato; or The Philosopher" in *Representative Men*; cf. *JMN* 10: 482).

[19]The two entries were made three weeks apart but are closely enough linked in subject matter to suggest that Emerson probably reread the first just before or while writing the second.

[20]*Autobiography*, p. 148.

[21]As in "The American Scholar."

notes the value of the "habit of being sometimes alone, the habit of reading, the habit of abstraction in order to find out what his own opinion is, the habit of controlling his conversation, the habit of praying, or referring himself always to God." For Emerson, of course, piety ultimately transcends practicality. But the respect for a discipline which recognizes the close relationship of body and mind, appetite and morality, remains somewhat Franklinesque. He ends the passage with a sentence which sounds like something Franklin might have written had he tried to get transcendental resonances into Poor Richard's maxims: "Order has a good name in the world for getting the most sweetness out of time" (*JMW* 3: 200).[19]

Thirty years later the phrase, "the conduct of life" surfaced as the title of a book by Emerson in which the essay "Wealth" holds a position somewhat comparable to that of "Discipline" in *Nature*. Or, more accurately, "Wealth" is like an expanded merger of "Commodity" and "Discipline." It is crucial because it makes clear that the Emersonian ethic was the Protestant ethic in a highly exalted form, an effort, like the one implicit in Franklin's life and writings, to fuse piety and practicality, to maintain that work, virtue, salvation, and enjoyment of the world are functions of one another.[22] As the first two paragraphs quickly demonstrate, "Wealth" is an elaboration of the basic Puritan idea of the calling:

> As soon as a stranger is introduced . . . , one of the first questions which all wish to have answered is, How does that man get his living? And with reason. He is no whole man until he knows how to earn a blameless livelihood. Society is barbarous until every industrious man can get his living without dishonest customs.
>
> Every man is a consumer, and ought to be a producer. He fails to make his place good in the world unless he not only pays his debt but also adds something to the common wealth. Nor can he do justice to his genius without making some larger demand on the world than a bare subsistence. He is by constitution expensive, and needs to be rich. (*W* 6: 84)

Already Emerson's conception of the calling has become exorbitant and implies an openness to enjoyment which, like Franklin's, we do not ordinarily associate with Puritanism. With an expansiveness that suggests Whitman, he is soon saying that man "is born to be rich. He . . . is tempted out by his appetites and fancies to the conquest of this and that piece of nature, until he finds his well-being in the use of his planet, and of more planets than his own. . . . The same correspondence that is between thirst in the stomach and water in the spring, exists between the whole of man and the whole of nature" (*W* 6: 88–89). But the connection between wealth and virtue or discipline is never laid by. "The subject of economy mixes itself with morals, inasmuch as it is a peremptory point of virtue that a man's independence be secured. Poverty demoralizes" (*W* 6: 90).

<hr />

[22]Kern suggests the connection between Emerson and the Protestant ethic in *New England Quarterly*, 13 (1940), 683.

To find the way to wealth—what Emerson would consider "true" wealth—is to acquire transcendental discipline. Character is formed by honest labor in a calling, since "wealth is in applications of mind to nature" and respect for the laws of nature. It necessitates the formulation of rules, the creation of "a better order." Emerson's observation in "Wealth" that the "counting-room maxims liberally expounded are laws of the universe" is an updating of his famous Aunt Mary's declaration, "I respect in a rich man the order of Providence."[23] In sum Emerson sees a legitimate pursuit of wealth as consistent with the natural order, part of Nature's functioning to fully humanize man. The concept of economy ultimately involves the satisfaction of moral and spiritual as well as material wants. Dishonest gain is thus not true wealth. To the charge that dishonesty pays, Emerson would reply, it is an illusion; in the long run fraud produces material and moral waste, which touches everyone.

Emerson is close here to a central perception in Franklin, which develops with his realization that he could dispense with revelation as far as morality is concerned. Both men assume an ultimate connection between self-interest and cosmic well-being. Franklin's secularization of morality begins with his daring to think, as he tells us in the *Autobiography*, that "vicious Actions are not hurtful because they are forbidden, but forbidden because they are hurtful, the Nature of Man alone consider'd." Applied only to success in business, his belief that "*Truth, Sincerity and Integrity* in Dealings between Man and Man" are "good" for one may seem naive. But when that belief expands suddenly to the far-reaching hypothesis that, "all the Circumstances of things considered," moral actions are beneficial to one, he brings us to the wisdom of a world in which if everyone behaved decently to one another, everyone would prosper.[24]

3. Franklin and Emerson: The Name of the Game

What tries the patience of the twentieth-century mind is the way in which Emerson and Franklin sometimes seem to take the connection between wealth and virtue too much for granted or interpret "wealth" too literally. We are skeptical when Franklin says that "no Qualities" are "so likely to make a poor Man's Fortune as those of Probity and Integrity."[25] *The Great Gatsby* is more real to us than *Poor Richard*. The pursuit of success demoralizes—as much as poverty: that is our fear. Commercialism distracts attention from the higher values in Emerson's economics and virtually guarantees waste and exploitation. Emerson's daring is apt to startle us more than he intended when in "Wealth" he says, "I have never seen a rich man. I have never seen a man as rich as all men ought to be." For metaphor most of us would probably

[23]Quoted by Miller, page 29.—ED.
[24]*Autobiography*, pp. 114–15, 158.
[25]*Ibid.*, p. 158.

prefer Thoreau's curiously parallel observation, "I have never yet met a man who was quite awake. How could I have looked him in the face?"[26] Disinterestedness has its limitations, its proximity, through indifference, to callousness.

While Franklin and Emerson are polar figures, each is polarized within himself between the attractions of practicality and contemplation. There is a certain remoteness or splendid isolation—some call it complacency—in both, Franklin's gregariousness notwithstanding. He is much more involved in the day-to-day world than Emerson, but, as Miller and Becker maintained, not completely so. There is a casualness about him that sometimes disappoints us. Promising as the *Autobiography* is, for instance, as a record of self-education and self-liberation in a society moving toward self-government, he shows no signs of wanting to push his awareness, particularly his self-awareness, any further than circumstances seem to require. There is a point in the consideration of moral issues beyond which he apparently does not want to get involved, perhaps on the assumption that in the long run the practical differences are negligible. Openmindedness, his greatest virtue, comes to seem at times an evasion of the responsibility of being serious down to the deepest level. Thus his mistakes remain mere "errata," typographical errors in the little book of his life.

The happy side of this failing, if such it should be called, is that he is a less somber, less pompous wise man, seer, or lay preacher than he is often taken to be—which is to acknowledge the depth of his sense of humor, its inextricable tie with his wisdom. The complex and subtle Franklin who emerges from recent scholarship and criticism has more in common with Emerson than did Franklin the plain-style Puritan or no-nonsense apostle of reason and utility.[27] We see his irony looking askance at his own moralizing out of a wry awareness of human (including his own) limitations lodged within a broad vision of human possibility. He preached as much as any Puritan, but no one was more aware than he that he was not better than he should be—as he shows at the beginning of the *Autobiography* by the pain he takes to call attention to his vanity: he is writing basically to please himself. When we see him in effect thanking God for his vanity "with all humility," we begin to see the man in his humor.[28]

Like Emerson, he is sententious in both the good and bad senses. Both lay down rules of conduct in aphoristic rather than legalistic language, aiming not

---

[26]Henry David Thoreau, *Walden* ("Where I Lived, and What I Lived For").

[27]J. A. Leo Lemay's "Franklin and the *Autobiography*: An Essay on Recent Scholarship," *Eighteenth-Century Studies*, 1 (1967–68), 185–211, gives some sense of the emerging Franklin. The essay calls particular attention to Franklin's virtues as a humorist (p. 195). In a more recent article, "Benjamin Franklin," in *Major Writers of Early American Literature*, ed. Everett Emerson (Madison: University of Wisconsin Press, 1972), pp. 205–43, Lemay depicts a writer of great artfulness and subtlety, thoroughly accustomed to directing and controlling the attitudes and emotions of his readers through sophisticated fictional contrivances which frequently obscure or mask his real identity or motive.

[28]*Autobiography*, pp. 44–45.

so much for precision as for provocation, to startle the reader or listener into sudden awareness. Franklin's interest in rules, law, and order was perhaps fundamentally, though he scarcely realized it himself, a function of an aesthetic awareness, of his recognition that the way something is said determines what is said, that admonition or prohibition, effectively conceived or formulated, is liberating, not restrictive, illuminating, not stupefying.

A sage with a high sense of drama, he may be as much artist as scientist. It is true that as a man of affairs he generally took a practical view of the arts, in theory writing to inform, instruct, and persuade, putting a high premium on the most directly communicative qualities in style. *"Heavenly Father,"* he argues, "is more concise, equally expressive, and better modern English" than *"Our Father which art in Heaven."*[29] His devastating criticism of a song by Handel[30] puts so much stress on the words coming through clearly that one may wonder what, if anything, he heard in the music, whether he conceived of artistic expression as anything more than the direct transference from one brain to another of a few simple ideas—the utilitarian aesthetic, essentially, of the *Bay Psalm Book.* Yet obviously Franklin did not always mean business when he wrote. One finds him too often taking a delight in forms and formality that quite belies the virtual philistinism of his insistence on the purely didactic function of literature.

Consider, for instance, the artfulness with which he contrives a letter of condolence:

> We have lost a most dear and valuable relation, but it is the will of God and Nature that these mortal bodies be laid aside, when the soul is to enter into real life; 'tis rather an embrio state, a preparation for living; a man is not completely born until he be dead: Why then should we grieve that a new child is born among the immortals? A new member added to their happy society?

One may doubt the strength of Franklin's faith in death as a new birth, but something in him rises to the occasion. Having decided to use a conventional form of commiseration, he works the whole letter out with neat precision. The elegance of his final image of death—an invitation to an eternal "party of pleasure"—has the authentic ring of something he would have liked to believe.[31]

He uses standard flourishes like the letter of condolence or congratulations to help him define himself in various social roles, personalizing the gestures, of course, often giving new life to shopworn sentiments. On happy occasions, he sometimes mocks rituals that threaten to turn into empty formalities. Standard forms and models, neoclassic formality, rather than a sense of organic form, moved him. Yet he could tell when a form did not fit a subject and could play on the discovery, often making fun of himself in the process.

[29]*Benjamin Franklin: Representative Selections, with Introduction, Bibliography, and Notes,* ed. Frank L. Mott and Chester E. Jorgenson (New York: American Book Co., 1936), p. 415.
[30]Ibid., pp. 351–54.
[31]*Papers,* VI, 406–7.

Gallantry was his forte, especially with women much younger than himself in whom his interest was supposed to be more or less paternal. In response to a letter received during a winter storm he writes, "Your Favours come mixd with the Snowy Fleeces which are pure as your Virgin Innocence, white as your lovely Bosom, and—as cold:—But let it warm toward some worthy young Man."[32] Another time the "fatherly Advice" he offers this lady becomes not only slightly risqué self-mockery, but also a parody of the advice-giving routine on which *The Way to Wealth* was later to be based. "Be a good Girl," he writes.

> Go constantly to Meeting . . . till you get a good Husband. . . . You must practise *Addition* to your Husband's Estate, by Industry and Frugality; *Subtraction* of all unnecessary Expenses; *Multiplication* (I would gladly have taught you that myself, but you thought it was time enough, and wou'dn't learn) he will soon make you a Mistress of it. As to *Division,* I say with Brother Paul, *Let there be no Divisions among ye.*[33]

For Franklin the conduct of life, as commentators are fond of noting, seems to have involved his self-dramatization in appropriate roles as much as it did the daily discipline of forming steady habits. We may see "cosmetic" image-making in his acting out the diligent tradesman for all Philadelphia to see or his playing the homespun American in Paris. Perhaps Emerson would have scented hypocrisy or self-deception in his shifting roles, or at any rate interpreted concessions to public opinion as inconsistent with a self-reliant nonconformity. But Emerson's conception of self-reliance was not withdrawal into a narrow privacy. He knew about complicated selves from personal experience. Given his sense of the self as so much of the time shifting, oscillating in a world of illusion, self-reliance becomes for him something more than a routine discipline. The Franklin who self-consciously plays social roles, who "loves," as Benjamin DeMott says, "to stage virtues,"[34] and who as a writer speaks through numerous personae seems ultimately a compatriot in cunning of the philosopher who in "Self-Reliance" warns against a "foolish consistency," who in the same essay admits his willingness, if need be, to speak from the devil and who alternately identifies with representative men of such radically different persuasions as Montaigne and Swedenborg, the democrat and the aristocrat, the slayer and the slain.

From the immediate or existential point of view both Emerson and Franklin see chaos in experience almost as often as order and harmony. In theory, however, they regard the world from another viewpoint as well—from the aspect of eternity. And the two views blending together at times transform confusion into mystery and surprise. The world becomes an infinitely intricate and entrancing work of art. Or to shift to, and at the same time recast, Carl

---

[32]*Papers,* V, 503.
[33]*Papers,* VI, 225.
[34]Benjamin DeMott, *New York Times Book Review,* 5 July 1964, p. 19.

Becker's image of Franklin looking at public affairs as a game,[35] life in general becomes for both of these shrewd observers a game, in which the object is to discover the rules—and they are infinitely complex. It is a game in which one does the best one can on proverbial wisdom and fresh observations of nature—a parcel of partial, relative insights—and with some part of the mind enjoys watching oneself play, surprised by the tricks life plays and excited by sudden discoveries and occasional tricks of one's own. In this game fair play and trickery are assumed to be ultimately compatible.

Trial-and-error is the name of the game. Both Emerson and Franklin are empiricists, trying to learn from an experience which has its endless complications. In the *Autobiography* Franklin observes himself making his picaresque way through life, sometimes in control of himself and the situation, sometimes simply running in luck, sometimes being victimized or remaining largely passive—though willing—lacking a sure sense of direction, having to respond to events he has scarcely anticipated. And this life, even with all its spectacular success, has more than a little in common with the experience which Emerson analyzes in terms of fate, polarities, and illusions.

Given the nature of this experience, both men take refuge in cosmic optimism. The serenity or tranquility of Franklin seems more actual, Emerson's more theoretical. In both, however, there is an oft-commented-on coldness. Too much has probably been made of it in both cases, yet the coldness still seems an important link between the two. For if, as Miller maintains, Franklin's "boredom with humanity" is what makes him Jonathan Edwards' brother,[36] then it must make him Emerson's great-uncle as well. And Yankee reticence will perhaps come to be seen as an indication that the split in Puritanism divides the individual within himself as much as it divides man from man. While the outward eye is alert to the practical, the would-be "transparent eyeball" of the inner self, alone with what circulates as "currents of the Universal Being" winks (*CW* 1: 10). On the verge of becoming nothing while seeing everything, the Yankee knows enough to smile—as Becker sensed Franklin smiling at the signing of the Declaration of Independence—and hold his peace.[37]

[35]Carl Becker, in *Dictionary of American Biography*, VI (1931), 597.
[36]Perry Miller, "Benjamin Franklin, 1706–1790, Jonathan Edwards, 1703–58," I, 97.
[37]Becker, *D. A. B.*

Emerson in His Cultural Context

Lawrence Buell

To move from Edwards or Franklin to Emerson is surely an Emersonian way of doing history, however faithful it may be to history itself. For Emerson, institutions were the lengthened shadows of single men (W 2: 61); "a personal ascendency" was "the only fact much worth considering" (W 1: 263); and the import of history was summed up by the "representative" figure, the figure who represented humankind at large by embodying this or that exemplary trait of character in memorable form. In his major work on this subject, *Representative Men* (W 4), Emerson could easily have substituted Jonathan Edwards for Emanuel Swedenborg as "the mystic" and, with just a little more forcing, could have made Franklin stand in for Goethe, the "writer" as omnicompetent citizen of the world.

But he didn't. Although Emerson refers here and there to both great colonial precursors, he never accorded them extended treatment, nor would it have occurred to him to do so. If the triangulation seems more inevitable to us, that is because we have recreated the Transcendentalist moment as one episode in a narrative of the unfolding American and more specifically New England consciousness, featuring the handful of great individuals who have cast the longest shadows. This myth then becomes our history. Perry Miller's "From Edwards to Emerson" and William Hedges', "From Franklin to Emerson" can be seen as two stages in the construction of this myth. Miller's essay did not invent but was crucially influential in perpetuating the thesis that Puritanism was Transcendentalism's dominant gene. Hedges did not so much dispute this thesis as remedy its most obvious defect—Miller's relegation of the Enlightenment phase of American history to a negative influence only: to that which stripped Puritanism down to the bare essentials—by offering a New Englandish Franklin as a counterbalancing father-figure. Hedges' Franklin is a secularized Puritan transported to Philadelphia rather than an Age of Reason *philosophe* who happened to grow up in Boston. Miller was the father of what is now called Puritan legacy studies, the working premise of which has been that Puritanism contributed the main ingredient of American civil religion.[1] The form of Hedges' dissent shows the continuing appeal of the premise.

The purpose of this essay is not to rebut the Miller-as-modified-by-Hedges thesis but to supplement it by characterizing Emerson more particularly in relation to his own historical moment. Viewed in this way, he looks both more provincial and more cosmopolitan: a nineteenth-century Bostonian with a very limited, indeed quasi-amnesiac memory of American history who displayed at most intermittent interest in the major Puritan thinkers and in the founding fathers of the American nation, yet with an intellectual range positively global in scope—comprehending for example Persian and Indian literary and intellectual culture as well as Judaeo-Christian, Greco-Roman, and European. I hope to connect these two dimensions and show that the paradox of amplitude and myopia was to be expected of Emerson's immediate cultural context: the culture of Unitarian liberalism.

I

Emerson grew to maturity without leaving the greater Boston area, attending the predictable approved schools and entering the ministerial profession elected by his father and his grandfathers for six generations back. Though a mediocre student as a Harvard undergraduate and a seminarian at its Divinity School more conspicuous for taking sick leave than for his academic prowess, Emerson had connections good enough to secure the position of colleague pastor in a Unitarian church in Boston, the denomination's (and the region's) capital. In later years he was severe on Unitarianism's "pale negations" (W 10: 204) and its mercantile sponsors. Yet even after he seemed to have made a clean break with his past by resigning his pulpit and moving to Concord, he continued to remain within his original cultural environment. Although like Thoreau after him Emerson liked to think of Concord as a rustic seat apart from the metropolis, part of its attraction was precisely its nearness to Boston. Moreover, Concord was ancestral ground for him, the "fields of my fathers" (*JMN* 4: 335). Its senior Unitarian minister was Emerson's step-grandfather; Emerson's first abode there was with him at a family home, the "Old Manse" made famous in literary history by a later tenant, Hawthorne. Emerson's first major publication was a historical oration for the town bicentennial (W 11: 29–86). Most of his closest intellectual associates, the Transcendentalist literati, were also refined liberal religionists with strong Unitarian and/or Harvard links. The person who anonymously served as the model of bad preaching in Emerson's Divinity School Address, his most vocally anti-establishment dis-

[1]For a (somewhat jaundiced) review and critique of Puritan legacy studies, see Russell Reising, *The Unusable Past: Theory and the Study of American Literature* (New York: Methuen, 1986), 49–91.

course, was, just as Emerson soon became, one of the Concord gentry with whom he remained on good social terms.[2]

In short, Emerson maintained throughout his life strong and cordial ties to his region and its class of cultural confreres, although he somewhat belied and offset these by maintaining a wry, sometimes even shrill, critical distance. He is famous for having stated of his father's generation that "from 1790 to 1820 there was not a book, a speech, a conversation, or a thought, in the State" of Massachusetts (*JMN* 13: 115)—a pronouncement that, as Lewis Simpson argues, helped perpetuate a myth of the region's intellectual decline after Puritanism and thus pave the way for the Miller thesis.[3] (It is amusing to imagine Emerson helping to invent Miller, who then turned the tables on Emerson by using the Transcendentalist revival as an example of debased Puritanism gone wild.) But Emerson could not have imagined being brought up or living in any other state. In his mature work, a repeated leitmotif is the futility of traveling. "The soul is no traveller; the wise man stays at home" (*W* 2: 81)—that is his consistent doctrine.

Anyone who has lived awhile in a small, relatively self-contained community has met at least a few long-term residents, true thinking people, who are acutely aware of local pathologies both systemic and personal, yet have achieved a certain sage-like detachment on that spectacle—and on themselves, knowing themselves also to be deeply rooted there, partaking of and at times even relishing a good bit of what in other moods they satirize. Emerson seems to have been such a person, both as a cantankerous outlying member of Boston's intellectual leadership and as a participating citizen of Concord. Indeed, Anglophone literature throughout the world has often drawn upon this mentality: Jane Austen, Henry David Thoreau, Flannery O'Connor, Alice Munro, R. K. Narayan.

It would be easy to get carried away by this charming picture of the provincial sage, which is after all only one of many possible snapshots of Emerson, or any complex person. But it may help to bring into focus the central paradox to which I have referred: that Emerson's essays in effect constantly try to dislodge their audiences by transporting them throughout realms of space and time even as they keep urging us to stay put. A spectacular example of this is the first essay in Emerson's first book of essays, "History"—an essay that Emersonians too often skip in order to get to the more famous "Self-Reliance" that follows. On the one hand, "History" jabs at the consumeristic excesses of what Emerson calls modern nomadism. Ancient pastoralists wandered for their survival, but "in America and Europe" today "the nomadism is of trade and curiosity; a progress, certainly, from the gad-fly of Astaboras to the Anglo and Italo-mania of Boston Bay" (*W* 2: 22). Yet the

---

[2]Conrad Wright, "Emerson, Barzillai Frost, and the Divinity School Address," *The Liberal Christians* (Boston: Beacon, 1970), 41–61.

[3]Lewis P. Simpson, "The Myth of New England's Intellectual Lapse," *The Federalist Literary Mind*, ed. Lewis P. Simpson (Baton Rouge: Louisiana State University Press, 1962), 3–9.

discourse of "History" partakes of that same mania. "Boston Bay" is the only local reference in an otherwise heady catalogue of globe-circling names, places and world events, as Emerson skitters from Hastrubal to Caesar Borgia, Solomon, Alcibiades, Shakespeare, Burke, Thucydides, Xenophon, Pindar, Zoroaster, Menu; and transports us to London, Rome, Greece, Peru, Assyria, St. Helena. The pinwheel moves so quickly that its shape starts to look more solid once one gets used to the constant motion; and indeed the essay reassures us that every individual contains the universal mind and thus the whole residue of history within him or her. Each life reenacts the history of the universe. So why worry if we don't catch all those allusions to remote places, periods, actors?—Especially when Emerson tells us flatly that nobody "will read history aright who thinks that what was done in a remote age, by men whose names have resounded far, has any deeper sense than what he is doing to-day" (W 2: 8). Yet "History" is not on quite the same wavelength as "Self-Reliance." It is equally important to Emerson to keep the reader anxious with his dazzling array of historical instances; for the corrolary to Self-Reliance is the doctrine that "every mind must know the whole lesson for itself,—must go over the whole ground. What it does not see, what it does not live, it will not know" (W 2: 10).

In short, Emerson advocates a life-style of intellectual self-decentering here, of intellectual nomadism as it were, even as he encourages us to believe that the end of this wandering will be to bring us back home to ourselves. What is more, the journey that this and other Emerson essays model for us is not a regional or even national journey, not like Walt Whitman's tramps through "these states," but an international one, to Europe, Asia, and Egypt. To broaden oneself intellectually was to go to the eastern hemisphere. That was axiomatic for Emerson. A visitor to the Emerson household would have felt this immediately: its adornments were almost all replicas of European artifacts, like the engraving of Guido Reni's *Rospigliosi Aurora* that Emerson mentions in the essay (W 2: 16, 382–83). It probably would never have occurred to Emerson to include an American in *Representative Men*; that is the most basic reason for considering the arguments of Miller and Hedges as not quite historical.

To be sure, Emerson was quite capable of playing the cultural nationalist. Even fledgling Emersonians know that his address on "The American Scholar" ("our intellectual Declaration of Independence," as it is now often called, following Oliver Wendell Holmes)[4] contains the ringing prophecy that "Our day of dependence, our long apprenticeship to the learning of other lands, draws to a close" (W 1: 82). But such jingoistic effusions cannot be taken too seriously. Considering the typical posturings of early nineteenth-century American scholar discourses (the topic was shopworn well before Emerson took it up), Emerson's essay is more notable for its refusal to wave the flag.

[4]Holmes, *Ralph Waldo Emerson, John Lothrop Motley* (Boston: Houghton, 1906), 88.

Consider what he *might* have said about the triad of resources he ascribes to the scholar: first nature, then books ("for the scholar's idle times" [W 1: 91]), then action. This *looks* like a quite American recipe: (1) *nature*, the great American resource; (2) *books*, placed behind nature in recognition of the brash anti-scholasticism of a pragmatic people; (3) *action*, reflecting a democratic erasure of class boundaries such as to prescribe "the hoe and the spade, for learned as well as for unlearned hands" (W 1: 100). "The American Scholar" *could* have been overtly nationalized in this way. Yet it is not. The Americanness of Emerson's recipe, its special pertinence to his countrymen as opposed to European intellectuals, its potential value as a reformation program for democratizing the scholasticism of Europe—none of these ideas are brought out at all explicitly. On the contrary, to the extent that he does localize his remarks, Emerson speaks of his three-point regimen as if it were part of a wave of international democratization emanating from Europe: the spirit of the age rather than of his own nation or place.

Emerson's poetry, which experiments with personae much more than with meter or language, provides an interesting side-exhibit here. Emerson ventriloquizes a number of different voices besides his "own" authorial voice. Most of them seem exotic: the sphinx, Alphonso of Castile, Mithridates, Xenophanes, Brahma, the World-Soul. Only once does he use a local vernacular speaker, the voice of a Concord farmer, and then only to correct it at once in the voice of "Hamatreya," the earth-god (W 9: 35–37). Emerson's subject matter, often also the loyalties, may be local ("Because I was content with these poor fields, / . . . The partial wood-gods overpaid my love" [W 9: 141]); but the voices are cosmopolitan. Emerson is not content merely to stand by the "rude bridge" of his hymn commemorating the Concord Fight; he must encircle the world, as in his vision of the shot fired there (W 9: 158).

Emerson's contemporaries, particularly his local adversaries, realized better than we do how he sought to distance himself critically from his proper milieu. That is why the Transcendentalists came to be called the Transcendentalists: a name snickeringly applied to mean "German nonsense"—"the crabbed and disgusting obscurity of some of the worst German speculatists," as Harvard professor Andrews Norton put it, in the most strident denunciation of Emerson's Divinity School Address.[5] Emerson was steeped enough in provincial Anglophile Boston culture, whose philosophical discourse was founded on the terms and taxonomies of Locke's Scottish rationalist successors, to be well aware of the disruptively exotic connotations of "Germany" to the stolid Bostonian mind, and to feel comfortable about playing with that stereotype, as when he casually remarks in *Nature* that "broad noon shall be my England of the senses and the understanding: the night shall be my Germany of mystic philosophy and dreams" (W 1: 17). These allusions to the

---

[5]Andrews Norton, "The New School in Literature and Religion" (1838), rpt. *The Transcendentalists: An Anthology*, ed. Perry Miller (Cambridge, Mass.: Harvard University Press, 1950), 193.

German chimera sounded all the more ominous in view of Emerson's readiness to make his writing *sound* "German" by introducing unfamiliar terms or contorting familiar ones (like his revisionary interpretation of "miracle" in the Divinity School Address) and his reliance on an associative, "poetic" style in preference to a deliberate linear rhetoric.

It is notable that when discussing the key cultural influences of his age, Emerson was not inclined to do what most American historians of Transcendentalism of the past half-century have done: namely, stress its character as a homegrown product, as if still anxious to ward off the old charges of unAmericanism. On the contrary, Emerson was careful despite or because he knew it might affront to gesture toward foreign sources. In his lecture on "The Transcendentalist" (1842), his most direct—although still oblique—account of the mentality of the movement dating from its heyday, Emerson brusquely cites it as a well-known fact that Immanuel Kant coined the term "Transcendental" in retort to Locke (W 1: 339–40). This overstates Kant's anti-Lockeanism, and by implication Emerson's own closeness to Kant as model, for the sake of acknowledging the suspect German authority over against the Anglo-American one. This device of citational provocation starts a half-dozen years earlier, in *Nature*, Emerson's first book. The texts Emerson here quotes at greatest length are from Shakespeare and George Herbert, both unexceptionally safe icons although Emerson proceeds to do strange things with them. But when it comes to citing more contemporary figures, Emerson invokes for example "a French philosopher" (the mystic Guillaume Oegger), DeStaël (author of a popular account of German culture), Goethe, Coleridge, Swedenborg, the charismatic German healer Hohenlohe, as well as a nameless "Orphic poet" (W 1: 35, 43, 73, 70–72). From a contemporary Bostonian standpoint, these choices ranged from the controversial to the bizarre.

At times, Emerson's eclectic heterodoxy seems quite gratuitous. At the end of his 1842 lecture on "Man the Reformer," for instance, after charging that Americans "rely on the power of a dollar" and lack idealism (W 1: 249), Emerson cites as an unexpected counter-example the spread of Islamic power after Mahomet, "who, in a few years, from a small and mean beginning, established a larger empire than that of Rome," conquering much of its former empire although "miserably equipped, miserably fed" (W 1: 251). This decision to ignore the familiar repertoire of Greco-Roman or Judaeo-Christian anecdotes of heroic achievement for the sake of featuring the Arabs who brought the classical era to an end seems a deliberate unsettlement of standard American historical mythography. Emerson does hold out at this point the hope that America will achieve "a nobler morning than that Arabian faith" (252), but he sticks with Oriental exempla until the end of the lecture: an Egyptian proverb (253), an Arab quatrain (255), as he complains about "this great, overgrown, dead Christendom of ours" (255). Imagine an American writer of the 1990s appealing in the pages of *Time* or *The Christian Science Monitor* to Islamic fundamentalism rather than to the Puritan heritage as a way of purifying American national feeling. This Emersonian stroke in the Age of Manifest Destiny might have been intended to have some of the same disconcerting effect. Ironically, today's Emersonians are more apt to recall Emerson's invocation of the spirit of pristine New England at the end of another 1841 oration, "The Method of Nature" (W 1: 220–21), because it is a quintessential example of the Puritan jeremiad persisting into the nineteenth century, than the peroration of "Man the Reformer," whose eclecticism is actually more typical of him. In fact, "The Method of Nature" itself goes on to cite Swedenborg and "Ali the Caliph" as its two final authorities (W 1: 222).

It should be emphasized that Emerson did not confine himself to puncturing American provincialism by reference to exotica. At those times in his life when he literally went around the world, his instinct was to decenter *it*. On his first trip to Europe in 1833, Emerson saw several of his literary heroes. As he prepared to leave for home, he coolly declared to his journal that "not one of these is a mind of the very first class," and that "I shall judge more justly, less timidly, of wise men forevermore" (*JMN* 4: 78). As he wrote up his second visit for *English Traits*, Emerson praised England with subtle deprecation as "the best of actual nations" (W 5: 299)—meaning, in effect that England was (1) the country of the past and present only and (2) a country of the "understanding" rather than the "reason," its special forte being material progress. Emerson intimates that America, not England, is to be the country of the future (W 5: 287–88). Here and elsewhere, Emerson's temperamental bias was to let an influence act upon him to a certain degree and relish its magnetism, but then withdraw critically from it and strip it bare. (Young literati like Thoreau and Whitman whom he initially admired and then criticized were especially disoriented by this syndrome.) Had Emerson been a European writing for European audiences, he might have adopted a position like Thomas More's in *Utopia* or Montesquieu's in *lettres persanes* that would have permitted him to diagnose his culture from an Olympian perspective. Yet it would be misleading to suggest that his habit of assuming a critical distance from his cultural roots was merely a personal trait that would have manifested itself similarly no matter where those roots were laid. For it was a habit that can be seen as growing out of the same Boston Unitarian milieu that produced in its more radical form his fellow-Transcendentalists and in its more conservative form the Harvard worthies who wondered whether the ex-minister had taken leave of his senses.

II

For a certain self-decentering had been built into liberal Congregationalist culture from the start. Unitarians differentiated themselves from Orthodox conservatives by the greater degree of cosmopolitanism they tolerated: accepting belles-lettres as a potential source of spiritual inspiration, studying other religious traditions for their anticipations of rational Christianity, sending the first New Englanders to Germany to complete their training as prospective academics. Indeed, one of the rallying cries of the sect was anti-sectarianism—to the discomfiture of the more practical strategists within their ranks. Emerson hints at the local state of things in his 1841 "Lecture on the Times":

> I remember, some years ago, somebody shocked a circle of friends of order here in Boston, who supposed that our people were identified with their religious denominations, by declaring that an eloquent man,—let him be of what sect soever,—would be ordained at once in one of our metropolitan churches. To be sure he would; and not only in ours but in any church, mosque, or temple on the planet; but he must be eloquent, able to supplant our method and classification by the superior beauty of his own. (*W* 1: 263)

At first glance, it seems that Emerson is drawing a simple contrast here between local fuddy-duddies and the enlightened avant-garde, intellectual radicals like himself. But then Emerson's own prudence becomes clear from his last qualifying phrase (only *true* eloquence would succeed); and beyond that, the careful reader will extract from the anecdote a point Emerson suppresses, namely that there must have been an exceedingly open, nonsectarian liberalism percolating through the churches of Boston to allow an anecdote like this one to circulate: an openness quite at odds with the rigidity of the "friends of order." This openness is not necessarily creditable; it could have arisen from complacency or apathy, which by no accident are also Emersonian charges against the Unitarian establishment. But the point holds that for reasons either worthy (broad-mindedness) or unworthy (torpor), or a mixture of both, the Unitarian culture of Emerson's boyhood was more latitudinarian and relativized in its values than New England Congregationalism had ever been before. Emerson grew up in an intellectual culture for which doctrinal and liturgical niceties counted for less than eloquence: a culture that can be said to have produced the young Emerson's hope to "thrive" in the field of divinity because success therein rested especially on the power of the "moral imagination" (*JMN* 2: 238); a culture quite capable of listening with interest if not with uncritical assent to mosque and temple representatives.[6] Against that background, Emerson can be seen as undertaking the self-appointed mission of stretching the range of Unitarian urbanity and, in his more zealous or mischievous moments, to see if he could get a rise out of the "friends of order" by exposing their limits. Although sometimes hesitantly, Unitarianism led all American sects in pioneering the study of

[6]For further information about the place of cosmopolitan (self-)culture in Unitarian thinking and practice, see especially Daniel Howe, *The Unitarian Conscience: Harvard Moral Philosophy, 1805–1861* (Cambridge, Mass.: Harvard University Press, 1970), Chapter 7; and David Robinson, *Apostle of Culture: Emerson as Preacher and Lecturer* (Philadelphia: University of Pennsylvania Press, 1982), Chapter 1. Howe points out that mainstream Unitarian culture remained strongly Anglophile and Christian-moralistic; its liberalism is much more evident in what it gave rise to (e.g., Transcendentalism) than in what it achieved under its own aegis.

comparative religion and in its interest in the spiritual wisdom of non Judaeo-Christian traditions.[7]

Emerson's boldness in pushing Unitarian liberalism to anti-sectarian, relativist extremes repudiated by middle-of-the-road Unitarians owed much to European Romanticism, especially his friend Carlyle, whom one scholar calls "the pioneer of Comparative Religion in England."[8] In his early essays, Carlyle undertook a deparochializing mission in Britain similar to Emerson's in New England. Scoffing at the sectarian view "that no mortal can be a poet unless he is a Christian," Carlyle queries, Is this "not inviting the simple-minded . . . to ask, when Homer subscribed the Thirty-nine Articles; or whether Sadi and Hafiz were really of the Bishop of Peterborough's opinion?"[9] From this we begin to see why Emerson was called "the American Carlyle": Emerson too displays a whimsical brusqueness, a fondness for intellectual caricature, a Euro-Asian bibliographical razzle-dazzle. But Emerson's receptivity to Carlyle's comparatist critique of provincial sectarianism owed much to his Unitarian background.

The clearest demonstration of this is the work of Unitarianism's boldest thinker, William Ellery Channing, whom Emerson cites in the aforementioned journal entry as the model of the moral imagination. The church's most charismatic minister, who delivered Unitarianism's first major manifesto ("Unitarian Christianity," an 1819 ordination sermon), Channing was almost compulsively resistant to being categorized: "I have little or no interest in Unitarians *as a sect*," he wrote in late life. "I have hardly anything to do with them. I can endure no sectarian bonds." Such declarations, which Channing's Transcendentalist nephew assiduously extracted for his official biography,[10] help explain why Emerson called Channing "our bishop" (*W* 10: 576). Channing's essay "On National Literature" (1830) gives us a quite specific glimpse of how the paradox of provincialism versus cosmopolitanism inhered in Unitarian thought.

Channing dares to express higher hopes for American literature than Emerson asserts in "The American Scholar," for "Juster and profounder views of man may be expected here, than elsewhere." Yet its present output is puny: "the few standard works which we have produced, and which promise to live, can hardly, by any courtesy, be denominated a national literature." Apart from Franklin and Edwards (with severe deductions for his "vassalage to a false theology"), the American slate is virtually a blank. Committed to self-culture

[7]Carl Jackson, *The Oriental Religions and American Thought* (Westport, Conn.: Greenwood, 1981); Jerry Wayne Brown, *The Rise of Biblical Criticism in America: The New England Scholars* (Middletown: Wesleyan University Press, 1969).

[8]Ruth apRoberts, *The Ancient Dialect: Thomas Carlyle and Comparative Religion* (Berkeley: University of California Press, 1988), 3. See also Chapter 3, "The Perspective of Universal History," which helps explain Emerson's vision in his essay on "History."

[9]Carlyle, *Critical and Miscellaneous Essays*, rev. ed. (1869; Boston: Dana Estes, n.d.), 1: 27.

[10]Channing's remark appears in William Henry Channing, *The Life of William Ellery Channing* (Boston: American Unitarian Association, 1882), 427.

as he is, and believing that "the mind is not a local power" but contains "its spring" "within itself," Channing is not disposed to knuckle under to European fashions; "for example, we think that the history of the human race is to be re-written" in the light of republican principles. At the same time, Channing urges American readers to avail themselves of all the inspiration the old world has to offer, cautioning in particular that "our reading is confined too much to English books," and that "we should be able to compare the writings of the highest minds in a great variety of circumstances"—in which spirit Channing recommends for example Victor Cousin, whose "rash generalizations" he actually dislikes, since Cousin's "metaphysics" is at least provocative, "a better presage than the lethargy which prevails on such topics in England."[11] Channing anticipates Emerson in building his case from the following set of mutually inconsistent polemic gestures: valorization of the enlightened individual American's perspective; deprecation of the American cultural result thus far; and commendation of an international program of study that is to extend far beyond the customary British models, combined with an "American Scholar"-like warning against intellectual dependence. By turns, the American scene Channing describes looks like the hope of the world or a cultural wasteland; and the recipe for cultural achievement, by turns, looks like self-reliant intuitionalism or a course of universal learning. As in Emerson's essay on "History," "home" is a place of great theoretical and emotional importance for Channing, yet it appears almost as a blank spot on the cultural map; its resources are ideological rather than bibliographic. Foreign cultures are theoretically dangerous, but they supply the catalysts for American self-realization and are thus of immense strategic importance. So Channing urges as wide an acquaintance with them as possible, while at the same time counseling against undue influence. Indeed, as we see from Channing's ambivalent commendation of French eclecticism, a gesture Emerson aggressively extends, Channing is ready to extend the frontiers of American reading in directions normally thought dangerous.

Perhaps the most exciting feature of Unitarian liberalism, for Channing and Emerson both, was its power as a kind of omnipurpose anti-dogmatic solvent to loosen the grip of precedents of all sorts. As Miller puts it, with characteristic panache, "Unitarianism rolled away the heavy stone of dogma that had sealed up the mystical springs in the New England character" (page 25). The problem with this assertion, however, is that it insists that we imagine Unitarian liberalism as the agent that recaptured Emerson for Puritanism, instead of making possible an escape from the whole Congregational enclave into something much closer to eclectic pluralism. True, Emerson never did completely escape sectarian confines at the social level; but doctrinally his mature thought is best described as a mystical humanism jerry-built from disparate sources (Goethe, Coleridge, Carlyle, Swedenborg, Platonism,

---

[11]Channing, *Works* (Boston: Munroe, 1845), 1: 267, 252, 267, 269, 276, 277.

Christianity, and a digest of eastern wisdom), at best post-Christian, consciously privileging no one tradition.

The broader, partially accidental, consequence of Miller's intepretation is to make not only the figure of Emerson but also—insofar as Emerson symbolizes the beginning of developed American literary culture—to make American literary history as a whole look like a quite ethnogenetic, isolationist enterprise. Such was not Miller's intent. He wrote his essay at a moment when Puritanism had not yet been redeemed from the obloquy of H. L. Mencken and other critics of the previous generation. He wrote, furthermore, at a time when Emerson's European geneaology was taken for granted, and the claim of an Edwards-Emerson connection was the harder case to argue. Miller signals this at the outset in the way he frames his question: "Was New England's trancendentalism wholly Germanic or Hindu in originage?" (page 14) Miller's later work on Transcendentalism takes a more balanced view.[12] The vehement emphasis on Emerson's Puritan origins in the balance of "From Edwards to Emerson" probably reflected Miller's sense of occupying an extreme position. Today, however, that position has become the norm. Americanists today, in literary studies anyhow, are more accustomed to thinking Edwards-Emerson and Franklin-Emerson than to thinking Goethe-Emerson or even Carlyle-Emerson.[13] This is the result not simply of the influence of Miller and his progeny but, more fundamentally, of a division of labor within academe that has led Americanists to concentrate on American materials more exclusively than a generation or two ago. We need to be reminded that this form of amnesia was the opposite of Emerson's and Channing's: that Emerson and Channing felt much more at liberty to forget about the colonial period, much more anxious, despite their commendations of Self-Reliance, to know the cultural news and the ancient traditions of the eastern hemisphere.

The Emersonian paradox I have been describing in this essay—a pertinacious insistence on the benefits of one's own time and place versus an anxiously eclectic quest for conceptual models far afield is—of course a "postcolonial" condition, a mark of the hopeful anxiety of the intellectual in a new nation aware that "our American letters are in the optative mood" (*JMN* 7: 364), and determined to remedy that lack by an independent-minded ransacking of all available traditions that will not succumb to any form of traditionalism and least of all to provincialism.[14] Emerson was hardly alone

[12]For example, in his editorial "Introduction" to *The Transcendentalists: An Anthology* (Cambridge, Mass.: Harvard University Press, 1950) Miller states that the religious revival that he identifies as the essence of Transcendentalism found its forms of expression in "Cousin, Wordsworth, Coleridge, and Carlyle" (p. 9), though he also insists that "the youngsters had reached back into an older Puritan manner" (p. 11).

[13]For recent affirmations of the importance of these European links, see Kenneth Marc Harris, *Carlyle and Emerson: Their Long Debate* (Cambridge, Mass. and London: Harvard University Press, 1978); and Gustaaf Van Cromphout, *Emerson's Modernity and the Example of Goethe* (Columbia, Mo., and London: University of Missouri Press, 1990).

[14]"Postcolonial(ism)" is a recent coinage used with special reference to recently independent third world cultures, but a good deal of what is covered by the term/concept applies to the post-

among the major writers of the period in this respect. Thoreau, Whitman, Melville, Longfellow are cases in point. We see the kinship, for instance, in their shared practice of juxtaposing wildly different cultural frames of reference. A Native American saga written in a Finnish epic form (Longfellow's *Hiawatha*), a divine figure that collages Jehovah, "Saturnius," and "Old Brahm" (Whitman's "Chanting the Square Deific"), a totem animal redolent of Hindu, Zoroastrian, and Egyptian as well as Judaeo-Christian symbolism (Melville's *Moby-Dick*), a critique of Christianity from the standpoints of Greek mythology and Sanskrit scripture (Thoreau's *A Week*)—these are some characteristic results. These just-cited works strive to create new world artifacts out of original collages incorporating old-world traditions.

These traditions are not valued so much for their own sake as pragmatically: for their use-value in making an American story more resonant, though at the same time (and we can often see this in the casualness of Emerson's lists of foreign references) the Americans often like to handle exotic frames of references with deliberate roughness, even parodically, as if to guard against the charge of pedantry or derivativeness. So it is that John McWilliams, surveying the history of the American epic from the neoclassical dinosaurs of the Revolutionary era through the American Renaissance, finds that "American heroic literature succeeded only after" the failure of "serious imitative epics. . . . It was the eventual combining of laughter with sublimity, familiarity with awe, folly with heroism, neoclassic knowledge with the provincial's scorn for it, that enabled Melville and Whitman to achieve splendid serio-comic works of prose and poetry."[15] In more modern postcolonial times, roughly the same can be said of Wole Soyinka's adaptation of Euripides in his version of *The Bacchae*, of Tayeb Salih's use of Joseph Conrad's *Heart of Darkness* in *Season of Migration to the North*, of Derek Walcott's dialogue with Homeric and British imperial narrative in *Omeros*. The notorious casualness of Emerson's deployment of learning is another instance of this: "as crabs, goats, scorpions, the balance and the waterpot lose their meanness when hung as signs in the zodiac, so I can see my own vices without heat in the distant persons of Solomon, Alcibiades, and Cataline" (W 2: 5). This sentence grandly reaches out to tally the universe twice: first, the heavens, then the universe of discourse, in fulfillment of the epic quest Emerson has enjoined on the provincial reader: "We, as we read, must become Greeks,

---

independence phase of the United States and other ex-colonies. For a general study that provides the beginning of a framework within which to study American literature of the early nineteenth century in the context of emerging forms of literature in European languages worldwide, see Bill Ashcroft, Gareth Griffiths, and Helen Tiffin, *The Empire Writes Back: Theory and Practice in Post-Colonial Literatures* (London and New York: Routledge, 1989). For a recent application to nineteenth-century America, see Lawrence Buell, "American Literary Emergence as a Postcolonial Phenomenon." *American Literary History*, 4 (1992), 1–32. For a useful precontemporary study, see Benjamin Spencer, *The Quest for Nationality: An American Literary Campaign* (Syracuse: Syracuse University Press, 1957).

15McWilliams, *The American Epic: Transforming a Genre, 1770–1860* (Cambridge: Cambridge University Press, 1989), 6–7.

Romans, Turks, priest and king" (W 1: 5). But in the process of yielding himself to these potentially vast and awesome images, the speaker bends them to his will by the incongruity of vernacularizing Aquarius into "water-pot" and banging it against King Solomon.

Nonetheless, the postcolonial's conflicted quest to appropriate foreign models has a certain shamefaced quality to it. "All that Greek manure under the green bananas," complains Walcott's persona; "when would I not hear the Trojan War / in two fishermen cursing in Ma Kilman's shop?"[16] The imaginative power displayed in this quest to poetize one's native land is threatened by the borrowed vocabulary. Emerson knew this problem well. He lamented it especially under the guise of deploring modern man's refusal to speak his own mind. "He dares not say 'I think,' 'I am,' but quotes some saint or sage" (W 2: 67). Yet Emerson also wrote an essay in at least qualified praise of quotation that comes close to declaring allegiance to intertextuality ("Language is a city to the building of which every human being brought a stone; yet he is no more to be credited with the grand result than the acaleph which adds a cell to the coral reef which is the basis of the continent") (W 8: 199). There is no way to get around the contradictoriness of perspective here, the vision of an entirely original expression versus the vision of a global discourse, except to recognize that its prominence as a motif in Emerson was no mere personal mannerism but a predictable concomitant of an era of intellectual emergence and of the culture within which he grew to maturity, which itself was a symptom and harbinger of that emergence—sectarianism in the process of achieving a deprovincialization that rejoiced, to quote Channing again, in "the increasing intellectual connexion between this country and the old world," yet stood behind the proposition "let others spin and weave for us, but let them not think for us."[17]

From the standpoint of a much later era, with American literature long since matured into a force of its own, it is tempting to resolve Emerson's and Channing's troubled paradox for them, to answer in the affirmative Emerson's outcry, "Can we never extract this tape-worm of Europe from the brain of our countrymen?" (W 6: 145) So we retell the story of his era, relieving Miller's astringency with a dose of American optimism, as a chapter in the narrative of American cultural emergence that had its origins deep in the New England past. Nor is that narrative entirely wrong, despite the fact that Emerson and Channing sought to distance themselves from their native heritage as much as to align themselves with it. But this myth of history becomes more wrong than right as an explanation of Emerson's genius when it is not offset by the awareness of Emerson as an ardent bibliographical omnivore, earnestly believing that not New England alone but the whole world was to be his workshop.

---

[16]Derek Walcott, *Omeros* (New York: Farrar Straus & Giroux, 1990), 271.
[17]Channing, 1: 261.

The Dream of Greatness

Stephen E. Whicher

The best-known statement of the radical self-dependence Emerson required is, of course, his essay 'Self-Reliance,' in which he wove together an anthology of passages on this theme from his lectures and journals of the previous eight years. A childlike security in the dominion of Good is here scornfully rejected.

> Cast the bantling on the rocks,
> Suckle him with the she-wolf's teat,
> Wintered with the hawk and fox,
> Power and speed be hands and feet.
> (W 2: 44)

Security begins when a man cuts loose from dependence on any foreign force and lives wholly from within. 'The man must be so much that he must make all circumstances indifferent' (W 2: 61). Emerson's imagination is stirred with the thought of a radical recovery of natural freedom, a vigor of wild virtue released from the inhibitions of a society entrenched in establishments and forms. The essay is a Spartan fife to rouse the hearer from dreams of needed help and throw him back on his wild Gentile stock of courage and constancy. Virtue in this context is not purity but *virtus*, the manliness proper to man in his integrity.

The basis for his belief in the possibility of recovering such manliness is still, of course, the doctrine of the God within. The Trustee is 'the aboriginal Self, on which a universal reliance may be grounded' (W 2: 63). The essay calls on man to ground his life on this aboriginal Self and in this way to render himself invulnerable to all the exterior life. 'He who knows that power is inborn, that he is weak because he has looked for good out of him and elsewhere, and, so perceiving, throws himself unhesitatingly on his thought, instantly rights himself, stands in the erect position, commands his limbs, works miracles; just as a man who stands on his feet is stronger than a man who stands on his head' (W 2: 89). With this Power to draw on, men are 'not minors and invalids in a protected corner, not cowards fleeing before a revolution, but guides, redeemers and benefactors, obeying the Almighty effort and advancing on Chaos and the Dark.'

Such Self-reliance (the capital letter must always be understood) is clearly not the same in mood as the religious sentiment, the glad submission to the dominion of the law that we examined in the last chapter, even though both are mutually reconcilable inferences from the same doctrine. According to the second, the Soul within is the Universal, the One Mind that unites all men, the Reason or moral nature of mankind, in which all private peculiarities are forgotten; in so far as man obeys it he leaves his individuality behind. According to the first, on the other hand, it is an original intuition of the private man, a principle of independence, creativity and youth, the main-spring of all heroism and greatness; in this sense, 'the Individual is the World' (*EL* 2: 214). If the one stresses the divinity of the Soul, as opposed to the weakness of mortal nature, the other stresses the subjectiveness of the Soul, as opposed to all external power or authority.

'The subject is the receiver of Godhead . . . ; nor can any force of intellect attribute to the object the proper deity which sleeps or wakes forever in every subject' (*W* 3: 77). Thanks to his proper deity, the individual is free, entire, sovereign, master of the finite. In the past the Church—society—had been the mediator between God and the erring private man; now, with God within man, the 'me of me,' Church and society became a cumbersome distraction, useful, if at all, only in the way the State, perhaps all nature, was useful, as a means of educating the soul drenched in time to step into his heritage. Properly, the man is all.

This radical egoism is expounded with unusual sharpness in Emerson's characterization of 'The Transcendentalist,' his degree of dramatic disengagement in that lecture permitting him to dispense with protective qualification.

> . . . His thought—that is the Universe. His experience inclines him to behold the procession of facts you call the world, as flowing perpetually outward from an invisible, unsounded centre in himself, centre alike of him and of them, and necessitating him to regard all things as having a subjective or relative existence, relative to that aforesaid Unknown Centre of him.
> . . . All that you call the world is the shadow of that substance which you are, the perpetual creation of the powers of thought, of those that are dependent and of those that are independent of your will. . . . You think me the child of my circumstances: I make my circumstance. (*W* 1: 334–35)

Though less often dwelt on, in the whole body of his public writings, than his more moralistic and reverential reflections, this transfer of the world into the consciousness is the secret key that unlocked his energies. The revelation of what it meant to be a Man, of the unlimited resources of spiritual energy inherent in his separate and independent self, is the vision that charges his three challenges of the 1830's—*Nature, The American Scholar,* the Divinity School *Address*—with their immense store of force, and creates the unsettling impression they manage to convey that a revolutionary reversal of values is just about to take place. The magnitude and direction of the challenge may be shown by an analysis of *Nature*, his most sustained and serious attempt to formulate his philosophical and religious position.

Since *Nature* is written under several strong and not always harmonious influences—Coleridge, Swedenborg, and various varieties of Platonism—and since it discusses such an array of elaborately subdivided topics, one cannot always easily penetrate its rapid criss-cross of ideas and see its underlying intention. A comparison with the contemporary journals, however, makes plain that Emerson's inquiry into the meaning and purpose of nature is at bottom an effort to assimilate nature into himself, to reduce the NOT ME to the ME. The effort took two directions: one, toward the conquest of nature intellectually, by achieving her Idea or theory; the other, toward a practical conquest, a kingdom of man, by learning the lesson of power. Through most of the book the first is dominant; the aim of the book is to indicate an answer to the question, To what end is nature? His chief weapon for this conquest of nature is idealism, a word he uses in two senses: the Ideal Theory of the Locke-Berkeley-Hume tradition; and a more Platonic conception.

The first five chapters are designed to establish the dominion of Platonic Ideas over nature. A soon discarded Swedenborgian notion of nature as a kind of divine cryptogram, a mute gospel which man is to decipher, somewhat obscures this purpose in *Nature*, but it emerges clearly in a summary entered in his journals at about the time he was putting the book together for the press. 'The delight that man finds in classification is the first index of his Destiny. He is to put nature under his feet by a knowledge of Laws. . . . The moment an idea is introduced among facts the God takes possession. . . . Thus through nature is there a striving upward. Commodity points to a greater good. Beauty is nought until the spiritual element. Language refers to that which is to be said. Finally; Nature is a discipline, and points to the pupil and exists for the pupil. Her being is subordinate; his is superior; Man underlies Ideas. Nature receives them as her God' (*J* 4: 33).

Up to this point Emerson has not gone much farther than a Cambridge Platonist or a Unitarian might have gone, though he has undoubtedly expressed himself differently. He has asserted the primacy of Ideas, has called this world a place of discipline, and has read man's moral values into his environment. He portrays a man, however, still in a state of pupilage, environed with a parentally superior nature, even if she is centered on him; and he has done little to suggest that the common God of man and nature is not the familiar external Creator, playing his master role in the drama of Christendom. From this subordination he breaks loose in the last three chapters, using the sceptical sense of idealism as a lever. Here he accomplishes his real revolution. Outside is subjected to inside; the huge world comes round to the man.

First, by means of the Ideal Theory, he would lead us 'to regard nature as phenomenon, not a substance; to attribute necessary existence to spirit; to esteem nature as an accident and an effect' (*W* 1: 49). Nature is brought within the sphere of the self; man is finally cut adrift from the belief in any reality external to himself. But to affirm the lack of a reality outside was only half the truth, unless reality were rediscovered inside; so Emerson moves from idealism to spiritualism. 'The Idealist says, God paints the world around your soul. The spiritualist saith, Yea, but lo! God is within you. The self of self creates the world through you. . . .' (*J* 4: 78). Thus the final revelation, reached in the chapter 'Spirit,' is the oneness of man and the self of self, so that man, the self, can be considered in a certain sense not merely the pupil or the observer but the creator of nature. Here, of course, the distinction springs up between the universal man and the individual; as things are, the self of self seems infinitely to transcend the capacities of the individual. But the distinction is a secondary or relative one, between possibility and actuality, and not between two separate things; the thought that stirs Emerson is that God is essentially self, and that ideally or poetically the two should and can be identical.

This ultimate assimilation of God into the self is the vision of the orphic poet in 'Prospects.' Whatever the relation of these passages to the conversation of Alcott, they are clearly integral to Emerson's book and Emerson's thought. The orphic poet is a device for expressing certain of Emerson's insights too bold and visionary to be asserted in his own person. Where expository prose, tied down to common sense, falters, the freer and more irresponsible speech of the poet can complete the thought. And the thought the orphic poet expresses for his creator is the ideal identity of man and God.

'Nature is not fixed but fluid. Spirit alters, moulds, makes it. . . . Every spirit builds itself a house, and beyond its house a world, and beyond its world a heaven. . . . Build therefore your own world. . . . The kingdom of man over nature, which cometh not with observation,—a dominion such as now is beyond his dream of God,—he shall enter without more wonder than the blind man feels who is gradually restored to perfect sight' (*W* 1: 76–77). At the same time the poet spins a myth of the fall of man, to account for man's present compound nature. Emerson regularly moves into mythology when speaking of this duality—necessarily, since his philosophy denies it. Why is man not divine in fact as well as in nature? There is no answer from philosophy, but the poet can interpose a fable. 'A man is a god in ruins. . . . Once he . . . filled nature with his overflowing currents. Out from him sprang the sun and moon. . . . But, having made for himself this huge shell, his waters retired; he no longer fills the veins and veinlets; he is shrunk to a drop. . . . Yet sometimes he starts in his slumber, and wonders at himself and his house, and muses strangely at the resemblance betwixt him and it' (*W* 1: 71–72).

In this chapter, also, the intellectual and the practical conquests of nature come together. Why can we not discover the secret of nature? 'The reason why . . . is because man is disunited with himself.' We shall find a theory of nature when we achieve the redemption of the soul. And the same self-fulfillment will solve the question of power. The momentary exhibitions of man's proper dominion over things that we now glimpse in acts of heroism, in art and poetry, in 'many obscure and yet contested facts, now arranged under the name of Animal Magnetism; prayer; eloquence; self-healing; and the wisdom of children,' will become steady and habitual when the work of culture is complete, and 'you conform your life to the pure idea in your mind' (W 1: 73–74, 73, 76). Then will come about, intellectually and practically, the kingdom of man that, to the eye of Reason, is no mythological prophecy sung by a poet to beguile the understanding into faith, but is now.

The full revolutionary force of what Emerson in these later chapters is saying is obscured by his Platonic and moralistic language, even in the exposition of his least orthodox thoughts. He himself, perhaps, does not fully appreciate the newness of what he is trying to say and wavers ambiguously between transcendental egoism and Platonic idealism. His originality remains impressive. One cannot demonstrate any important influence of Fichte or of any other source of German idealism on Emerson, although hints and echoes of this way of thinking were of course in the air. Though presumably he would not have moved in this direction if he had not been prompted to do so by some indirect Germanic influences, he still comes to this faith independently, his will to believe such doctrine allowing him, without altogether understanding his own thought, to expand a few imperfect hints into a whole world-view.

His contemporary Theodore Parker knows little of this egoism, nor Hedge, nor Ripley, all three good German scholars; the two latter cling to what vestiges of historical faith their Unitarianism and intuitionism together may leave them; the former is simply an intuitionary *philosophe,* deploying all his scholarship in support of his grand design to try the creeds of the churches and the constitutions of the states by the nature of mankind and the constitution of the universe. Brownson again, even at his most transcendental, has a social consciousness quite foreign to this self-centeredness. Nor is there anything really similar in Alcott's high-souled talk of Lapse and Birth and Personalism, nor in Margaret Fuller's enthusiasms, nor even in Thoreau, whose sensuous and spiritual self-immersion in nature is quite unlike Emerson's desire to put nature under his feet.

Though Coleridge more than anyone else helped him to this faith, his own religious experience and feeling is very different. Perhaps Carlyle, heavily influenced by Fichte, provides the closest parallel, but even he sees a call to duty and discipline and *Entsagen* where Emerson, for all his moralism, sees the emancipation of man. Borrowing hints and phrases from all around him, responding with his uncanny sense for the key thought to the intricate cross-influences of his time, Emerson yet strikes one of the most startlingly new notes, all circumstances considered, ever to be struck in American literature, while hardly appearing to be aware that he has said anything unusual. The lesson he would drive home is man's entire independence. The aim of this strain in his thought is not virtue, but freedom and mastery. It is radically anarchic, overthrowing all the authority of the past, all compromise or coöperation with others, in the name of the Power present and agent in the soul.

This revolutionary reading of his discovery of the God within, as it is the most unsettling, so it is the most unstable. It could come into being at all, one feels, only because of his peculiar craving for self-dependence. And it is protected also by the very fact that it is not the only element in Emerson's faith, but one member in an ambiguity. He could proclaim self-reliance because he could also advocate God-reliance; he could seek a natural freedom because he also sought a supernatural perfection; he could challenge society with his heresies because he considered himself closer to the true faith than they; he could assert that the individual is the world because, thanks to the moral law, we know that nothing arbitrary, nothing alien shall take place in the universe; the huge world, which he dared to defy, was really on his side and would not, as it were, spoil his game. The dual necessity, at once divergent and identical, to be free and invulnerable shapes much of his thinking.

We are now in a position to chart, not too seriously, the controlling geography of Emerson's mind. His favorite image of a polarity is inescapable here, for the rationale of fluid, poetic thinking like this, which affirms without thought of consistency the truth of the present insight, must be dynamic rather than systematic, a statement of the controlling opposites between which, by some organic law of undulation, his mental life swung. It is only the avoidance of a tight little dogma, the preservation of its negative capability, that makes such a mind interesting, and the student must be careful, as the hostile critic conspicuously is not, to avoid in his turn reducing him to easy formulas.

I propose, as a rude scaffolding for this analysis, the sufficiently difficult image of two crossed polarities. The north and south poles, the major axis, are the conceptual poles of the One and the Many, the Universal and the Individual, faith and the rest of experience, Reason and Understanding, between which Emerson saw man suspended. And across this lies a minor axis, whose poles, shifting and blending into each other, are harder to define, the temperamental west and east poles of pride and humility, egoism and pantheism, activity and passivity, Power and Law, between which, again, Emerson's nature was divided. Most of his central convictions can be plotted in some manner in relation to such coördinates. At the top of the chart belong the quasi-mystical moments in which, as he put it, he is dissolved in the Mind; self-reliance is a northwest idea; the moral law lies northeast; what Santayana called 'normal madness,' and Emerson 'exaggeration,' is southwest in quality; the idea of fate, perhaps, southeast.

The game is easy and not very profitable, nor do I hold any brief for the number or definition of these coördinates; yet they have a certain value. Chiefly I would stress the analogy of a polar field. As with Whitman, Melville, and Henry Adams, we are dealing with a mind that makes any assertion of belief against the felt pull of its lurking opposite, the two forming together a total *truth of experience* larger than the opposing *truths of statement* of which it is composed. Such a mind of course has 'double vision,' but it has a unity, too, though the unity of the poet's world rather than of the philosopher's system—the organic unity of the whole field as it is successively explored in thought. Only as we feel behind Emerson's rapt affirmations of the Soul, for example, the world of practical fact, which they deny *because it is also true*, can we gauge the quality of his thought. In the same way the vigor with which he insists today on freedom derives in part from his anticipation of the vigor with which tomorrow he will insist on law.

'Be yourself.' 'Be genuine.' 'My life is a May game, I will live as I like.' 'I would write on the lintels of the door-post, *Whim*' (*J* 5: 215; *W*: 2: 51). Such declarations of unconditional independence best express the deepest drive of his nature, a drive he felt was sanctioned by the discovery of his proper deity. Yet his egoistic rebellion in the 1830's could not have announced, as did Whitman's,

> I harbor for good or bad, I permit to speak at every hazard,
> Nature without check with original energy.[1]

'Be yourself' meant to Emerson 'Be your potential self.' The old longing for a change of nature, prompted by the early clash of his exorbitant ambition and his incapacity, was only intensified by his discovery that the grace and power of God, from which he had been taught to expect a rebirth to spring, was part or parcel of his own soul by nature. The principle on which he set out to base his life—'Live from within'—was not a means of carefree liberation, but of strenuous and radical self-renewal.

We feel, then, for all the release they hail, a continuing tension stiffening his journals and lectures of the period. To be a 'true and free man' was a challenging, a heroic undertaking. 'The air . . . invites man with provoking indifference to total indolence and to immortal actions. . . . the vast Eternity of capacity, of freedom, opens before you, but without a single impulse. . . . It demands something godlike in him who has cast off the common yokes and motives of humanity, and has ventured to trust himself for a taskmaster. High be his heart, faithful his will, vast his contemplations, that he may truly be a world, society, law to himself; that a simple purpose may be to him as strong as iron necessity is to others.' Generally, as was his habit when under pressure, the effort received moralistic formulation, particularly in the first years after he left the Second Church. '. . . to govern my passions with absolute sway is the work I have to do,' he wrote in 1831, and repeatedly his

---

[1]Whitman, "Song of Myself," *Leaves of Grass* (1892 edition), section 1.—Ed.

language later is reminiscent of this Unitarian aspiration, through rectitude, to 'Likeness to God' (J 3: 319, 285; 2: 386).

Yet his true goal was not really a Stoic self-mastery, nor Christian holiness, but rather something more secular and harder to define—a quality he sometimes called *entirety*, or *self-union*. His aim, in Thoreau's terms, was to live deliberately, to seize the nick of time. The common experience of life, for him as for us, was of a succession of occasions, routine or unexpected, that overtook the individual like the scenes that follow one another outside the window of a moving train. The initiative lay with what he called 'the exterior life,' the twin deities of Time and Chance; the individual adapted himself to them as best he could, in an eternal improvisation, formlessly strewn with half-forgotten themes and abandoned developments (J 4: 14). To Emerson, as to Thoreau, this was superficial and unnecessary. The individual should somehow dominate his destiny, live so entirely from within himself that he, as it were, initiated each new occasion as it arrived. Only then, no longer 'drunk with the opium of Time and Custom,' would he, as he once put it, ascend above his fate and work down upon his world (J 4: 243).

This self-sufficient unity or wholeness, transforming his relations with the world about him, is, as I read him, the central objective of the egoistic or transcendental Emerson, the prophet of Man created in the 1830's by his discovery of the extent of his own proper nature. This was what he meant by 'sovereignty,' or 'mastery,' or the striking phrase, several times repeated, 'the erect position.' To enter for good the sanctuary of a free and absolute self-direction, such as he glimpsed in creative moments of insight and enthusiasm, was then his consuming ambition. 'We are very near to greatness: one step and we are safe: can we not take the leap?'

To take the leap into greatness he had to overcome two radical difficulties: the inconsecutiveness of his own moods, the impossibility of preserving the moments in which he felt his unity with the power within him; and the necessity of dealing with an outside world that remained obdurately independent of his will. . . .

'Society is, as men of the world have always found it, tumultuous, insecure, unprincipled. Society is cajoled and cowed and betrayed. . . . Society must come again under the yoke of the base and selfish but the individual heart faithful to itself is fenced with a sacred Palisado not to be traversed or approached unto, and is free forevermore' (*EL* 2: 186). The opposite and enemy of the sovereign self, as Emerson recognized in 'Self-Reliance,' is the community. The voice of cherub scorn for society that speaks in the above lecture of 1837 could be matched or exceeded by many similar passages dating from about that time. The shock of the 1837 depression, in particular, seems to have moved him to an open defiance. Himself sheltered from the worst of the blast, as it turned out, he responded to the stir in the air with a kind of holy joy. 'I see a good in such emphatic and universal calamity as the times bring[:] That they dissatisfy me with society. . . . Behold the boasted world has come to nothing. Prudence itself is at her wits' end.

'Pride, and Thrift, and Expediency, who jeered and chirped and were so well pleased with themselves, and made merry with the dream, as they termed it, of Philosophy and Love,—behold they are all flat, and here is the Soul erect and unconquered still. What answer is it now to say, It has always been so? . . . Let me begin anew; let me teach the finite to know its master. Let me ascend above my fate and work down upon my world' (*J* 4: 241–43).

Phrases from this passage in his journal appear in the address he made, in Alcott's place, at the Greene St. School in Providence in the summer of 1837, and in the first lecture of his next winter's course on *Human Culture* he spoke out sharply and publicly against the tyranny of society.

> Man, upright, reasoning, royal man, the master of the lower world, cannot be found, but instead—a deformed Society which confessedly does not aim at an ideal integrity, no longer believes it possible, and only aims by the aid of falsehoods at keeping down universal uproar, at keeping men from each other's throats. . . . A universal principle of compromise has crept into use. A Routine which no man made and for whose abuses no man holds himself accountable tyrannizes over the spontaneous will and character of all the individuals. . . . We are overpowered by this great Actual which, by the numbers, by the extent, by the antiquity lost in darkness of its arrangements, daunts our resolution and though condemned by the mind yet we look elsewhere in vain for a realized reform and we say, This is the way of the World, this is necessary, and we accept the yoke and accommodate our feet to the treadmill. . . .
>
> [But] Before the steady gaze of the Soul, the whole life of man, the societies, laws, and property and pursuits of men, and the long procession of history, do blench and quail. Before this indomitable soul ever fresh and immortal the aged world owns its master. . . . And the clear perception of a single soul that somewhat universally allowed in society is wrong and rotten, is a prophecy as certain that sooner or later that thing will fall, as if all creatures arose and cried out, It shall end. (*EL* 2: 218–20)

Although, in sounding this radical note, Emerson was certainly not alone— was, indeed, caught up in a rising wave of social ferment in his region—in his case it had deep personal roots. It grew from and continued the controversy he began with his society—or, more accurately, with the idea or phantom of society within himself—when he resigned his Boston charge. His journals record a long struggle between his ingrained sense of dependence on, and obligation to, society, and his stubborn resolve at all costs to be his own master. His resignation, though already stemming from this conflict, did not resolve it. On the contrary, that single overt act of self-reliance, as it determined the course of his outward life, so it had long repercussions in the recesses of his own mind. Not until 1842, at least, ten years after his apostasy, could he be said to have achieved a real inner equilibrium; and it is possible to argue that not until the flattering invitations that resulted in his second trip to England in 1847–48, and that busy tour itself, had demonstrated to him beyond doubt that he *had* achieved a leading position in society, was he able at last to rest from his old anxiety.

His rebellion against the dominion of society encountered two main inner obstacles: his fear of solitude, and his sense of responsibility.

Balancing his centrifugal drive is a centripetal one, a craving for unanimity and affection. As John Bard McNulty has brought out,[2] there is a latent warmth of humanity, and a concealed reference to many actual passages of friendship, beneath the surface coldness of his essay 'Friendship,' for all its austere conclusion that we walk alone in the world. So, after transcribing his essay 'Love' for the printer, Emerson confessed its inadequateness. 'I, cold because I am hot,—cold at the surface only as a sort of guard and compensation for the fluid tenderness of the core,—have much more experience than I have written there, more than I will, more than I can write' (*J* 5: 411). Against Emerson's lofty dismissal of the half-gods we must set his loyalty to the old affections of family—his devotion to his brother Charles, to Ellen Tucker, to his son Waldo, the long and loving companionship with 'mine Asia,'—all of which amply demonstrate his capacity for affection, at least within his own clan.

Beyond the family circle, however, his craving for friendship and love seldom found adequate satisfaction. His relations with Alcott, with Carlyle, with Caroline Sturgis, let alone Thoreau or Margaret Fuller, were all disappointing at last, and he could only conclude sadly, 'Baulked soul! . . . Man is insular and cannot be touched' (*J* 4: 238). For all the fluid tenderness at the core, invisible repulsions usually constrained him to awkwardness and aloofness with other men and denied his wish for companionship adequate overt expression, until by revulsion he felt like the transparently anonymous humorist in 'Society and Solitude' who, as he quotes him, is 'only waiting to shuffle off my corporeal jacket to slip away into the back stars, and put diameters of the solar system and sidereal orbits between me and all souls. . . .' (*W* 7: 5)

But the love at the heart, checked in one place, broke out elsewhere. For human relations Emerson substitutes ideal relations. The essay 'Friendship,' for example, in the end paints an ideal of friendship scarcely any human relation could realize and can end only with the 'sublime hope . . . that elsewhere, in other regions of the universal power, souls are now acting, enduring and daring, which can love us and which we can love.' So the essay 'Love,' for all its initial deification of persons, teaches, as the conclusion of 'Friendship' put it, 'True love transcends the unworthy object and dwells and broods on the eternal . . .' (*W* 2: 213, 216). The pattern these essays obey is habitual to Emerson. From the particular, the personal, the actual, he moves to the general, the impersonal, the ideal; the love unsatisfied on the level of persons is devoted to thoughts.

---

[2]"Emerson's Friends and the Essay on Friendship," *New England Quarterly*, 19 (1946), 390–94.—ED.

The Emerson the world encountered was therefore usually half and the lesser half of the man. Apart from men he lived an intense emotional life they could seldom see or share, except as he brought its fruits to them in his lectures and essays, or as they obscurely felt its aura surrounding his uncompanionable presence. Yet he also felt, often acutely, that such solitude, rich though it was, still cut him off from reality, was even not real living at all. Beside the life of thought in which he was at home was another life of association with other men from which he was debarred. A proper life would unite the two, but in his experience they were antithetical. *The American Scholar,* for example, written to demonstrate the social importance of 'Man Thinking,' betrays in its praise of action an underlying dissatisfaction with the scholar's life of solitary thought. 'I run eagerly into this resounding tumult. I grasp the hands of those next me, and take my place in the ring to suffer and to work. . . .' (W 1: 95). Unless the scholar acts, he wrote in 'Literary Ethics,' he is 'incomplete, pedantic, useless, ghostly' (W 1: 177). Recurrently Emerson felt the loss of reality inherent in his detachment and repudiated his ghostly life for one in contact with real men.

But his wish for independence clashed also with his sense of obligation to be useful to the society he repudiated. He was not merely, by vocation, a sauntering poet, but a teacher, with grave social responsibilities to discharge. After leaving the ministry, for all the welcome he gave his promised freedom, he was deeply disturbed at the threatened loss of a recognized place among his fellows, and balanced his acknowledgment of his organic solitude with repeated attempts to demonstrate to his own satisfaction that, for all that he obeyed only his instincts, he still possessed an organic relation to society and was not an outcast or egotist, shirking his responsibilities in some private palace of art.

This concern was the price he paid for rejecting an established vocation, a rebellion that left him, even in his own eyes, without an evident place in New England life and so called into question the basis of his self-respect. A man's life could fairly be judged, he agreed, by the answer he was able to give to the question, 'Where is the fruit?' (W 3: 83). If by 1844 he thought he had learned to find a private fruit sufficient, less than seven years before he still felt a demand for an overt effect, a life of active usefulness.

This sense of an obligation to serve, clashing with his wish for freedom, generated characteristically a preoccupation with 'great action.' A life in union with the Soul would flood him with a power of heroic performance that would sweep him and his society together along new paths. His inner freedom, he felt, could be guaranteed only by outward capacity. The duality of his life did not then, as it did later, seem to lie between a busybody activity and a passive worship of Ideas, but between a habitual existence as a 'surprised spectator and learner' and inspired moments in which, in his phrase, 'I am a Doer' (J 4: 248–49). His imagination became filled with images of past doers—Napoleon, for example, fascinated him—and with various large-scale abstract character-types—The Reformer, The Scholar, The Hero—shadowy outlines of the possible great emancipating roles he felt he had it in him to play, with God his prompter. Gazing into the magic mirror of his intuition, Emerson beheld Man in his native power, a great responsible Thinker and Actor, whose 'victorious thought' one after another 'comes up with and reduces all things, until the world becomes at last only a realized will,—the double of the man' (W 1: 40).

No task so caught Emerson's imagination as that of drawing the portrait of the great man. He ransacked the pages of history for examples of greatness and devoted an early lecture series, and eventually a book, to the characters of great men. The example of the heroes and leaders of the past gave some color of actuality to his vision of great action. 'In a century, in a millennium, one or two men; that is to say, one or two approximations to the right state of every man. . . . Each philosopher, each bard, each actor has only done for me, as by a delegate, what one day I can do for myself' (W 1: 106, 108). The use of great men was to reveal us to ourselves. 'We wish to hold these fellow minds as mirrors before ourselves to learn the deepest secret of our capacity.' 'Then I dare; I also will essay to be' (W 1: 161).

One quality they all shared was force. The great man 'is effective, generative; . . . he is constructive, fertile, magnetic. . . .' (W 4: 7). He has tapped the springs of power. This is a quality shared by all the great, that makes them such, whatever the particular variety of possible greatness they illustrate; they are primary or affirmative men. In his early lecture series on *Biography* Emerson flatly ascribes this force to the moral sentiment. Luther is great, for example, because 'He achieved a Spiritual revolution by spiritual arms alone,' by a 'sublime reliance on the simple force of truth.' So the lecture on Fox, the most personal of the five, portrays a man who, trusting wholly to the religious sentiment, outstripped the gifted, the cultivated, and the powerful and shook, by virtue of 'this enormous assertion of spiritual right, all the tyrannies, all the hierarchies, all the artificial ranks of the world.' It is an early sketch of the American scholar.

Yet he could not entirely overlook the evident distinction between the religious sentiment and the power to act. The moral sentiment could certainly inspire, but to conquer and prevail took more than ecstasy. To be a doer demands the knack, or character, or magnetism, or whatever personal force it is that gives one man ascendancy over another. Rationalized here and elsewhere as moral supremacy, in the end it could seem to him simply an arbitrary gift of destiny.

> I hold it of little matter
> Whether your jewel be of pure water,
>
> .   .   .   .
> But whether it dazzle me with light.
> (W 9: 32)

In his reflections on heroism we find his clearest recognition of the unsanctified aspect of practical power.

In a review in 1850 of *Representative Men*, Émile Montégut defined Emerson's idea of greatness as *antique*, a celebration of the great soul by nature, and rejected this easy greatness in favor of the Christian ideal of greatness by achievement and suffering, like that of Christ, an ideal he believed he found in Carlyle's *Heroes and Hero Worship*.[3] Whatever the justice of this comparison, there can be little question that the antique Roman was the original model of Emerson's natural hero. The 'Doctor and historian' of heroism was Plutarch (*W* 1: 248). 'I must think we are more deeply indebted to him than to all the ancient writers. . . . A wild courage, a Stoicism not of the schools but of the blood, shines in every anecdote, and has given that book its immense fame.'

Emerson's clearest celebration of this antique Stoicism of the blood is his essay 'Heroism,' originally one of a diptych of lectures portraying respectively 'Heroism' and 'Holiness.' The subject of the second lecture was the saint, 'the state of man under the dominion of the moral sentiment.' 'The saint . . . is a man who, accustomed to revere the moral sentiment as a law, discriminates it in his thinking from his private self; cuts it off; puts it far from him; calls it by another name; and attributes to himself none of its infinite worthiness; but contrasts the animal tendencies in him, with this overpowering worth; and so, is divided; and calls one, God, and worships it, and calls the other, himself, and flouts it' (*EL* 2: 340–41). The hero, on the other hand, was 'a concentration and exaltation of the Individual.' Heroes 'have never discriminated between their *individual* and what philosophy denominates their *universal* nature. . . .' The hero is man active, not philosophical; he is will without thought. 'There is somewhat not philosophical in heroism; there is somewhat not holy in it; it seems not to know that other souls are of one texture with it; it has pride; it is the extreme of individual nature' (*W* 2: 250). Thus the spiritual perception of the scholar is eliminated by definition from Emerson's portrait of the hero, which becomes in its very partiality a clearer picture of the active element in Emerson's ideal of greatness, provided we bear in mind Emerson's own reservation, that '[holiness] overlooks [heroism], and gives a more precise account of it.'

'. . . [man] is born into the state of war' (*W* 2: 249). There is a certain ferocity in nature—Emerson mentions lock-jaw, hydrophobia, insanity, war, plague, cholera, and famine—which a man must withstand; and there is, more real to Emerson, a ferocity in society, too, toward its nonconformists, which a man worth his salt must face and defy. The saint transcends these evils through faith. But most men need something of the saint and something of the hero to see them through all the crises of their active life. For them a sufficient faith is a matter of a very few hours in a lifetime; for the rest they must fall back on their own resources of character. The hero is one whose own resources are all he needs.

[3]Émile Montégut, "Du culte des Heros selon Emerson et Carlyle," *Revue des Deux Mondes*, 20, n.s., vii (1 July 1850, suppl. 15 August 1850), 722–37.—ED.

His leading trait is an unshakable will. The opposition of men will not turn him aside from his purposes; the hero judges for himself. So he scorns all that men call prudence. Most men lead lives of petty calculation and low aims, pursue worldly prizes and creature comforts, dote on health, or wealth, or reputation. The hero lives on a plane above all this, where such practical discretion has no meaning. Heroism 'is a selftrust which slights the restraints of prudence, in the plenitude of its energy and power to repair the harms it may suffer.' Emerson cannot make too sharp the distinction between the heroic and the common life. 'There seems to be no interval between greatness and meanness. When the spirit is not master of the world, then it is its dupe' (W 2: 250, 252).

Above all, heroism is power: the hero is master of the world. He has the promptitude, the energy, the instinct of success that allows him to set aside ordinary prudence and bend events to his will. The ease and hilarity of the hero, of which Emerson makes a particular point, is a symptom of his mastery; in an Age of Reflection the hero 'feels and never reasons, and therefore is always right. . . .' (W 2: 250). Emerson had been reading a good deal about Napoleon before he wrote this lecture, and his later essay on that man of the world is his most extended tribute to those attributes of greatness which were polar to his own.

Now these traits of the hero, and particularly his practical mastery, bear no obvious or necessary relation to virtue. Though the hero is a doer, it does not follow that he must be a do-gooder. Napoleon, Emerson came to concede, was a great man, but he never called him a good one. The hero's secret impulse need not be virtuous, it need only be successful. Nevertheless, the instinctive act of faith by which he defines the hero as the soldier of virtue is central to his idea of heroism: 'The essence of greatness is the perception that virtue is enough' (W 2: 255). Generally, outside this essay, he does not make such a sharp distinction between heroism and holiness. The hero's impulse, he usually holds, is in fact one with the moral sentiment; in the last analysis, 'an able man is nothing else than a good, free, vascular organization, whereinto the universal spirit freely flows. . . . The hero is great by means of the predominance of the universal nature. . . .' (W 1: 165). Beneath what we might call his 'good conduit' theory of heroism, however, we can see the sayer's envy of the doer's power. The Nietzschean Superman is already half explicit in Emerson's hero.

It is evident, I would assume, that Emerson's whole dream of practical power through Self-reliance is just that—a dream. Through it he attempted to meet the pressures of his actual world by creating, in his mind, a heroic personality endowed with a supreme power before which they would vanish. The product and expression of his personal tensions, it is clearly less a genuine program of action than what he afterwards called it, a romance. Miraculously, as it seemed, the discovery of the God within opened a door of escape from the trap of mortality, and the imprisoned spirit rushed to pass through.

Meanwhile, life went on, and with it its mundane difficulties. While Emerson's greatness originates in the power of faith that turned him aside from the path of convention, he retains our respect for him as a man by his capacity to recognize the facts of his condition, even while most enraptured by his romance of infinitude. Through and under the vast claims of his faith runs a common-sense realistic perception of the actual state of affairs, as an intermittent recognition of the waking world offsets the prodigious dream of *Finnegans Wake*.

We see this, for example, in the way he both admired and condemned all that he called prudence. His common sense revolted at any foolish neglect of the practical conditions of life in the name of heroism. No one is exempt from the laws of life. Promptness, thrift, industry, forethought, temperance, courage are virtues for us all alike. It is all very well to be 'the helpful giant to destroy the old or to build the new' (W 1: 99), if you can manage it; but imprudent genius dies 'exhausted and fruitless, like a giant slaughtered by pins' (W 2: 233). A scrupulous attention to such things as health, bread, climate, and social position is the first practical condition of freedom, and an indispensable school of character. Common sense teaches that nothing great can be expected from a man who cannot learn to manage little things.

And yet such prudence is unideal; it is the virtue of the senses. He could try, in such essays as 'Prudence,' to show how prudence and heroism could and should be reconciled, but one moment's renewed *experience* of the ideal was apt to shatter his case. The holy times of insight and moral sentiment were memorable partly because they seemed to raise him above the whole realm of being which made prudence necessary. Prudence was god of this world; but man was great and happy, Emerson's faith insisted, only as he set his foot on this world and lived in the spirit, above prudence.

Inescapably, common sense said, his was the bifold life of the scholar, part contemplation, part routine daily living, And yet his faith promised so much more! Its whole point and force was the revelation of a new life-principle which would redeem him from routine. To concede, with common sense, that life *must* be dual was as much as to concede the emptiness of the liberation his discovery of the omnipotence of the Soul had seemed to open to him, and was therefore something he came to slowly, partially, and with the utmost reluctance. If freedom lay only in the total self-trust of greatness, and if in fact he could be great only in inceptions and not in act, how did his new faith free him? The duality of his experience, condemning him to glimpses of a kingdom to which he was entitled by his constitution, yet which he could not enter, seemed to him at first a vanishing anomaly, then a wild and bewildering contradiction, and finally an absurdity of fate which he must learn to accept as best he might.

The enthusiastic vision of a rebirth into greatness, in the might of the God within, that would inaugurate a spiritual revolution in society also is thus the dynamic element in his early thought. As it takes hold, around 1833, the succession of his journal entries falls into an erratic alternating movement of aspiration and retreat, as fresh gusts of hope catch his imagination and then subside. A greatness that would conquer and prevail seemed to him at first his great opportunity and somehow his obligation; every man should 'live a life of discovery and performance' (W 1: 221). Yet he also knew all the time that such ideas were simply an extravagance of faith, and that the scholar's life with which he was familiar would always be his fate. The chief problem he had to solve in these years was not so much how to achieve greatness, as how to bring his dream of great action into some kind of contact with facts and square it with experience.

The Making of an American Prophet: Emerson, His Audiences, and the Rise of the Culture Industry in Nineteenth-Century America

Mary Kupiec Cayton

. . . The case of Ralph Waldo Emerson, one of the most celebrated of American intellectuals, can shed light on the ways in which meanings are made in intellectual discourse and what those meanings have to do with those people not filling the role of intellectual within the culture. Historians have never known precisely how to categorize Emerson. Perry Miller saw him as the heir and transformer of Edwardsian Puritanism. F. O. Matthiessen saw in him the founder of American literary romanticism and termed his the "age of Emerson." Others (notably Stanley Elkins) have seen him as a prime mover in a generation of reformers, with Transcendentalism being a dangerously uncompromising Emersonian movement for social reform. He was also, according to various scholars, a democratic philosopher, an incipient Darwinist, and a pragmatic mystic.[1] Reception theory suggests that Emerson's cultural impact may have depended less on what he intended than on what key communities of interpreters made of him.

If reaction in the popular and religious press and in the journals of the literary community is any gauge, Emerson attained a limited, local notoriety in his native new England during the 1830s. He was born in Boston in 1803,

From *American Historical Review*, 92 (1987), 598–620 (first three paragraphs omitted). Reprinted by permission of the American Historical Association.

[1]Perry Miller, "From Edwards to Emerson," *New England Quarterly*, 13 (1940): 589–617; F. O. Matthiessen, *American Renaissance: Art and Expression in the Age of Emerson and Whitman* (New York, 1941); Stanley M. Elkins, *Slavery: A Problem in American Institutional and Intellectual Life* (Chicago, 1976). For a variety of views on Emerson spanning 150 years, see *Critical Essays on Ralph Waldo Emerson*, Robert E. Burkholder and Joel Myerson, eds. (Boston, 1983). Some of the major biographies of Emerson include Ralph L. Rusk, *The Life of Ralph Waldo Emerson* (New York, 1949); Joel Porte, *Representative Man: Ralph Waldo Emerson in His Time* (New York, 1979); Maurice Gonnaud, *Individu et société dans l'oeuvre de Ralph Waldo Emerson* (Paris, 1964); Stephen E. Whicher, *Freedom and Fate: An Inner Life of Ralph Waldo Emerson* (Philadelphia, Pa., 1953); Gay Wilson Allen, *Waldo Emerson: A Biography* (New York, 1981); and John McAleer. *Ralph Waldo Emerson: Days of Encounter* (Boston, 1984).

the son of a prominent Unitarian minister who died young. Prior to 1825, Emerson seems to have viewed himself (to judge by his journals and letters) primarily as a fledgling poet who hoped to make his mark on the world of *belles-lettres*. In need of both money and a socially sanctioned way of indulging his proclivities for philosophizing, he entered upon the study of the ministry, eventually assuming the pastorate of the Second (Unitarian) Church, Boston. He resigned in 1832: his ministerial colleagues and his congregation interpreted the role of the Lord's Supper celebration in the spiritual life of the church in a way he had come to view as intolerable. After a period of travel, he returned to his ancestral home of Concord, lecturing occasionally, substituting for local ministers, and preaching from time to time in vacant pulpits. Freed from immediate financial pressure by his wife's legacy, he also spent time during the period 1834–36 reading, thinking, and writing his challenge to the epistemology of the time, *Nature*.

Prior to 1836, Emerson seems to have been viewed by his contemporaries much as one might expect: a somewhat unorthodox clergyman whose eccentricities and devotion to literature were within the bounds of acceptability for the Unitarian ministry. Joel Myerson and Robert Burkholder, in their comprehensive Emerson bibliography, have listed fifteen published works, mainly in the religious press, that speak of or implicitly refer to Emerson during the period 1829–35. Nearly all refer to ecclesiastical, literary, or civic activities that would have been well within the province of a Unitarian minister of the day. With the publication of *Nature*, attention to Emerson increased but remained within the elite circles of institutional Unitarianism and its literary adjuncts, the Harvard-dominated literary journals of the Boston area.[2] Part of a culture in which literature still functioned principally as a mode of spiritual discourse, the reviewers of *Nature* analyzed something they named philosophical and aesthetic discourse, but, clearly, they meant to read through these in order to see its religious and moral implications.[3]

Emerson emerged as a recognizable national figure in the decade and a half following the publication of *Nature* because his message shifted from being heard in religious and literary terms to being heard as discourse pertaining to something else. That something else seemed to move beyond the conventions of religious or literary discussion and provide a framework that included both. It would not be entirely accurate to call Emerson's message "secular" in contrast to "religious," since both he and his audiences perceived something spiritual in his utterances. Nor am I willing to use the term "popularization," since the process was not necessarily one of simplification and homogenization of a complex, determinate message for a non-expert audience. Rather, some-

[2]Robert E. Burkholder and Joel Myerson, *Emerson: An Annotated Secondary Bibliography* (Pittsburgh, Pa., 1985).

[3]See Burkholder and Myerson, *Bibliography*, 12–27; and selected reactions to *Nature* in *Emerson's Nature—Origin, Growth, Meaning*, Merton M. Sealts, Jr., and Alfred R. Ferguson, eds. (New York, 1969), 74–110.

thing happened from 1836 to 1850 that made Emerson accessible and appealing to a new audience who, because of its own circumstances, was able to hear him in a new and different way.

In lyceums and Mechanics' Institutes, knowledge that had formerly been defined only as religious, literary, or scientific began to be defined also as practical or pragmatic. The lyceum movement in its early days depended mostly on local speakers who had regional reputations. As Donald Scott has noted, early lyceum speakers were usually people with training and connections in other areas of public performance—law or the ministry, for instance—and their drawing power may have been proportional to the audience's familiarity with their other public roles.[4] Some speakers may also have been known through locally printed and distributed sermons, speeches, essays, or textbooks. Speakers not immediately familiar to the audience were probably arranged for by local ministers, lawyers, and other intellectuals, who tended to be part of networks that, in some cases, crossed regions. Emerson's course on "The Times," in New York, 1842, for instance, was arranged by his brother William, a New York lawyer. The new "popular" audience for the lyceums grew out of preexisting networks of intellectuals who began to be heard in new contexts.[5]

The existence of a new popular press, growing in conjunction with a burgeoning commercial economy, eventually provided a vehicle that made these early word-of-mouth connections superfluous and masked the origins of the speakers in the religious or legal communities. At first, in the major publishing centers of Boston and New York, coverage of lecturers in newspapers was minimal, lest summaries of lectures steal the speaker's "product" and render it unusable with other audiences. The only evidence in the Boston *Daily Advertiser* of Emerson's lecture course on "Human Life" in Boston in the winter of 1838 took the form of paid advertisements: two in October announcing a course of "ten or more Lectures" and soliciting subscriptions; and individual announcements printed the day of each lecture, advertising its topic, time, location, and price.[6] This neglect of Emerson was neither unique

---

[4]Donald M. Scott, "The Popular Lecture and the Creation of a Public in Mid-Nineteenth-Century America," *Journal of American History*, 66 (1980): 791–809. On the lyceum movement, see Carl Bode, *The American Lyceum: Town Meeting of the Mind* (New York, 1956); and David Mead, *Yankee Eloquence in the Middle West: The Ohio Lyceum, 1850–1870* (East Lansing, Mich., 1951).

[5]Until 1835, even publication was predominantly a local matter, with few materials marketed outside the area where the bookseller had printed and bound them. Of the lecturers during the first decade of the lyceum in Salem, Massachusetts, for example, fewer than half resided in Salem itself. The rest included locally prominent politicians, ministers, and college professors, such as William Sullivan, Edward and Alexander H. Everett, and Henry Ware, Jr. See William Charvat, "James T. Fields and the Beginnings of Book Promotion, 1840–1855," *Huntington Library Quarterly*, 8 (1944–45): 76; and *Historical Sketch of the Salem Lyceum, with a List of the Officers and Lectures since its Formation in 1830* (Salem, Mass., 1879), rpt. in Kenneth Walter Cameron, ed., *The Massachusetts Lyceum during the American Renaissance* (Hartford, Conn., 1969), 15–17.

[6]*Boston Daily Advertiser*, 21, 22, and 26 October 1838.

nor the consequence of his late notoriety over the "Divinity School Address." Wendell Phillips's lecture in 1839 at the Boston Lyceum on "The History of Inventions" was announced with much the same lack of fanfare.[7]

Before long, the situation changed, at least in some newspapers. An article in the Boston *Daily Advertiser*, reprinted from the New York *Evening Post*, commented that other newspapers had responded to the public's desire for press coverage of lectures. The *Post* spoke of "the practice which certain newspapers have recently adopted, of reporting the lecture made before the different societies of the city" and felt compelled to explain why it had not covered lectures.[8] The *Post's* misgivings notwithstanding, a number of New York newspapers and literary periodicals began to afford Emerson significant coverage in the mid-1840s. New York controlled the publishing market, and what New Yorkers wrote about, other parts of the country usually read about. "The eastern papers had said much of Mr. Emerson, and we get an eastern mail every day," wrote a Cincinnati correspondent on Emerson's first visit there in 1850.[9] Perhaps the most important paper to cover lectures was Horace Greeley's New York *Tribune*, said to be "the most influential newspaper in the country."[10] Greeley's coverage of the "isms" of the day, sensational in their own way, sold newspapers and rocketed the *Tribune* to a position of importance in the world of the New York press.[11]

In Boston, the *Daily Advertiser* wholeheartedly endorsed the New York *Evening Post's* position and refused to publish accounts of lectures. Perhaps in recognition of Emerson's rising popularity as a lecturer, it nevertheless accorded *Essays, First Series*, themselves print versions of the lectures, a lengthy front-page review.[12] This article treated Emerson as part of a literary

---

[7]*Boston Daily Advertiser*, 21 February 1839.

[8]To publish accounts of lectures, or even to describe the lecturer so as possibly to misrepresent him, the *Post* argued, was tantamount to robbing him of his daily bread, because it precluded his right to give the lecture again and to receive remuneration for it. Excerpts from this article are reprinted in the *Boston Daily Advertiser and Patriot*, 7 December 1841.

[9]*Salem Register* (Massachusetts), 3 June 1850, p. 2, rpt. in Kenneth Walter Cameron, ed., *Literary Comment in American Renaissance Newspapers* (Hartford, Conn., 1977), 19.

[10]William Alexander Linn, *Horace Greeley* (New York, 1912), 71.

[11]Emerson met Greeley in 1842; throughout the decade, Greeley published sympathetic reports of what had come to be called "transcendentalism." In 1844, Emerson's stock undoubtedly rose further as Greeley hired Margaret Fuller as his regular literary editor. Her first piece for the *Tribune* was a review of Emerson's *Essays, Second Series*. George Ripley, late of Brook Farm, followed her as the *Tribune's* literary critic in 1849. See Linn, *Horace Greeley*, 71–109; Greeley, *Recollections of a Busy Life* (New York, 1869), 169–91; James Parton, *The Life of Horace Greeley* (Boston, 1855), 219–28; and Glyndon G. Van Deusen, *Horace Greeley: Nineteenth-Century Crusader* (Philadelphia, Pa., 1953). Charvat indicated that, during the period of the commercialization of the book trade (1840–55), an author's "literary and social contacts"—and those of the publisher—were instrumental in getting books reviewed in the popular press ("Fields and the Beginnings of Book Promotion," 77–78). Hence the contact of Emerson's friends with the influential world of New York periodicals seems particularly significant. Charvat's *Literary Publishing in America, 1790–1850* (Philadelphia, Pa., 1959) provides a fuller description of the way in which publishing networks in the United States operated during this period.

[12]*Boston Daily Advertiser*, 7 December 1841.

community and evaluated *Essays* in literary terms. The review was far from flattering; the writer found Emerson's *Essays* tough, distorted, inharmonious, opaque, ponderous, and labored. Yet he expended time and attention on the book, he explained, because, "from its intellectual tendencies, it may be viewed as the representative of a class of works (chiefly of foreign importations) which have met with some success in 'Young England.' "[13]

The British connection the *Advertiser* refers to provides a second clue to the sources of Emerson's early notice as a public figure in the United States. Although Emerson had enjoyed substantial popularity among a certain group of educated, patrician, Unitarian-bred young men in New England, a transatlantic connection contributed significantly to the furthering of Emerson's reputation as a literary figure. The Boston reviewer who took Emerson to task for *Essays*, for example, began his article by noting that the preface to Emerson's book had been written by Thomas Carlyle. Emerson "is brought before the reading public by one of the 'observed' of the day," the reviewer remarked, "and may thus gain a degree of notice, which, we will venture to affirm, he would not else have attracted."[14] Emerson had done Carlyle the service of overseeing the American publication of Carlyle's works and ensuring that he received royalties for them; Carlyle in turn arranged for the publication of a British edition of 750 copies of the *Essays* and wrote a preface. The anonymous reviewer of the *Advertiser* was responding not to the American edition of Emerson's work but to the British edition, published almost half a year after its American counterpart under the patronage of an established British literary figure. The British edition of Emerson's work proved popular enough to be pirated. Beginning with the British publication of *Essays, First Series*, British periodicals began to review Emerson, frequently pairing his name with that of Carlyle. ("A Yankee pocket edition of Carlyle," some called him.)[15] Although the reviews in Great Britain were far from uniform, Emerson was generally noted, whatever his faults, to be a characteristically American product.[16]

Emerson's lecture tour of Britain in 1847–48 increased his standing as a

[13]*Boston Daily Advertiser*, 16 December 1841.

[14]*Boston Daily Advertiser*, 16 December 1841.

[15]See, for example, George Gilfillan, "Ralph Waldo Emerson; or The 'Coming Man,' " *Tait's Magazine*, rpt. in *Littell's Living Age*, 17 (April 1848). This article is in turn reprinted in Kenneth Walter Cameron, ed., *Emerson among His Contemporaries* (Hartford, Conn., 1967), 15–19.

[16]In addition to Gilfillan's article, see "Emerson," *Blackwood's Magazine*, rpt. in *Eclectic Magazine*, 13 (February 1848): 145–58, in turn rpt. in Cameron, *Emerson among His Contemporaries*, 8–14; "Mr. Emerson's Lectures," *Jerrold's Newspaper*, rpt. in *The Daguerrotype*, 2 (12 August 1848): 467–73, and in Cameron, 20–24; "The Emerson Mania," *The English Review*, 12 (September 1849): 139 and following, rpt. in *The Eclectic Magazine*, 23 (December 1849): 546–53, in *Littell's Living Age*, 25 (6 April 1850): 37–38, and in Cameron, 38–39; "Review of Representative Men," *British Quarterly Review*, 11 (1 May 1850): 281–315, rpt. in *Littell's Living Age*, 26 (6 July 1850): 1–16, and in Cameron, 45–56. On the wide notice taken of Emerson in British periodicals from 1840–50, see William J. Sowder, *Emerson's Impact on the British Isles and Canada* (Charlottesville, Va., 1966), 1–28.

public figure there, and British periodicals took note of him, for better or worse. The several American periodicals that reprinted British literary gleanings—the *Eclectic* or *Littell's Living Age*, for example—picked up the British literary assessments.[17] Emerson made no money from any of his books until after his celebrated tour of England; *English Traits*, published in 1850, was the first to make a profit. An anecdotal example of the role of British publicity in expanding Emerson's reputation beyond his region appears in the autobiography of Moncure Daniel Conway, the young Virginian who became Emerson's hagiographer and his publicist in Cincinnati. Studying law in Warrenton, Virginia, in December of 1847, Conway stumbled on an article about Emerson with extracts from his essays in *Blackwood's*, the Scottish literary review.[18] Conway traveled to a bookstore in Fredericksburg, where a copy of Emerson's "Arithmetic" was in stock but Emerson's *Essays* unheard of. Ordering a copy and remarking on his new literary find to his cousin John, Conway learned that the increased attention to Emerson had prompted John to write an article about him for the Richmond *Examiner*.[19]

Between a growing notice in the New York press, whose literary editors were often originally from New England, and a reputation in British literary periodicals, which persisted in influencing American literary opinion, Emerson's name was becoming familiar by the late 1840s to a class of readers who kept up with literary affairs. Characterization of him in the British popular press during his 1847–48 lecture tour, however, provided him with an image more readily transferable to popular American audiences. Townsend Scudder's work contains substantial evidence that the British press, in presenting Emerson to audiences of the Mechanics' Institutions, substantially de-emphasized the literary and religious aspects of his discourse in order to portray him as an already highly acclaimed American of prophetic stature. He was a man who spoke directly to the heart, not subject to the ordinary canons of logic. Both literary and religious criticism of Emerson continued to be produced, and, in fact, critics frequently evaluated his writing in either negative or decidedly mixed fashion. Even these appraisals, however, began to betray the influence of the popular press: this man was not to be evaluated strictly according to the rules defining literary or theological discussion. Rather, he was to be seen as a radical of some sort, whose message was to be judged according to some new, and as yet unarticulated, rules governing "feeling" and "spirit," and whose exemplary American-ness was defined as somehow crucial to audience reception of his message.[20]

[17]E. Douglas Branch, *The Sentimental Years, 1836–1860: A Social History* (New York, 1934), 111.

[18]The article is almost certainly "Emerson," *Blackwood's Edinburgh Magazine*, 62 (December 1847): 643–57. This was the first article on Emerson published in *Blackwood's*.

[19]Moncure Daniel Conway, *Autobiography, Memories and Experiences*, 2 vols. (London, 1904), 1:68–70.

[20]Evidence is both summarized and quoted at length in Townsend Scudder, "Emerson's British Lecture Tour, 1847–1848," *American Literature*, 7 (1935): 166–80.

Although dissenters and young Oxford intellectuals formed part of Emerson's audience, by far the majority of those who heard him in Mechanics' Institutions were not mechanics at all, but "clerks, shopkeepers, apprentices, &c . . . professional men, merchants, warehousemen, schoolboys."[21] The new commercial classes coalesced around Emerson despite the fact that they remained relatively oblivious to his notions of theology, metaphysics, society, and government. What such an audience made of Emerson is a perplexing question. Its primary concern lay neither with literature nor theology. Yet, to understand the making of Emerson as a "popular" intellectual, it is crucial to know the mind of his audience. Between 1840 and 1855, Emerson began to be seen not primarily as a religious or literary figure but as something else, and the coalescence of a bourgeois mercantile audience via the press had much to do with this redefinition of role.

The importation of eastern lecturers such as Emerson in the 1850s marked a new phase of the lyceum and lecturing movement in the midwestern United States. The formation of audiences for these lecturers suggests a good deal about the ways in which the emerging American commercial classes "made" Emerson and gave a cultural imprimatur to particular aspects of his message. Over time, various parts of Emerson's message became obscured through the sheer inability of his listeners to comprehend them as relevant to their own situations. Other parts became exaggerated, probably beyond anything Emerson ever intended, as a result of the coalescing audience's ability to fit them into discourse patterns and experiences that it brought to its experience of the speaker. Emerson's audience had come to a sense of group identity long before his arrival, and hearing him seems to have played a part in heightening its self-consciousness as a group. Before examining in detail how this audience heard his message, it is important to look closely at who his listeners were and the common experience they brought to their interpreting.

Nearly every town had its own lyceum by the mid-1830s. Cincinnati's lyceum was founded in 1830, Cleveland's in 1832; the Columbus Reading Room and Institute was organized in 1835, and the one in Indianapolis sometime before that year.[22] These lyceums were part of the national movement begun by Josiah Holbrook in 1829 to promote dissemination of useful

---

[21]Robert Chambers, "Mechanics' Institutions," *Papers for the People* (Philadelphia, Pa., 1851), 3: 197–228, quoted in Scudder, "Emerson's British Lecture Tour," 35. For more extensive remarks on the nature of Emerson's British audiences, see Scudder, 15–36; see also David D. Hall, "The Victorian Connection," in *Victorian America*, Daniel Walker Howe, ed. (Philadelphia, Pa., 1976), 84.

[22]John J. Rowe, "Cincinnati's Early Cultural and Educational Enterprises," *Bulletin of the Historical and Philosophical Society of Ohio*, 8 (1950): 304–06; Elbert Jay Benton, *Cultural Study of an American City: Cleveland*, Part II (Cleveland, Ohio, 1944), 38–39; William Alexander Taylor, *Centennial History of Columbus and Franklin County, Ohio*, 2 vols. (Chicago and Columbus, 1909), 1: 241; W. R. Holloway, *Indianapolis: A Historical and Statistical Sketch of the Railroad City* (Indianapolis, Ind., 1870), 50. Mead, *Yankee Eloquence*, provides the fullest account of the growth of the lecture system in Ohio.

information, discussion, and debate. Lyceums began to languish within a decade, however, and were forced to change their form of organization. It was to the second form of this lyceum movement that Emerson was eventually invited to speak, and in the character of these newer organizations lie the clues to the nature of Emerson's audience in the Midwest.

Throughout the young cities of the region, Literary Societies, Young Men's Societies, and Young Men's Mercantile Libraries rapidly displaced lyceums, These new organizations were explicitly established by and for the young mercantile classes of the cities. The urban centers of the newer region contained a disproportionate number of young, unmarried men, most of whom lived in boarding houses. In Chicago in 1850, for example, 94 percent of the male population was under the age of fifty, two-thirds were under thirty, and half ranged from fifteen to twenty-nine years of age.[23] Mostly migrants from rural areas, these young clerks, salesmen, bookkeepers, and banktellers were potentially cut off from the influences of family, friends, and church that might have held them in the path of virtue at home. Many writers saw these young men in danger of slipping into vicious habits such as gambling, drinking, theater-going, brothel-visiting, and Sabbath-breaking. A steady stream of advice manuals and tracts poured forth to advise them on the formation and maintenance of character and the path to social acceptability in their new environment.[24] In the cities of the Midwest, the Young Men's Societies provided an alternative gathering-place to taverns and theaters for the young members of the mercantile class. These groups also afforded young men the opportunity to acquire the practical knowledge and debating and speaking skills necessary for social and professional advancement.[25]

The Young Men's Associations, like the lyceums themselves, were anchored in the tenets of the self-culture movement. Self-culture as an ideal originated in urban centers, from the desire of artisans and mechanics to acquire an education in practical and theoretical knowledge of scientific and technical matters. The notion of self-culture quickly took on wider implications: the apostles of the self-culture movement began to advocate the cultivation of an internalized system of morality especially fitted to the newly commercialized portions of the country, particularly, urban areas. Introspective self-examination of conduct would provide highly mobile young men of

[23]Paul Boyer, *Urban Masses and Moral Order in America, 1820–1920* (Cambridge, Mass., 1978), 109.

[24]See Boyer, *Urban Masses*, 108–20; Irvin G. Wyllie, *The Self-Made Man in America: The Myth of Rags to Riches* (New Brunswick, N.J., 1954), 34–54; and Karen Halttunen, *Confidence Men and Painted Women: A Study of Middle-Class Culture in America, 1830–1870* (New Haven, Conn., 1982), 1–32. On the moral dangers inherent in the theater, see Claudia D. Johnson, "That Guilty Third Tier: Prostitution in Nineteenth-Century American Theaters," in Howe, *Victorian America*, 111–20.

[25]William Ellery Channing, in *Self-Culture* (1838) noted the importance of "Utterance"—not only because he considered speaking in public a prime way of improving one's intellect but also because "to have intercourse with respectable people we must speak their language." He noted that social rank and social advancement depended on this fluency. See *Self-Culture* (rpt. edn., New York, 1969), 27–28.

the urban centers, isolated from traditional institutional bolsters of morality, the means for maintaining character in a disorienting environment.[26] Within the philosophy, however, a tension existed: the young man had to be self-reliant and independent of external influences but only so that he could remain true to a collective standard of morality in time of trial. "Self-culture" was, in short, an articulation of the *process* whereby moral character might be maintained. The "culture" that succeeded it—and that Emerson's lecturing did its part to promote—focused on the *definition* of collective standards of morality and acceptable behavior.[27]

The self-culture movement in the Midwest was intimately linked to city boosters and businesspeople, those who had the greatest interest in maintaining moral order among the young male migrants to the city. In the Midwest, the gradual commercial development of eastern cities was compressed into a few years, as cities rapidly appeared out of the prairie. As a result of this rapid economic development, the midwestern merchants played a larger part in civic affairs than their counterparts in the East. Because the merchant—not the minister, the lawyer, the politician or the college professor—was the representative civic figure, the culture movement in the Midwest was, almost from its inception, dominated by the merchant classes.[28] Over and over in their official biographies, successful merchants had their good fortune attributed to self-education and self-culture.[29] It is not surprising that they domi-

[26]Wyllie, *Self-Made Man*, 21–54 and 94–115; and John G. Cawelti, *Apostles of the Self-Made Man* (Chicago, 1965), 39–98.

[27]On character as a defense of virtue against the corrupt, see Halttunen, *Confidence Men and Painted Women*, 1–55.

[28]This is not to suggest that the mercantile classes of eastern cities were not also influential in the establishment of its cultural institutions. The leisure and professional classes nevertheless seem to have been more strongly represented there than in the West. See Ronald Story, "Class and Culture in Boston: The Athenaeum, 1807–1860," *American Quarterly*, 27 (1975): 178–99. An example of mercantile leadership in cultural affairs that I take to be fairly typical in the Midwest was the organization of the St. Louis Mercantile Library Association, the organization that sponsored Emerson's visit in 1852. It was established and funded by merchants and businessmen. Convinced by mercantile journals such as *Hunt's Merchant Magazine* that their young clerks needed to be educated beyond practical matters of business to do their jobs well, merchants took pride in the "inestimable value" that the new association would offer "the young men connected with commerce" by sponsoring lectures and discussions as well as providing books. *Missouri Reporter* (St. Louis), 6 January 1846. The typical founder of the association tended to be an older and established merchant involved in business dealings with the New York financial market and with markets outside St. Louis. He had probably migrated to St. Louis in his youth in search of "a wider field of enterprise," as the stock phrase for the sort of ambition that was positively evaluated went. He looked on himself as a self-made man whose thirst for self-culture led to his success. A canny businessman as well as a morally responsible employer, he took personal responsibility for promoting the reputation of his city as a cultural center. See Brad Luckingham. "A Note on the Significance of the Merchant in the Development of St. Louis Society as Expressed in the Philosophy of the Mercantile Library Association, 1846–1854," *Missouri Historical Review*, 57 (1963): 184–98.

[29]For the St. Louis case as one example, see Richard Edwards and M. Hopewell, *Edward's Great West and Her Commercial Metropolis, Embracing a General View of the West, and a Complete History of St. Louis, from the Landing of Ligueste, in 1764, to the Present Time* (St. Louis, Mo., 1860), 389, which lists thirty-six individuals instrumental in the establishment of the Mercantile Library Association.

nated the foundation of a new lecture movement in the Midwest designed to inculcate certain moral values in their protégés. When Emerson came to Pittsburgh in 1851, merchants closed their shops early so that young clerks could go to hear him.[30] The sorts of messages he and other eastern lecturers brought to the platform fit the aims of a mercantile version of the self-culture ideal. In it, recommended activities and ways of thinking led not only to improvement of character but directly to business success.[31]

While sponsoring self-culture activities such as debating, public speaking, and literary study, the Young Men's Organizations also served to consolidate the young business class of a city by introducing them to one another and giving them a common set of cultural activities that, by their very definition, built "character." The reading rooms that flourished with these organizations were regarded as "a pleasant resort and an agreeable place to introduce one's friends and also respectable strangers who visit the city."[32] These organizations provided the setting for Emerson's lectures in the Midwest during the 1850s. Although they shaped the character of popular response to him, he in his turn acted as a catalyst for the cultural consolidation already underway in the region. Emerson's reception in one important midwestern city—Cincinnati— illustrates how these business-oriented audiences helped create an Emerson in line with commercial values.[33]

---

[30]Anne Louise Hastings, "Emerson's Journal at the West, 1850–1853" (Ph.D. dissertation, Indiana University, 1942), 8.

[31]This is the traditional notion of the self-made man, as opposed to the ideal of self-culture. It is discussed at length in Wyllie, *Self-Made Man*; and Cawelti, *Apostles of the Self-Made Man.*

[32]Taylor, *Centennial History,* 241.

[33]Although the responses to Emerson's visits to Cincinnati had at times their own character, they are, so far as I can tell, fairly typical of the range of reaction he received elsewhere in the region. I base this judgment mainly on a wealth of accounts of Emerson's lecture tours in the Middle West and his reception there that rely heavily on local periodicals for documentation: Mead, *Yankee Eloquence,* 24–61; Willard Thorpe, "Emerson on Tour," *Quarterly Journal of Speech,* 16 (1930): 19–34; Samuel P. Orth, *A History of Cleveland, Ohio,* 3 vols. (Chicago and Cleveland, 1910), 1: 491–93; Owen Philip Hawley, *Orient Pearls at Random Strung: Mr. Emerson Comes to Marietta* (Marietta, Ohio, 1967); C. J. Wasung, "Emerson Comes to Detroit," *Michigan History Magazine,* 29 (1945): 59–72; Russel B. Nye, "Emerson in Michigan and the Northwest," *Michigan History Magazine,* 26 (1942): 159–72; Donald F. Tingley, "Ralph Waldo Emerson on the Illinois Lecture Circuit," *Journal of the Illinois State Historical Society,* 64 (1971): 192–205; Paul Russell Anderson, "Quincy, An Outpost of Philosophy," *Journal of the Illinois State Historical Society,* 34 (1941): 54–57; Robert R. Hubach, "Illinois, Host to Nineteenth Century Authors," *Journal of the Illinois State Historical Society,* 38 (1945): 454–59; Hubert H. Hoeltje, "Ralph Waldo Emerson in Iowa," *Iowa Journal of History and Politics,* 25 (1927): 236–76; Hubert H. Hoeltje, "Notes on the History of Lecturing in Iowa, 1855–1885," *Iowa Journal of History and Politics,* 25 (1927): 62–131; Luella M. Wright, "Culture through Lectures," *Iowa Journal of History and Politics,* 38 (1940): 115–62; Brad Luckingham, "The Pioneer Lecturer in the West: A Note on the Appearance of Ralph Waldo Emerson in St. Louis, 1852–1853," *Missouri Historical Review,* 58 (1963): 70–88; "Emerson in Indianapolis," *Indiana History Bulletin,* 30 (1953): 115–16; Lynda Beltz, "Emerson's Lectures in Indianapolis," *Indiana Magazine of History,* 60 (1964): 269–80; Hubert H. Hoeltje, "Emerson in Minnesota," *Minnesota History,* 11 (1930): 145–59; and C. E. Schorer, "Emerson and the Wisconsin Lyceum," *American Literature,* 24 (1953): 462–75. Louise Hastings, "Emerson in Cincinnati," *New England Quarterly,* 11 (1930): 443–69, focuses on Emerson's reception in this city.

The primary impetus for Emerson's first trip to Cincinnati in 1850 was literary. Emerson's reputation at this time still rested principally on his print production. In October of 1849, twelve young men—lawyers, clerks, and teachers, none of whom were over twenty-five years of age—formed the Cincinnati Literary Club. These men lived close together and gathered on Friday nights in the rooms of Ainsworth Rand Spofford, a clerk at a Cincinnati bookstore, to eat, drink, and debate slavery, the tariff, and free will. The group combined the aims of self-culture and conviviality that typically characterized Young Men's Associations. It met weekly "to promote the wider culture of our intellectual, moral, and social powers," with one night a month set aside for formal debate and another for the "Informal": songs, light verse, and drinking.[34] As was the case with Young Men's Organizations elsewhere, the young men of the Literary Club could not afford to guarantee Emerson's expenses, so they turned to the "solid men of Cincinnati," lawyers, ministers, and merchants, to underwrite his expenses. The merchants responded by pledging one hundred and fifty dollars toward the course of lectures.[35]

Emerson came to deliver his course of lectures in May of 1850, to a city decidedly unclear as to what to believe about him. He already had a large enough reputation for the *Daily Cincinnati Gazette* to note on 15 May that "the movement for a course of lectures from RALPH WALDO EMERSON, to which we alluded sometime since, has proved successful, and . . . Mr. Emerson will arrive in Cincinnati in a few days, and commence a course of five lectures here early next week." The *Gazette* thought he would have " 'a few' people to hear him, at least."[36] "In this don't-care-much-for-genius sort of latitude," a Cincinnati correspondent of the Salem *Register* wrote after Emerson's first lecture, "the town was on tip-toe of 'look out' to see what kind of reception would be extended to him, what class of people would attend, and, finally, what would be thought of him. No one could come to any conclusion upon either point from what the daily papers said in advance; for it was observed that they had not been *paid* in advance, and consequently the 'Locals' were as silent as an oyster, excepting so far as they felt called upon to draw attention to his advertisement, &c.—and that, by the way, with the same adjectives that informed us that a *notable* fat boy was exhibiting at the Museum, &c."[37] For the majority of Cincinnatians outside the small literary and professional circles that issued the invitation, the popular attitude was

---

[34]Cincinnati Literary Club, Minutes, vol. 1, MS., Cincinnati Public Library. On the Cincinnati Library Club, see Hastings, "Emerson's Journal at the West," 6–7; James Albert Green, *The Literary Club and Cincinnati in 1849* (Cincinnati, Ohio, 1931), 3; and Eslie Asbury, "The Literary Club," *Cincinnati Historical Society Bulletin*, 32 (1974): 105–21.

[35]Ainsworth Rand Spofford, "Address Delivered at the Literary Club's 50th Anniversary," *Minutes of the Literary Club*, 28 October 1899, quoted in Hastings, "Emerson in Cincinnati," 443.

[36]*Daily Cincinnati Gazette*, 15 May 1850.

[37]*Salem Register*, 3 June 1850.

one of wait-and-see. Emerson was but one more presumably famous name, of whom many might have heard but from whom few knew what to expect.

Press reception of Emerson on his first appearance in Cincinnati is significant both because it illustrates the process of public image-making and because it set the tone for Emerson's visits to the region throughout the decade that followed. In the race with other growing cities of the region for resources, midwestern newspapers, which were even more intimately connected with the mercantile community than those of the East, became "civic cheerleaders."[38] Extensive journalistic treatment of the individual lecturers, including Emerson, contributed toward the shaping of a corporate response to the speaker, as had been the case in Britain during Emerson's 1847–48 tour there.

By far the most common response to Emerson was to wonder why all the fuss about his transcendentalism. "Judging Mr. Emerson's matter and manner, by this single lecture," the *Gazette* reporter wrote, "we should write so differently of both, from what we have seen written by others, that the same man could not be recognized as the subject of the several descriptions . . . [H]e is so far, in his intellectual and oratorical lineaments, from resembling the newspaper portraits above which we have at various times seen his name written, that we half incline to think the wrong man has come along, and attempted to play off a hoax upon us backwoods people." "Gothamite scribes have certainly mistaken Mr. Emerson for somebody else, and given descriptions of him which will not be recognized in this region," the *Gazette* concluded, referring to descriptions of Emerson that emphasized his religious deviation and his impractical and unintelligible philosophy.[39] Another reviewer, "perfectly satisfied by the Lecture of Wednesday evening," insisted that "a great deal more nonsense has been written about him by Gilfillan and others, than they have written about other people." George Gilfillan reviewed Emerson in 1848 for *Tait's Magazine*, a British periodical, and the *Gazette* reviewer's familiarity with the British review is perhaps as significant as his disagreement with Gilfillan, who attacked Emerson for triteness, mistiness, and worship of man disguised as nature.[40]

Although Cincinnatians persisted in looking for evidence of Emerson's vaunted unorthodoxy and fuzzy philosophical doctrines, they could not find it. "In that portion of the discourse which might be placed under the didactic head," wrote the correspondent for the Cincinnati *Daily Commercial*, after Emerson's second lecture, "no theory was introduced which would appear to present the lecturer in the character of a 'new light.'" He was "as unpretending as . . . a good old grandfather over his Bible," the *Gazette* reported, and "his most remarkable trait is that of plain *common sense.*" The *Columbian and Great West* reported that "the *transcendentalism* didn't come, longingly as we looked for it from the beginning, and stoutly as many, who professed to have heard the course before, declared that it would be along by-and-by." When Emerson's planned course of lectures met with success, he was persuaded to give a second course of three, "The Natural History of Intellect," "The Identity of Thought with Nature," and "Instinct and Inspiration." In these, it was judged, "our people will get something more of what is *peculiar* in Mr. Emerson's mind, and philosophical views, than was obtained from the first course." Still, newspapers found no sign of a threatening religion or philosophy.[41]

A comparison of the print essays "Aristocracy," "Eloquence," "Books," and "Instinct and Inspiration" with reportage of the lectures that formed their basis offers some idea of what Emerson's audiences thought they heard if it was not transcendentalism. It is noteworthy that in none of his lectures of the first course did Emerson speak directly about religious or philosophical opinion as he had in lectures of the late 1830s and early 1840s. Rather, he adapted his philosophy to the needs of the popular audience by choosing topics that communicated through concrete and homely metaphors his attitude toward these subjects without ever approaching them directly. His audience believed itself to be getting "common sense, humor, and truth; the second time, humor, truth, and common sense; the third time, truth, common sense, and humor."[42] The texts of the essays show that the audiences of the lectures were still receiving, albeit indirectly, the characteristic Emersonian depiction of the universe as a series of laws that transcended social convention, tradition, or proscriptive statute. In other words, Emerson's underlying philosophy and his religious stance in these lectures had not changed substantially from the more controversial *Nature* and "Divinity School Address," but Emerson was no longer explicitly using the languages of philosophy or religion to make his points.

By applying those laws to subjects that were ostensibly nonpolitical and nonreligious, Emerson seemed to his listeners to be merely passing along practical advice on practical subjects—the epitome of self-culture. In Cincinnati, the talks that received the most enthusiastic responses included "Eloquence" and "England." "Eloquence" contained what conventionally came to be called "gems" or "pearls of wisdom": aphoristic sayings that encapsulated the practical laws of human life in a novel way. "England" was praised as "one of the most graphic and interesting pieces of descriptive narration that we

[41]*Cincinnati Daily Commercial*, 23 May 1850; *Daily Cincinnati Gazette*, 24 May 1850, *Columbian and Great West*, 1 June 1850; *Daily Cincinnati Gazette*, 30 May 1850.
[42]*Columbian and Great West*, 1 June 1850.

have listened to."[43] It was treated as a catalogue of observations rather than as a coherent piece of thought. If the audience was pleased by Emerson's "common sense," it was because his compelling images drawn from everyday life could be understood in a practical, materialist way as well as in the metaphorical, idealist sense in which Emerson probably intended them. Emerson "don't *say* at all—he *hints* or *intimates* or walks around about what he *would* say but *don't* say," the young Rutherford B. Hayes, a member of the Cincinnati Literary Club, astutely observed in a letter to a friend.[44]

Ironically, one of the least successful of Emerson's lectures in Cincinnati was concerned with literary culture itself, the area in which Emerson had presumably made his mark. "Books" was pronounced "above the range and without the best of the great majority of the auditory." His lectures on "The Natural History of the Intellect," of a more overtly philosophical character, were "of too abstruse a nature, and altogether too comprehensive in their method, to be characterized in a newspaper paragraph or two, at all events from a single hearing." "Instinct and Inspiration," which the printed text shows to be one of the most overtly philosophical and least anecdotal of his lectures, flowed right past the audience. It was what the British and American reviewers would have called "misty"; the Cincinnati audience, at least, the commercial elements of it whose opinions tended to be reflected in newspapers, were by that time prepared for a frontier philosopher rather than a dangerous transcendentalist. Listeners found the lecture difficult and waited for something more to their liking. As Emerson's lectures grew more philosophical and the novelty of having him in town wore off, attendance at his lectures fell.[45]

Throughout the 1850s, midwestern newspapers that reported on Emerson's discourses exhibited some difficulty in summarizing his lectures as coherent wholes. Although audiences were described as "strongly impressed" or "profoundly attentive," reporters often found it "impossible to give a synopsis of the lecture," no matter how favorably impressed.[46] The organizing principles escaped them. Of "The Conduct of Life" in Cincinnati in 1857, for example, the *Daily Enquirer's* front-page story stated: "The lecture was listened to with profound attention, though, from its epigrammatic and somewhat abrupt and disconnected style, it was a matter of extreme difficulty to follow the thread of the discourse."[47] Rutherford Hayes's description of his impression of an Emerson lecture echoes the responses of most newspaper reviewers. "Logic and method, he has none," Hayes wrote, "but his bead-string of suggestions, fancies, ideas, anecdotes, and illustrations, delivered in a subdued, earnest

[43]*Daily Cincinnati Gazette*, 30 May 1850. For a complete text of "Eloquence," see W 1: 59–100.

[44]*Diary and Letters of Rutherford Birchard Hayes*, Charles Richard Williams, ed., 5 vols. (Columbus, Ohio, 1922), 1: 315.

[45]*Daily Cincinnati Gazette*, 30 May 1850, 3 June 1850. For the printed essay versions of these lectures, see W 7: 187–222 ("Books"), and 12: 65–89 ("Instinct and Inspiration").

[46]*Chicago Tribune*, 23 January 1857.

[47]*Cincinnati Daily Enquirer*, 28 January 1857.

manner, is as effective in chaining the attention of his audience as the most systematic discourse could be."[48] Emerson's philosophy of composition, natural law, and organic growth are clearly articulated elsewhere, and his treatment of individual subjects in the western lectures are without a doubt illustrative of his philosophical framework as he had sketched it in earlier writings. Because he focused on concrete topics for the popular audience, however, the system behind the anecdotes remained implicit and suggestive rather than explicit and logically developed. Audiences frequently reached the conclusion that, in his talks, there was no point at all.

When reporters did summarize Emerson's lectures for their readers, the result was frequently a disjointed series of remotely connected sentences. The following selection, taken from the Cincinnati *Gazette's* summary in 1852 of Emerson's "Wealth," conveys some of the difficulty listeners had in finding an overarching framework in which to put Emerson's anecdotes and aphorisms:

> One of the most natural enquiries about a person, but partially known, was "what has been his *success* in life?" The first question asked with regard to a stranger is, *"How does he get his living?"* All men are consumers, and all ought to be producers. Man is an expensive animal and ought to be rich. Wealth has its source in the application of mind to nature. The most intimate ties subsist between thought and nature. The art of getting rich consists, not in industry, but in being at the right spot for such getting, and in the right application of forces. Steam was as abundant 100 years ago as now, but it was not put to so good a use as now. (Applause.) The grass and wheat rots in Michigan, until the active men screw steam power to that hay and flour and whirl it into New York and London. Coals have been rightly called black diamonds. Coal is a portable climate and transports itself. (Applause.) But coal and water were useless in England, till Watt and Stephenson and Brunel came, and then how quickly transformed to wealth![49]

This summary also affords an interesting comparison of what the audiences heard and what the speaker actually said. The essay "Wealth" from *The Conduct of Life* parallels the lecture in every respect, yet it is fascinating to notice how the newspaper interpretation compares with this printed text:

> As soon as a stranger is introduced into any company, one of the first questions which all wish to have answered, is, How does that man get his living? And with reason. He is no whole man until he knows how to earn a blameless livelihood. Society is barbarous until every industrious man can get his living without dishonest customs.

---

[48]*Diary and Letters of Hayes*, 301. For a similar reaction, see the commentary of William Cullen Bryant a decade earlier, who, as he listened to Emerson in New York, explicitly listened for transcendentalism: "In regard to the peculiar doctrines of Mr. Emerson, we hardly consider ourselves qualified to judge. We cannot say that we precisely apprehend what they are. Now and then, in listening to his discourses, or reading his essays, we have fancied that we caught glimpses of great and novel truths"; *New York Evening Post*, 3 March 1842, rpt. in Charles I. Glicksberg, "Bryant on Emerson the Lecturer," *New England Quarterly*, 12 (1939): 530–34.

[49]*Daily Cincinnati Gazette*, 13 December 1852.

Every man is a consumer, and ought to be a producer. He fails to make his place good in the world unless he not only pays his debt but also adds something to the common wealth. Nor can he do justice to his genius without making some larger demand on the world than a bare subsistence. He is by constitution expensive, and needs to be rich.

Wealth has its source in applications of the mind to nature, from the rudest strokes of spade and axe up to the last secrets of art. Intimate ties subsist between thought and all production; because a better order is equivalent to vast amounts of brute labor. The forces and the resistances are nature's, but the mind acts in bringing things from where they abound to where they are wanted; in wise combining; in directing the practice of the useful arts, and in the creation of finer values by fine art, by eloquence, by song, or the reproduction of memory. Wealth is in applications of mind to nature; and the art of getting rich consists not in industry, much less in saving, but in a better order, in timeliness, in being at the right spot. One man has stronger arms or longer legs; another sees by the course of streams and growth of markets where land will be wanted, makes a clearing to the river, goes to sleep and wakes up rich. Steam is no stronger now than it was a hundred years ago; but it is put to better use. A clever fellow was acquainted with the expansive force of steam; he also saw the wealth of wheat and grass rotting in Michigan. Then he cunningly screws on the steam-pipe to the wheat-crop. Puff now, O Steam! The steam puffs and expands as before, but this time is dragging all Michigan at its back to hungry New York and hungry England.[50]

Some immediately apparent differences between the two texts include a treatment of material facts (steam, wheat, grass, coal) as a more prominent part of the message in the lecture summary and as the substance of the message rather than as illustrative of higher theory. The audience appears to have been expecting instruction in empirical truth, and that is what they found in Emerson's address. The applause would indicate that the audience responded more readily to the illustrations than to the point of those illustrations: that wealth, both material and moral, consists in the discovery of a "better order" to the one currently in use. Moreover, the newspaper's concern with success is as a how-to proposition rather than as a moral issue having a bearing on one individual's relationship to the social order. For Emerson, the issue is how "every industrious man can get his living without dishonest customs." For the reviewer, it is merely the issue of getting a living. Finally, the newspaper account flattens the double sense of Emerson's utterances. "Every man is a consumer, and ought to be a producer," says Emerson, echoing themes introduced in "The American Scholar," the "Divinity School Address," *Nature*, and "Self-Reliance." In the newspaper summary, the question becomes purely a material one. Emerson's "He is by constitution expensive, and *needs* to be rich," becomes "Man is an expensive animal and *ought* to be rich" (emphasis added). For Emerson, "rich" stands as material metaphor for a spiritual and moral state; in the context in which the reviewer places it, it seems to have predominantly material and economic references.

50W 6: 85–86.

Emerson meant to inculcate moral reformation through his lecture topics, and he proposed to draw in his audience through a choice of topics that seemed familiar and practical. Some of the titles in his western course, "The Conduct of Life," indicate the nature of the audience to whom he was accommodating himself stylistically—"Power," "Wealth," and "Culture." Each title can be read as praise of the commercial culture as practiced in the United States or, as Emerson intended, a subtle indictment of its shortcomings. Emerson's attempt to restructure his mercantile audience's vision of the institutions they were creating to define their lives might easily be mistaken for endorsement of the existing order. For example, when Emerson says in his lecture on "Power" that "life is a search after power," the audience who heard common sense but no organizing idea may have interpreted the comment as sanction for an aggressive economic expansionism they could readily recognize as a part of their current practice. The organizing idea of the lecture is, however, Emerson's advocacy of a power that derives from a moral understanding of the laws of nature and a "sympathy with the course of things."[51] His larger message has little to do with economics. His analogies, which include much practical advice to young men, are nevertheless taken from the realm of affairs with which his audience was familiar—business.

Emerson may have been systematically misconstrued by his audience. Several instances of newspaper reportage of lectures reveal the same tendencies as are apparent in the Cincinnati *Gazette's* report on "Wealth": a summary of the individual propositions from the lecture without a sense of underlying structure, an inclination to take Emerson's statements at face value as common sense, and a failure to acknowledge Emerson's reasoning by analogy from the material to the moral sphere.[52] Other newspapers flatly refused to summarize Emerson's discourses and explained their failure to do so in terms that are very suggestive of misunderstanding. The Alton *Weekly Telegraph* (Illinois) is a case in point: "Concerning the matter of Mr. Emerson's lectures, we shall not attempt to speak, as a synopsis of anything so closely condensed would be almost impossible. Each sentence seemed separate and distinct, perfect in itself. On his views, however, of culture, that of polishing our manners so as to suppress all natural and spontaneous emotions—making men mere cultivated automatons—was rather in advance

---

[51]W 6: 55, 58.

[52]Instances in which parallel texts can be compared include reportage on "Power" in the *Daily Cincinnati Gazette*, 10 December 1852, with "Power" in *The Conduct of Life* (W 6: 51–82); and a summary of "Power" in *The Illinois Journal*, 13 January 1853, rpt. in Robert R. Hubach, "Emerson's Lectures in Springfield, Illinois, in January, 1853," *American Notes and Queries*, 6 (1947): 164–67. Compare a summary of "Books" in *The Independent* (New York), 4 April 1850, with "Books" in *Society and Solitude* (W 7: 187–221). Compare "Social Aims" and "Resources," summarized in *Boston Semi-Weekly Advertiser*, 30 November 1864, with the essays of those titles in *Letters and Social Aims* (W 8: 77–108, 135–54). Summaries of lectures for which I have not yet 30 November 1864; "The Man of the World," *Cincinnati Daily Gazette* [same periodical as *Daily Cincinnati Gazette*], 15 March 1867; "Economy," *Daily Cincinnati Gazette*, 14 December 1852; "Culture," *Chicago Daily Tribune*, 4 February 1854.

of his audience. They may be capable of being educated to such a point;— but we question its desirability."[53] The irony is, so did Emerson. The discussion either obscures or distorts Emerson's point; from the summary, it is not entirely clear which.

Audience claims that Emerson used no logic in constructing his lectures appear to have been another way of saying that his mercantile audiences could not see the logical structure of the discourses. Stephen Toulmin has analyzed the structure of an argument as consisting of claims (assertions about what is true), grounds (the underlying foundation that assures the claim to be solid and reliable), and warrants (the connection that exists between ground and claim).[54] Emerson's warrant for the assertions of his "common sense" lectures was the radically idealist cosmology sketched out in *Nature* and further elaborated in the spoken and published lectures of the early period. Whatever language or analogies he employed to reach his audience, he saw himself as preaching a message of moral reform whose warrant was a unique spiritual understanding of nature and nature's laws. His audience heard the warrant to be a set of already familiar, pragmatic, common-sense rules for attaining individual financial and social success. The Emerson whose anecdotes and aphorisms are understood but whose larger method is not becomes the epitome of the commercial values prized by the audiences who invited him.

Often presented in the same lecture series with such pragmatic materialists as P. T. Barnum, Emerson's lectures resembled in import, if not in style, Barnum's "Art of Money-Getting," or "Success in Life."[55] Emerson's presence and message became implicated in the expansion of the commercial culture that sponsored his visits. As the lecture system of which he was part became more solidly entwined with the making of the urban commercial order, his lecture performances came to be part of a canon of acquired learning that defined the parameters of knowledge and behavior within the new international bourgeois way of life, and he himself the representative *par excellence* of "culture."

The transition in the Midwest from institutions for self-culture to institutions for the spread of culture can be seen in microcosm in the transformation of the lecture into a form of popular entertainment. The process mirrored a larger one, in which "culture" was becoming a form of consumption necessary for the maintenance of one's class standing. Although originating in the ideals of personal empowerment implicit in the self-culture movement, the new

[53]20 December 1867, rpt. in Paul O. Williams, "Emerson in Alton, Illinois", *ESQ* [*Emerson Society Quarterly*], 47 (1967): 98. Among those who declined to synopsize because of the "condensed nature" of the utterance were the *Daily Cincinnati Gazette*, 5 June 1850; and the *Cincinnati Daily Enquirer*, 1 February 1857.

[54]Stephen Toulmin, Richard Rieke, and Allan Janik, *An Introduction to Reasoning* (New York, 1979), 25–26.

[55]On Barnum, see Neil Harris, *Humbug: The Art of P. T. Barnum* (Boston, 1973), 154–58, 193–95.

culture industry was signaled by appreciation of emerging icons of culture who apparently supported mercantile values. Emerson's reputation as American prophet became firmly established in tandem with the rise of a national culture industry that created and perpetuated obedience to social hierarchy.[56] Speakers like Emerson began to be publicized in newspapers and competed with the theater, concerts, panoramas, and wax museums for public audiences. Lecturers were introduced to the public in the same way as other performers.

One criterion that audiences increasingly used to evaluate the worth of performers was the national or international reputation of the performer or amusement in question. P. T. Barnum's extraordinary engineering of a public reception for Jenny Lind in the United States in 1850 illustrates the influence that journalistic coverage of a public figure could have on a career. Barnum distributed widely a biography of Lind emphasizing her international fame, her piety, character, and philanthropy. Crowds who had not heard of her a few months before mobbed her upon arrival in New York. "All of this extraordinary enthusiasm . . . had developed before Jenny Lind had sung a note in America," wrote Neil Harris. "In a sense the musical performances, tumultuously received as they were, formed only an anticlimax."[57]

Lind's remarkable success as a result of Barnum's promotion was one version of a national trend toward celebrity-making, which capitalized on gossipy anecdotes designed to reveal the inmost characters of performers. As Emerson entered a company of "distinguished performers and well known names" in Cincinnati, for example, he began to receive a familiar kind of attention in the local press heretofore rare. One "Anecdote of Mr. Emerson" the *Gazette* published during Emerson's visit to the city depicted Emerson as at once disingenuous, familiar, and eccentric—in short, as a "personality." His journal was called "a kind of intellectual and scientific rag-bag" in the popular press, his wife an amazed observer of a genius she little understood. The significance of stories such as these lies not so much in any real information they imparted to audiences as in the way their personification of Emerson and performers like him met the needs of audiences for personalities (not belief systems) with whom to identify and on whom to model themselves.[58]

Newspapers began to comment frequently on the physical appearance of the speaker as if it were equal in importance to anything he might say. Emerson surprised audiences with his gaunt and homely appearance, his narrow forehead, and his long, hooked nose. In his habitual "plain suit of ill-

---

[56]I have borrowed the term "culture industry" from Max Horkheimer and Theodor W. Adorno, *The Dialectic of Enlightenment* (New York, 1969), 120–67.

[57]Harris, *Humbug*, 121.

[58]*Daily Cincinnati Gazette*, 22 November 1852; 15 December 1852. On the tendency toward the creation of media personalities, see Richard Sennett, who, in *The Fall of Public Man* (New York, 1976), made the case that, by the nineteenth century in Western culture, privatization of experience led to a distorted emphasis on personality of public figures rather than attention to their social roles.

fitting black," he was "not unlike a New England schoolmaster." He was by turns bashful, ungraceful, embarrassed, and half-apologetic, but each designation only added to his mystique as an uncalculating soul of pure wisdom and character. "He rarely looks his hearers full in the face," the *Gazette* observed, "but at emphatic expression has a habit of turning his eyes backward as if to look in at himself." Here was no trickster or partisan but a single-hearted purveyor of truth.[59]

Response to great individuals became the index of culture in a city, and evidences of "cultured" responses to them became in turn proof of the speaker's own worthiness. The newspapers announced one of a new course of Emerson lectures in 1857 with the assurance that it had been "delivered with great effect before a very cultivated Boston audience." In Chicago, in February of 1854, the *Tribune* prepared the city for Emerson's arrival by reprinting a laudatory excerpt about him from the *Edinburgh Review*, for Chicago, a foreign literary journal of impeccable reputation. Such notices served a dual function: while drumming up interest in a particular speaker, they also reaffirmed for booster-conscious cities their connection with a larger world of "culture" outside the region. Awareness and appreciation of people who had captivated the better sort of audiences elsewhere testified to the tone and quality of the city itself.[60]

The emphasis on a speaker's wide reputation enabled the promoters to clear a profit and established the city's claim to fame as a member of the cultural *avant-garde* but led to the demise of speakers of purely local reputation. As a city's participation in a national system of culture grew, local notables declined in status and authority on the lecture circuit. When the Reverend Francis Vinton of New York came to Cincinnati to lecture on "The Gentlewoman," the *Enquirer* regretted the small crowd in attendance. "The reverend lecturer has not the particular kind of notoriety which, we regret to say, is most attractive here." Cincinnati's own Rev. C. M. Butler lectured on "Sir Philip Sidney" in his home city, and the *Enquirer* took the opportunity to fulminate on the pervasiveness of the celebrity lecture system and its "imported trash."[61] So prevalent did well-known, highly paid speakers become on the western lecture circuit that some newspapers began self-consciously to try to stem the tide and restore the old regional system. In 1855, the Sandusky *Register* and the *Genius of the West* both published lists of western lecturers in the hope that the region would begin to employ its own.[62] They were not

[59]*Daily Cincinnati Gazette*, 28 January 1857. Halttunen, *Confidence Men and Painted Women*, 56–152, has commented on the use of dress and mannerisms during this period to communicate an image of personal sincerity.

[60]*Daily Cincinnati Gazette*, 31 January 1857; *Chicago Daily Tribune*, 4 February 1854.

[61]*Cincinnati Daily Enquirer*, 25 January 1857.

[62]*Sandusky Commercial Register*, 24 October 1855. Mead, *Yankee Eloquence*, 194–95, discussed the growing disenchantment with eastern lecturers by the end of the 1850s; W. H. Venable, *Beginning of Literary Culture in the Ohio Valley: Historical and Biographical Sketches* (New York, 1949), 251–53, lists the eastern and western lectures being promoted by the various factions.

successful. Westerners continued for the most part to look to those of established reputation, that is, to easterners, to occupy their lecture platforms.

Along with describing visiting speakers in inflated terms, newspapers offered glowing descriptions of the audiences who partook of the high-toned intellectual fare. The more famous the speaker, the more elaborate the description of the audience. "The audience to-night will no doubt be the most brilliant and fashionable that has been drawn together for some time," ran the announcement of a Cincinnati concert of Ole Bull, a Norwegian violinist of renown, and Maurice Strakosch, a pianist, in 1852. Theodore Parker's fame attracted "the select many" to his lecture on "The Progress of Mankind." With Emerson, the praise awarded the audience grew with his national reputation. His first course of lectures in Cincinnati in 1850 attracted an "audience intellectual as well as large." "The literati and the fashion of our Queen city" were expected in December of 1852.[63] By 1857, Emerson's lectures were "largely and brilliantly attended," and it was apparent to the reviewer that "the intellectual aristocracy of the city has seldom been so well represented as in this audience." In Milwaukee, too, Emerson's audience was certified "very large and brilliant." After the Civil War, when Emerson had become a household word as literary figure and popular lecturer, newspaper accounts increasingly congratulated audiences on their wisdom in appreciating such a great man, "The literary public of Cincinnati honored themselves last night, in honoring perhaps the finest scholar and most profound thinker of the country," the *Gazette* reported in the first sentence of its review. "The most elegant assemblages we remember to have seen on any occasion in this city" welcomed him. When Emerson gave his final lecture in Chicago in 1871, it was the audience reaction, not the quality of the lecture, that was at issue. "It is needless to say that it [the lecture] was well received. The applause was discreetly timed, and bespoke the culture of the audience."[64]

The press continually reinforced the renown of the speaker before, during, and after his arrival and thus promoted the notion that the audience was cultured and brilliant. The "justly celebrated Emerson" was praised; journalists were certain that "the fame of the lecturer will undoubtedly draw a crowded hall"; "the poet and philosopher, who is universally recognized as one of the great thinkers of the age" was coming to speak.[65] This newspaper promotion could not have created talent where there was none, but it did

[63]Daily Cincinnati Gazette, 23 and 30 November 1852; 22 May 1850; and 8 December 1852. *Cincinnati Daily Times*, 8 December 1852, printed the only mixed description of an audience I have come across. The auditors were mixed in character, it observed, and "people who never had a Father, and do not possess a thousand dollars in the world to bless themselves and progeny" took the front seats.

[64]*Cincinnati Daily Commercial*, 3 February 1857; *Milwaukee Daily Sentinel*, 8 February 1854; *Daily Cincinnati Gazette*, 15 March 1867; *Cincinnati Daily Commercial*, 15 March 1867; *Chicago Tribune*, 28 November 1871.

[65]*Daily Cincinnati Gazette*, 10 December 1852; *Chicago Tribune*, 2 February 1854; *Cincinnati Daily Commercial*, 27 January 1857.

establish a cycle whereby the repute of the speaker drew self-defined "intellectual" and "cultivated" audiences, and "cultivation" itself began to be defined as attendance on and acquaintance with certain famous cultural figures. Self-culture, the active expansion of one's faculties and the promoting of self-awareness, was becoming transformed into culture, the conspicuous consumption of the performances of people who were nationally and internationally defined as important intellectuals. Emerson became one of the first symbols of this culture, newly defined as the awareness and mastery of a certain body of knowledge. Culture was a state to be achieved, a status to be acquired, no longer a process of self-awareness and introspection.[66]

Emerson the public personality contributed to a national system of culture that was effectually the consumption of well-known texts and performances. Indeed, his lectures, in an oft-repeated phrase, came to be known as "intellectual treats," tidbits of wisdom dispensed by the wise man to the public at large. Thomas Wentworth Higginson perhaps best expressed this representative image Emerson had come to hold for most midwesterners as he repeated the assessment of a booking agent for western tours: Emerson's continued popularity rested "not on the ground that the people understand him, but that 'they think such men ought to be encouraged.' "[67] "He impresses one with the idea of long years of study, of many nights of toil, of incessant diligence in the fields of art, science and literature," another commented.[68] Emerson had become the professional embodiment of Man Thinking, the archetype set forth in his own "American Scholar" address of 1837. Ironically, however, in becoming a representative man, he seemed set apart, superhuman—no longer an inspiration to individual thought but an embodiment of the best that had already been thought and was known to be true. As Emerson himself remarked of Horace Greeley, the people liked him because he did their thinking for them.[69]

Nearly half a century after Emerson's decade of western lecturing, Thorstein Veblen observed that, in all known civilizations, the people place an esoteric knowledge of truth and reality in the keeping of a select body of specialists; scientists, scholars, savants, clerks, priests, shamans, folk healers. "In the apprehension of the group in whose life and esteem it lives and takes effect," Veblen wrote, "this esoteric knowledge is taken to embody a systematization of fundamental and eternal truth; although it is evident to any outsider that it will take its character and its scope from the habits of life of

[66]This definition of culture as acquisition of a certain body of knowledge and style is suggested by Alan Trachtenberg, *The Incorporation of America: Culture and Society in the Gilded Age* (New York, 1982), 140–81; and Burton J. Bledstein, *The Culture of Professionalism: The Middle Class and the Development of Higher Education in America* (New York, 1976), 1–45.

[67]Thomas Wentworth Higginson, "The American Lecture-System," *Every Saturday*, 5 (18 April 1868): 494.

[68]*Cincinnati Daily Enquirer*, 1 February 1857.

[69]*Chicago Daily Tribune*, 4 February 1854.

the group, from the institutions with which it is bound in a web of give and take."[70] Even though Emerson had not necessarily intended to do so, even though, in fact, such a system of culture as an end in itself was at odds with some of the cardinal tenets of his philosophy, he became its high priest. By 1860, it was generally agreed that Emerson was "one of the most remarkable men in America." He embodied values that his audience took to be vital to their way of life. He was "original, self-reliant, bold in thought and utterance," yet he seemed to threaten none of the customs or institutions that had become comfortable. He was "unpretending and simple in manners," yet he became a standard by which to measure one's own intellectual and moral sophistication. "He says many things that the majority of people either misunderstand or intelligently disapprove," yet his audience could tell, from his impeccable character and apparent approval of the mores of society—of wealth, power, aristocracy—that he did not really mean these things.[71] He became the image of the seer and prophet whose double-edged moral message could be taken materially if it made more sense to do so. The embodiment of the democratic scholar, he helped to consolidate for an economically defined community a notion of culture that reinforced boundaries between the cultivated and the uncultivated. He represented the paradox of a dominant culture that claimed to be dedicated to self-improvement but that increasingly took self-improvement to mean adherence to an ever-more-clearly defined body of standards and behaviors sanctioned by the mercantile and professional groups who sponsored him.

Emerson could become this powerful national symbol because the structure of the lecture system encouraged speakers and audiences alike to view what happened on the lecture platform as unbiased and apolitical.[72] The moral knowledge dispensed from the platform by the guileless speaker could shape a national consensus. Especially in the Midwest, where the proliferation of religious denominations provided some measure of ideological division, Emerson's ideas were bled of any philosophical, political, or religious implications and used as the basis for a secular faith that focused on a materially defined progress, unlimited wealth, and conspicuous social achievement within the framework of a stable and proscriptive set of moral values. If professional and mercantile people dominated the values of this new consen-

[70]Thorstein Veblen, *The Higher Learning in America: A Memorandum of the Conduct of Universities by Business Men* (New York, 1957), 1.

[71]*Cincinnati Daily Gazette*, 2 February 1860.

[72]The Cincinnati Young Men's Mercantile Library Association, for example, took pains to prevent discussion of anything "political" in its lecture program. Orestes Brownson caused a ruckus in 1852 when he made inflammatory remarks about Louis Kossuth. See David Mead, "Brownson and Kossuth at Cincinnati," *Bulletin of the Historical and Philosophical Society of Ohio*, 7 (1949): 90–93. Henry Ward Beecher was invited to St. Louis in 1860 on the condition that he "eschew all subjects pertaining either to politics or religion"; *Daily Cincinnati Gazette*, 2 February 1860. He refused the invitation. Emerson himself received some difficulty in the press in Cincinnati after he had publicly spoken elsewhere in praise of John Brown. See *Cincinnati Daily Times*, 1 February 1860; and *Cincinnati Daily Commercial*, 2 February 1860.

sus, if the moral orientation of the mercantile community and its Young Men's Associations was generalized and taken to be impartial and unbiased knowledge, it was not through hypocrisy. The intentions of the groups were sincere, even if the result was to extend their own hegemony over American culture as a whole.

Certainly, this is not the whole story of Emerson or the whole story of what audiences made of him. There remains the question of what he may have thought of his audience's misapprehension of him. In general, he seems to have believed that a person had to speak the truth and maintain a studied oblivion toward what hearers might or might not make of it.[73] Other audiences contested for the right to interpret his words definitively, among them, religious scholars, philosophers, literary critics, historians, and radical reformers, who did not cease to appropriate his discourse to their own ends, despite the popular triumph of the mercantile Emerson. Because he claimed to speak a truth that transcended context, Emerson may also be a particularly blatant example of the process by which an intellectual may be "made" by the interpretive stance of a specific discourse community. With other intellectuals, the process may not be nearly so clear cut.

A view of the mercantile Emerson nevertheless helps sort out many of the apparent contradictions within Emerson scholarship, as scholars may belong to more than one discourse community at a time. It reminds us that there is one Emerson but many discourse communities to hear his message. It is not only the speaker who represents a battleground in which conflicting cultural tensions or differing discourse communities strive for reconciliation; the text itself is debated and interpreted by various publics. Groups that are catalyzed into new forms of self-consciousness as a result of hearing texts that resonate for them receive ways not only of naming the world for themselves but also of seeming to share a common vision with others who share the text. No matter that the same words may be recognized in a wholly different way by other communities of listeners or readers. If Emerson has come down to us as a cultural prophet, it is not necessarily evidence that we all share a common culture founded on a common intellectual philosophy—only that the words themselves are common to enough cultural groups that we are willing to overlook the sometimes radically different ways in which we hear them.

[73]On Emerson's attitude toward audience reception, see John H. Sloan, " 'The Miraculous Uplifting': Emerson's Relationship with His Audience," *Quarterly Journal of Speech*, 52 (1966): 10–15. Passages in Emerson's own writing that are illuminating include *L* 5: 4 and *JMN* 9: 10–11, 50, 225, 258, 430; 10: 315.

Emerson, Individualism, and the Ambiguities of Dissent

Sacvan Bercovitch

What we may be witnessing is . . . the end of history as such: that is, the end point of mankind's ideological evolution and the universalization of Western liberal democracy as the final form of human government. . . . [T]he victory of liberalism has occurred primarily in the realm of ideas or consciousness and is as yet incomplete in the real or material world. But there are powerful reasons for believing that it is the ideal that will govern the material world *in the long run*.

—Francis Fukuyama, "The End of History?" *National Interest* (1989), 4

Let me assure him, in case he's worried, that there certainly are ["journals on the left"]. One of them, now entering its 36th year and going strong, is *Dissent*, of which I'm co-editor; it speaks for liberal-democratic socialists. We do it on our own, "grubby" or not. And perhaps . . . we come closer to traditions of American individualism than the conservative journals.

—Irving Howe, "Letter to the Editor," in response to James Atlas's article on Fukuyama, *The New York Times Magazine* (Nov. 19, 1989), 14

My purpose in this essay is to offer a contextual reading of two journal entries by Ralph Waldo Emerson, the first philosopher of American individualism, whose major essays have become the locus classicus for American dissent. Part of that context is historical, involving a dramatic confrontation between socialist and liberal ideologies in Jacksonian America; another part is specific to Emerson, and involves a decisive change in his career. Still another part, pertaining to the "traditions of American individualism," speaks to the recent controversy about subversion and containment in American literature, and by extension in the culture at large.

The first of the two journal entries, recorded in late November or early December 1842, seems to have come in response to the utopian socialist schemes which had just eventuated in the founding of Brook Farm. It marks Emerson's first use of the term with which he has been most closely identified and, more broadly, the first formulation of radical individualism in the modern world:

> The young people, like [Orestes] Brownson, [William Henry] Channing, [Christopher A.?] Greene, E.P.P. [Elizabeth Palmer Peabody], & possibly [George] Bancroft think that the vice of the age is to exaggerate individualism, & they adopt the word *l'humanité* from Le Roux [Pierre Leroux], and go for *"the race."* Hence the Phalanx, owenism [sic], Simonism, the Communities. The same spirit in theology has produced the Puseyism which endeavors to rear "the Church" as a balance and overpoise to Conscience.[1]

Emerson's brief passage may be read as an index to the development of the concept of individualism in Jacksonian America. To begin with, it reminds us that that development was not intrinsic to liberal discourse but on the contrary grounded in the European socialist attack on free enterprise. In fact, "individualism" was coined in the 1820's by French radicals to designate the source of the various evils they saw as characterizing the modern bourgeois order: "ruthless exploitation," "civil anarchy," "spiritual rootlessness," "infinite fragmentation," "ruthless competitive . . . attitudes," "social atomization," "confusion of interests," "mean egoism." In this exclusively negative sense, signifying *the* vice of the age, individualism was adopted by virtually all nineteenth-century critics of liberal society. Some of these were ancien régime conservatives; others were moderates, such as Alexis de Tocqueville, who in the second volume of *Democracy in America* (1840) provided the era's most famous definition of the term ("individualism," he concludes, "at first only dams the springs of public virtues, but in the long run it attacks and destroys all the others also"). By far the majority, as Emerson indicates, were the radical sectaries whom Karl Marx labelled utopian socialists—the followers of Robert Dale Owen, for example, and the advocates of Charles Fourier's Phalanx, and above all the Saint-Simonians, the widely influential disciples of Count Claude Henri de Saint-Simon, "le grand seigneur sans-culottes," who shaped the pejorative nineteenth-century definitions of individualism: "system of isolation [or "of isolated selves"], in work or in undertakings, the opposite of the spirit of association"; "power without obedience, rights without duties"; "the exclusive domination of capital, the reign of the bourgeois aristocracy"; "theory by which the rights of the individual prevail over those of society"; "system of self-interest, as opposed to the public interest, or the general good." These definitions were aimed polemically, as an expression of class struggle, against the middle classes of Europe,

---

[1]Emerson, *JMN* 8: 249. Cf. Koenraad W. Swart, "Individualism in the Mid-Nineteenth Century," *Journal of the History of Ideas*, XXIII (1962), 81; Steven Lukes, *Individualism* (Oxford, 1973), pp. 4, 6; Joseph de Maistre, "Extrait d'une conversation" (1820), in *Oeuvres complètes* (Lyon, 1884–1887), XIV, 286; Félicité Robert de Lamennais, *Des Progrès de la révolution et de la guerre contre l'église* (1829), in *Oeuvres complètes* (Paris, 1836–1837), IX, 17–18; Alexandre de Saint-Cheron, "Philosophie du droit," *Revue encyclopédique*, LII (1831), 600.

and ethnographically, as cultural description, against the northern United States.[2]

Emerson's reference to "the vice of the age" plainly shows that he took "individualism" from the socialists. But his own sense of the concept remains ambiguous. I called it radical because he aligns individualism with "Conscience" against the systemic forces of church and state. However, as Emerson develops his thought, it turns out that *this* radical alignment (individualism as conscience) is directed not against a system—at least not that of the American North—but against European anti-liberals: primarily the socialists, well represented by Pierre Leroux, inventor of the term "socialism,"[3] whom Emerson associates with Edward Pusey, a leader of the Oxford Neocatholics. And to compound the ambiguity, Emerson apparently does not mean by this hostile alliance of secular and spiritual collectivism to justify the liberal state. To say that associationists like Channing and Brownson mistook the source of evil is not necessarily to argue the superiority of Jacksonian self-interest. What Emerson did conceive of as the good society he makes vivid in a second journal entry, several days later:

> The world is waking up to the idea of Union and already we have Communities, Phalanxes and Aesthetic Families, & Pestalozzian institutions. It is & will be magic. Men will live & communicate & ride & plough & reap & govern as by lightning and galvanic & etherial power; as now by respiration & expiration exactly together they lift a heavy man from the ground by the little finger only, & without a sense of weight. But this Union is to be reached by a reverse of the methods they use. It is spiritual and must not be actualized. The Union is only perfect when all the Uniters are absolutely isolated. Each man being the Universe, if he attempts to

[2]De Tocqueville, *Democracy in America*, ed. J. T. Mayer, trans. George Lawrence (Garden City, N.Y., 1969), p. 507; Frank E. Manuel, *The Prophets of Paris: Turgot, Condorcet, Saint-Simon, Fourier, and Comte* (New York, 1962), p. 105; Pierre Claude Victoire Boiste, *Dictionnaire Universel de la Langue Française*, Huitième Édition, rev. Charles Nodier (Paris, 1834); J. B. Millière, *Ann. Ass. Nat.*, XXV, 547 (1870), quoted in Jean Dubois, *Le Vocabulaire Politique et Social en France de 1869 à 1872* (Paris, 1962), p. 322; Maxmilien Paul Émile Littré, *Dictionnaire de la Langue Française* (Paris, 1869); Étienne Cabet, *Salut par l'union* (1845), quoted in Dubois, *Vocabulaire Politique*, p. 322.

[3]I refer to "socialism" in its modern radical sense, of course, as "opposed . . . to 'individualism' "; so conceived, Leroux's use of the term to criticize "bourgeois liberal capitalism [was] enormously influential and . . . generally representative of other socialist, communist, and [European] romantic critiques of the period" (Paul E. Corcoran, *Before Marx: Socialism and Communism in France, 1830–1848* [New York, 1983], pp. 3–4). Emerson refers in this sense explicitly to Leroux's widely-discussed treatise *L'humanité* (1840), but he was probably familiar with the arguments of an even more influential pamphlet of 1834, "De l'individualisme et du socialisme" (reprinted as an appendix to David Owen Evans, *Le Socialisme Romantique: Pierre Leroux et ses contemporains* [Paris, 1948]), one of seven remarkable visionary discourses, issued as *Sept Discours sur la situation actuelle de la société et de l'esprit humain* (Paris, 1841), which might be seen as the European utopianist counterpart of Emerson's *Essays: First Series* (Boston, 1841). Significantly, Leroux addressed his appeals "To the Bourgeoisie and to the Proletarians," precisely the sort of class identity that Emersonian individualism is meant to deny. For the impact during this decade of Leroux and his work ("one of the great men of France and the representative of an important school in philosophy and politics"), see Orestes Brownson, "Liberalism and Socialism," *Brownson's Quarterly Review*, 3rd ser., III (1855), p. 183.

join himself to others, he instantly is jostled, crowded, cramped, halved, quar-
tered, or on all sides diminished of his proportion. And the stricter the union the
less & more pitiful he is. But let him go alone, & recognizing the Perfect in every
moment with entire obedience, he will go up & down doing the works of a true
member, and, to the astonishment of all, the whole work will be done with concert,
though no man spoke; government will be adamantine without any governor.
    union ideal,—in actual individualism, actual union
    then would be the culmination of science, useful art, fine art, & culmination on
culmination. (*JMN* 8: 251).

This visionary company of separate cosmic Selves may be seen as Emerson's antidote to the vice of the age. But far from resolving the meaning of
individualism, it amplifies and complicates the ambiguity. It may be worth
remarking that my concern here is ideological rather than semantic. The
question is not whether Emerson got the word right, but why he adopted it
when and as he did. My interest, that is, centers on the cultural symbology
implicit in Emerson's effort to come to terms with "individualism." And so
considered, the journal passage seems to be a striking (if oblique) endorsement of systemic individualism. It is as though Emerson had decided, on
reconsidering the attacks on individualism, that the remedy was not to
abandon it, but to draw out its potential. I refer, first, to his emphatic
rejection of the European radicals—a wholesale repudiation of socialism
which he now expands to include Italian, Swiss, and German (as well as
English and French) examples, and the fields of philosophy, aesthetics, and
education, in addition to social reform. Secondly, I refer to the religious
context he provides for "the Church"-defying conscience: the tradition he
inherited of New England dissent, leading from the Puritan imitation of Christ
("entire obedience" made visible in spiritual non-conformity) through the
Edwardsean revivals, "concerts" of believers (each in himself an image of God)
advancing in mystic unity towards some millennial "culmination on culmination." Finally, I refer to the secular ideal towards which all this points and
which is all but explicit in Emerson's imagery. "The union is only perfect
when all the Uniters are absolutely isolated. Each man being the Universe
. . . let him go alone": it is a dream-vision of laissez-faire. To *go it alone* on
these terms is to be a *member*, not a fragment, and as a member to embody
the values of Jacksonian democracy: self-interest, balance of powers, and
minimal government. To federate in this sense as *uniters absolutely isolated* is
to enact the principles of group pluralism as set out in the very concept of a
"United States," from the Constitution through the Compromise of 1850. And
to progress into the end-time kingdom, so federated, is to conflate sacred
history with manifest destiny.

    In short, this is a vision of the liberal millennium. Logically, stylistically,
and substantively, "union ideal" requires a corresponding "ideal individualism." The concept is called for not only by the formulaic structure of Emerson's language—his "balanced antagonism" of terms—but by the argument

itself (*JMN* 11: 371; 372, 374). "Ideal individualism" would seem to be the prepared-for resolution of the basic questions he sets out, concerning means and ends, self and society, vice and its antidote. But at the verge of resolution, Emerson hesitates or recoils; and in a sudden leap of grammar and meaning, an incomplete sentence followed by a blank on the page, he leaves us instead with a fragmentary opposition: "union ideal,—in actual individualism, actual union."

That ambiguity, together with the lacuna or hiatus that surrounds it, lies at the heart of Emersonian dissent. If, on the one hand, the imagery of the journal passage points us toward a liberal millennium, on the other hand the absent "ideal individualism" bespeaks Emerson's resistance to Jacksonian ideology, his aversion to identifying the ideal with any system, including that of the liberal North. And by 1842 Jacksonian ideologues were beginning to effect precisely such an identification. Initiated three years earlier partly in hostile response to Tocqueville's *Democracy*, the Jacksonian apologia for individualism issued in a direct inversion of the term. Through the 1840's, in what amounted to a full-scale American counter-attack against European critics, "individualism" was unofficially but effectually redefined as "the last order" and "highest reach of civilization," a system destined to bring society to "ultimate perfection" by "correct[ing] abuses, one after another, until the nature of individual man is thoroughly emancipated." There is no need to elaborate the arguments: they have become something of a cultural metaphysics by now. But a couple of points deserve emphasis. The first pertains to the society at large. The Jacksonian apologia for individualism is perhaps the single most dramatic instance in American history of ideology in action. It would make for a model case-study of the means by which the advocates of a particular way of life translate social values into moral absolutes; interpret the difference between what is ("abuses" and all) and what ought to be (naturally and universally) as the distance between practice and theory; and on that basis transform complaints about the system into a confirmation of the principles that sustain it. By mid-century, in America as nowhere else, individualism was being promulgated as "the ultimate perfection of man."[4] To borrow Fukuyama's pseudo-Hegelian phrase, it augured the end of history.

My second point pertains to the difference between Emerson and the Jacksonian ideologues. The Jacksonians defend individualism as a social, economic, and political system (as in fact the term then required). Individualism is for them the natural condition of a new nation-state which is bringing to fruition, institutionally, the "great progressive movement" ascending from the "state of savage individualism to that of an individualism more elevated, moral, and refined."[5] For Emerson, individualism centers first and last on the

---

[4]Anon., "The Course of Civilization," *The United States Magazine and Democratic Review*, VI (1839), 211, 208, 209, 214, 209.
[5]*Ibid.*, p. 209.

independent self. Progress is a function of self-reliance working against the ubiquitous conspiracies of society:

> No love can be bound by oath or covenant to secure it against a higher love. No truth so sublime but it may be trivial tomorrow in the light of new thoughts. . . . I cast away in this new moment all my once hoarded knowledge, as vacant and vain . . . [and] make a new road to new and better goals. (*W* 2: 320)

This is the early, radical Emerson, of course, seer of "perpetual inchoation," prophet of the new as transition set against repose in any form, set against *telos* itself; "Champion of the Individual," as William James commemorated him, whose writings from *Nature* (1836) through *Essays: First Series* (1841) develop a utopian vision of the self which transforms earlier concepts of autonomy (Descartes's cogito, Locke's self-possessive individualism) into a self-emptying mode of visionary possession.[6] This radical Emerson requires us to discard in order to incorporate. He insists on risk at any cost, especially the cost of social stability. He invokes the personal meaning of "constitution" against the political:

> Nothing interests me of all an individual says but that which I perceive to be constitutional to him. Thereby he is strong, &, if unchecked . . . would be a plague to society. (*JMN* 7: 482)

He advocates self-reliance against all norms and conventions, especially those of liberal individualism (self-help, self-made, self-interest). He recasts the very concept of progress into an attack on social progressivism:

> Society never advances. It recedes as fast as it progresses—its progress is only apparent, like the workers of a treadmill. . . . Progress belongs to the Individual. . . . Society is, as men of the world have always found it, tumultuous, insecure, unprincipled. . . . Society must come again under the yoke of the base and selfish, but the individual heart faithful to itself is fenced with a sacred palisado. . . . And out of the strength and wisdom of the private heart shall go forth at another era the regeneration of society. . . . By myself, for myself, I can have faith, Ideas, Progress, God; but if I must apply all these to Society as we see it they become Philistery. (*EL* 2: 174, 176; *JMN* 5: 190)

The proper term for this outlook is individuality, the belief in the absolute integrity, spiritual primacy, and inviolable sanctity of the self. A number of scholars have discussed Emerson's thought from that perspective, but mainly from within the American context: the historian Yehoshua Arieli, for example, as a function of Jacksonian nationalism, and the political scientist George Kateb, as *the* theory of American liberal democracy, distinctive to the United States and embodied in its ripest intellectual form in Transcendentalism. It is therefore worth stressing that individuality in its modern sense is neither

---

[6]Richard Poirier, *The Renewal of Literature: Emersonian Reflections* (New Haven, 1988), p. 172, quoting Emerson; *Boston Evening Transcript*, May 25, 1903, p. 3 (this is the reporter's summary of James's address).

American nor liberal nor democratic, but European, radical, and anti-bourgeois: a trans-historical, trans-cultural concept which according to the anthropologist Louis Dumont derives from Christianity but which in its modern genesis, as a post-Renaissance, post-Reformation ideal of self-realization, was developed in Germany, France, and England in explicit antagonism, and later in programmatic antithesis, to the perceived defects of systemic individualism. The following extracts from continental polemics of the 1830's are representative:

Human societies are born, live, and die, upon the earth; there they accomplish their destinies. But they contain not the whole man. . . . There still remains in him the more noble part of his nature: those high faculties by which he elevates himself to God. . . . We, individuals, each with a separate and distinct existence . . . we have *a higher destiny than that of states.*

In [our present] society . . . individualism is enthroned and individuality is outlawed . . . [But] God has willed individuality and not individualism; He has confirmed the former and quelled the latter. . . . All constitutions, all political institutions pose a threat to individuality . . . [and yet] individuality will bring about the social restoration which is being called for on all sides.[7]

Through the Romantic period and beyond, individuality served as a utopian rallying point against liberal ideology for virtually all groups in the political spectrum, left, right, and center, from royalists to anarchists. Its influence helps explain the anti-bourgeois animus behind the European Romantic vision of the individual. Its effects extend from the widespread theological attack on free enterprise (in the name of "Gospel individuality") to Marx's contrast in *The Communist Manifesto* (1848) between capitalist alienation and "the free development of each [individual]," or as he elaborates this in the *Grundrisse*—speculating on the classless third stage of history—"free individuality, based on the universal development of individuals." Its radical implications are striking even in that marrow of liberal thought, John Stuart Mill's *On Liberty* (1859). Nothing is more detrimental to progress, Mill writes in his discussion "Of Individuality," than the pressures of popular government and middle-class conformity:

The majority, being satisfied with the ways of mankind as they now are (for it is they who make them what they are), cannot comprehend why those ways should not be good enough for everybody. . . . [But] whatever crushes individuality is despotism, by whatever name it may be called. . . . [T]here are but few persons . . . whose experiments . . . would be likely to be any improvement on established

---

[7]Arieli, *Individualism and Nationalism in American Ideology* (Cambridge, Mass., 1964); Kateb, "Thinking about Human Extinction (II): Emerson and Whitman," *Raritan*, VI (1987), 1–22; Dumont, *Essays on Individualism: Modern Ideology in Anthropological Perspective* (Chicago, 1986); Pierre Paul Royer-Collard, quoted in François Pierre Guillaume Guizot, *General History of Civilization in Europe* (New York, 1840) p. 31; Alexandre Vinet, *Essais de Philosophie Morale et de Morale Religieuse* (Paris, 1837), pp. 148, 152, 155.

practice. But these are the salt of the earth; without them, human life would become a stagnant pool. . . . At present individuals are lost in the crowd . . . in America, they are the whole white population; in England, chiefly the middle class. But they are always a mass, that is to say, collective mediocrity. . . . The progressive principle . . . is antagonistic to the sway of custom . . . and the contest between the two constitutes the chief interest of the history of mankind.[8]

By "contest" Mill does not mean revolution: he champions liberal democracy as the best of all possible "despotisms," and he warns specifically against "the sort of 'hero-worship' which applauds the strong man of genius for forcibly seizing on the government of the world and making it do his bidding." Still, the radical implications are unmistakable.[9] Mill's contrast between the "progressive principle" and middle-class "mediocrity" is symptomatic of a form of cultural relativism which applies to liberal democracy no less than to other ways of life. Individuality, he writes in *Political Economy*, is "a circle . . . which no government, be it that of one, of a few, or of the many, ought to be permitted to overstep," and he makes it plain here, as he does also in *On Liberty*, that the other side of this defense of privacy is a standing invitation to "antagonistic" "resistance." He also recognized, albeit reluctantly, that the revolutionary threat this entailed was most palpable in the most anti-liberal extremes: on the one hand, the elitism of the Übermensch, from Carlyle through Nietzsche; on the other hand, the left-wing egalitarianism that eventuated in the uprisings of 1848. "Beware of confounding individuality with individualism," warned the Saint-Simonian Alexandre de Saint-Cheron in 1831 (echoing a host of diverse European thinkers from Friedrich List to Henri Joncières and Max Stirner): "individualism [is] . . . mean egoism, lonely and disunited, which chokes all dignity . . . while the sentiment of individuality is the holy exaltation of man." So, too, the Swiss literary historian and theologian Alexandre Vinet, representing a Catholic-Romantic tradition that included such disparate writers as Sainte-Beuve, Victor Hugo, Balzac, and Lamartine: "individualism and individuality" are "two sworn enemies; the first an obstacle and negation of society; the latter a principle to which society owes all its savor, life, and reality. . . . The progress of individualism on the

---

[8]Vinet, *Essais de Philosophie Morale*, pp. 152–154; Marx, *Manifesto of the Communist Party*, in *The Marx-Engels Reader*, ed. Robert C. Tucker (New York, 1978), p. 491, and *Grundrisse: Foundations of Political Economy* (1857–1858), trans. N. Nicolous (New York, 1973), p. 158; John Stuart Mill, *On Liberty* (1859), ed. Currin V. Shields (New York, 1956), pp. 69, 77, 78, 80, 86.

[9]Raymond Williams's historical summary is pertinent to this opposition: "The emergence of notions of *individuality*, in the modern sense, can be related to the break-up of the medieval social, economic, and religious order. In the general movement against feudalism there was a new stress on a man's personal existence over and above his place and function in a rigid hierarchical society" (*Keywords: A Vocabulary of Culture and Society* [Oxford, 1976], p. 163). The affinities here to the emergence of the concept of individualism allowed European liberals (as I note below) to adopt that concept of individualism *within limits*, as a necessary interim stage of human development. The same historical affinities allowed Americans later in the century to absorb the concept of individuality, conversely, as an ideal within the larger ideological framework of individualism.

one side, and the gradual extinction of individuality on the other . . . constitute a double abyss . . . in which we are precipitated."[10]

Pierre Leroux, perhaps the leading socialist theorist of the time, offered the radical alternative to that looming liberal abyss. Individualism, he explained in 1832, serves only "for liberating the bourgeoisie": it leads to a political economy . . . [of] everyone for himself . . . all for riches, [and] nothing for the poor." Individuality, on the contrary, opens into a "system of association which would realize . . . equality and brotherhood," a system whose premises Leroux expounds in his 1840 treatise, *L'humanité* (to which Emerson refers) as well as in his influential tract, "On Individualism and Socialism" (1834):

> Every man is indeed a fruit on the tree of humanity; but being the product of the tree makes the fruit no less complete and perfect in and of itself. The fruit is also the tree, it contains the seeds of the tree which generated it. . . . Thus in his essence every man is a reflection of society at large . . . every man is the law for which laws are made and against which no law can prevail.[11]

On some basic level, this utopian vision underlies Emerson's reluctance in the 1842 journal to invest the ideal in individualism. It also contributes to his otherwise surprising endorsement of socialist ideas of the future. For Emerson's polemic there (as elsewhere) against the "Communities" turns on means, not ends. Although he insists "on a reverse of [their] *methods*," he embraces their "*idea* of Union." It is a profoundly radical gesture: a disavowal in potentia of all systems, individualistic as well as collectivist, capitalism and communism alike, Adam Smith's together with Fourier's, Owen's, and Pestalozzi's. The real point, Emerson seems about to say, is not my plan for society against yours. It is perfect union, a hope we both share, based on a dream of individuality—something "spiritual and . . . not [to] be actualized"—which by definition sets the individual at odds with society as it is, anywhere, at any time. In this perspective, the 1842 hiatus has in it the potential of an absolute separation of the actual America (individualism) from the ideal (individuality). We may read into the absent "ideal individualism"—or into the blank on the page that divides "actual individualism" from spiritual "culmination"—the most extreme positions of antebellum dissent: William Lloyd Garrison's, for example, in repudiating the Constitution, or Thoreau's in supporting the *armed* resistance of John Brown, or once again, Margaret Fuller's in joining the Italian socialists of 1848.

---

[10]Mill, *On Liberty*, ed. Shields, p. 81, *Principles of Political Economy with some of their Applications to Social Philosophy* (Boston, 1848), II, 514 (V, xi, 1), and *On Liberty*, ed. Shields, pp. 86, 90; Saint-Cheron, "Philosophie du droit," p. 29; Vinet, quoted in Swart, "Individualism," *Journal of the History of Ideas*, XXIII, 84–85.

[11]Arieli, *Individualism and Nationalism*, p. 233; Leroux, "De la philosophie et du Christianisme," *Revue encyclopédique*, LV (1832), 303, 308–319, and "De l'individualisme et du socialisme" (1834), reprinted as appendix in David Owen Evans, *Le socialisme romantique: Pierre Leroux et ses contemporains* (Paris, 1948), pp. 223–32.

The drama of the 1842 journal passage lies in the collision or uncanny convergence of this spirit of individuality on the one hand and, on the other, its cultural antithesis, the apologia for liberal society implicit in the imagery of laissez-faire. In retrospect, we may safely say that Emerson's hesitation about adopting or rejecting either extreme indicates a search for the proper ambiguous connective between the two. We may say further, I believe, that that search marks a turning point in his career—between the radical early essays and the conservative "later Emerson"—and that the key to the shift lies in his confrontation with the theory and practice of socialism.

I noted earlier that Emerson's commitment to individuality led him to embrace the socialists' visionary ends. I would now add that Emerson's antipathy to their methods bespeaks his deeper commitment to liberal thought. He had not worked this through by 1842; or more accurately, he had mystified his position through the ambiguity of "America." His early essays distinguish between Jacksonian society and the "true America," as between ideology and utopia. He critizes the defects of laissez-faire in the name of "the Spirit of America" (to which he dedicated his journals in 1822, at the age of 19) (*JMN* 2: 3). He retreats from the pressures of specialization and industrialization, as well as from his private griefs, into "this new yet unapproachable America I have found in the West" (*W* 2: 72). "The American Scholar" opposes the prospect of "a nation of men" in America to America's actual "iron-lid[ded]" market-place economy (*W* 1: 115, 81). Upon such distinctions— grounded in an absolute that gains substance from the metaphors of the American way while yet claiming, by rhetorical inversion, opposition, and reversal, to transcend the actual America—Emerson built his radical doctrine of the individual. "America" was for him alternately the facts of liberal individualism and the ideals of individuality—a symbolic polarity which appeared sometimes as sheer antagonism, sometimes as probational conflict, and whose divergent meanings he somehow combined, in the early essays (1836–1841), in his consummate figure of dissent, the representative/ adversarial American Self.

The socialist challenge forced the resolution of the ambiguity. I refer here neither to the theory nor to the practice of socialism per se, but to what these implied about Emerson's prior intellectual and imaginative commitments. In such implications—not in the programs for collectivist living, not in the affirmation of collectivist principles, not in the critique of individualism or its exaggerations, but in the denial of "the Spirit of America"—lay the problem of socialism for Emerson. What compelled his interest was his recognition of a different road to utopia, an alternative model of culture. Socialism repudiated the very rhetoric of "America." It contested not only the pragmatics of the market-place, but the very concept of the United States as "the country of the Future" (*W* 1: 371). As method and in theory socialism denied the new-ness of the New World (as against the outwornness of the Old); it denied the myth of the War of Independence (as the Revolution to end revolutions), the prophetic claims of manifest destiny, and the typology of the open, regenerative West. And it may be that in 1842 Emerson's belief in individuality, together with the mounting criticism of individualism (as "the vice of the age") brought him to the verge of a sweeping repudiation of his society, a total, unequivocal dissociation of the meaning of America from the United States, as Augustine had severed the city of God from the city of man.

To some significant extent, that crisis in cultural commitment and symbolic language contributes to the extraordinary volatility of *Essays: First Series*. I have in mind now Emerson's response to internal developments (rather than to the socialist challenge): his alarm at the 1837 Depression, his contempt for "King Andrew" Jackson (and for his "henchman" Martin Van Buren, elected in 1836 by a "cowardly majority"), his fears concerning the growing urban "rabble," and his horror of the self-made arrivistes who were threatening to bring down Boston's Brahmin Whig establishment. These and similar "twinings and tendrils of . . . evil" contributed to his disgust with the "depravity," "stupidity & corruption," "treacherous, short memoried, suicidally selfish, all illogical world" of Jacksonian free enterprise (*JMN* 7: 514; 4: 332; 8: 137). Essentially, Emerson shared the radical scepticism about institutions that Hester voices mid-way through *The Scarlet Letter*; basically, he felt the same outrage at political, social, and economic injustice that mobilized over fifty socialist communities in New England and other regions of the country through the 1840's. His journals of 1836, when *Nature* was published and "The American Scholar" begun, bristle with scorn for "this . . . era of Trade," with its "fever of Speculation . . . & restlessness of politicians" (*JMN* 5: 237, 238).

> [T]here is no Idea, no Principle. It is all scrambling for bread & Money. . . . (*JMN* 5: 260)

> When I spoke or speak of the democratic element I do not mean that ill thing vain & loud which writes lying newspapers, spouts at caucuses, & sells its lies for gold. . . . There is nothing of the true democratic element in what is called Democracy; it must fall, being wholly commercial. (*JMN* 5: 203)

In 1837 he elaborated his concept of true democracy through a critique of "Trades and Professions" which concludes that "Labor and not property is the source of real power" (*EL* 2: 124). Soon after he expanded this radical concept of power into a fundamental challenge to existing property and labor relations:

> the reliance on Property, including the reliance on governments which protect it, is the want of self-reliance. Men have . . . come to esteem . . . civil institutions as guards of property, and they deprecate assaults on these, because they feel them to be assaults on property. . . . But a cultivated man becomes ashamed of his property, out of a new respect for his nature. (*W* 2: 87–88)

The radicalism potential in such statements is especially conspicuous by contrast with reformist appeals of the 1830's, ranging from William Ellery

Channing's high-brow *Self-Culture* to the Loco-Foco exposés in William Leggett's *Plain-Dealer* and Theodore Sedgwick's *Public and Private Economy.* The difference between these attacks on Jacksonian free enterprise and Emerson's dissent, or for that matter between Emerson and the young dissenters of 1842, lies in the utopian intensity of Emerson's vision. By 1839, he had recoiled not only from the exaggerations of actual individualism but from the system itself, as from a vast commercial lie—had embraced a form of Romantic titanism that according to local Unitarians bordered on antinomian heresy, and according to Nietzsche on the doctrine of the Superman:

> The whole world travails to ripen & bear the sufficiency of one man. . . . He asks no vantage ground, no favorable circumstance. The obedient universe bends around him. . . . He needs no . . . church, for he is himself a prophet; no statute book, for he hath the Lawgiver. . . . (*JMN* 7: 331–32)

> What is the State?
> The Hero is the State
> The Soul should legislate. (*JMN* 7: 334)

On July 4, 1839, the journals record a personal "declaration of independence," apparently conceived during a walk that day in the woods around Walden Pond, which would become the cornerstone of "Self-Reliance":

> The doctrine of hatred must be preached as the counteraction of the doctrine of love when that pules & whines. I hate father & mother & wife & brother when my muse calls me & I say to these relatives that if they wish my love they must respect my hatred. I would write on the lintels of the door-post, *Whim.* . . . your nonsense of popular charity, the suckling of fools, the building of meetinghouses, the alms to sots,—though I confess with shame I sometimes succumb & give the dollar it is a wicked dollar which by & by I shall have the manhood to withhold. (*JMN* 7: 224)

Shortly after this, Emerson endorsed Garrison's disavowal of the state, and advised Americans to "[g]ive up the Government without too solicitously inquiring" about consequences. The United States, he explained, is just another "government of force. . . . We are accustomed to speak of our National Union & our Constitution as of somewhat sacred . . . but these bands are trivial in the comparison" with "Individual character": "Character is centrality, the impossibility of being displaced or overset. . . . Society is frivolous, and shreds its day into scraps, its conversation into ceremonies and escapes" (*JMN* 7: 281, 304; *W* 3: 99).

In this optative mood, Emerson decided to come to terms with the recent "sympathy for communistic experiments" and "considerable interest in social-ism," at home and abroad.[12] On August 4, 1840 he wrote to Margaret Fuller that he hoped to transform *The Dial* from a "papyrus reed" to "a fatal arrow":

> I begin to wish to see a different Dial from that which I first imagined. I would not have it too purely literary. I wish we might make a Journal so broad & great in its

---

[12]John T. Flanagan, "Emerson and Communism," *New England Quarterly,* X (1937), 243, 245.

survey that it should lead the opinion of this generation on every great interest & read the law on property, government, education, as well as on art, letters, & religion. A great Journal people must read. And it does not seem worth our while to work with any other than sovereign aims. So I wish we might court some of the good fanatics and publish chapters on every head in the whole Art of Living. I am just now turning my pen to scribble & copy on the subjects of 'Labor,' 'Farm,' 'Reform,' 'Domestic Life,' etc. (*L* 2: 322)

In the next year or two Emerson proceeded to publish "Fourierism and the Socialists," "English Reformers," and other essays in which, by implication at least, he welcomed the socialists' attack on individualism. Their methods he rejected at once, but at this point he was persuaded that "success depends on the Aim, not on the means. Look at the mark[,] not on your arrow. And herein is my hope for reform in our vicious modes of living. Let a man . . . fix his heart on magnificent life & he need not know the economical methods." What else *could* one do? "I see . . . that commerce, law, & state employments . . . are now all so perverted & corrupt that no man can right himself in them. . . . Nothing is left him but to begin the world anew." New England reformers were right to renounce a country in which "men are tools & not masters," a polity where "Things are in the saddle / And ride mankind," a region where "[t]he ways of trade are grown selfish to the borders of theft, and supple to the borders (if not beyond the borders) of fraud" (*JMN* 7: 350, 342, 436; *W* 9: 73; 1: 230).

What Emerson meant by beginning the world anew devolved then and always upon a vision of cosmic subjectivity, "the doctrine Judge for yourself[,] Reverence thyself" (*JMN* 4: 342). His journal entry of April 7, 1840 holds true for his entire career: "In all my lectures, I have taught one doctrine, namely the infinitude of the private man" (*JMN* 7: 342). And four months earlier, on January 1, 1840, he declared as his manifesto in "Politics" what we might consider to be a foreshadowing of his meditation three years later on "individualism": "the great antitdote and corrective in nature to this abuse of Formal Government is the Influence of Private Character, the growth of the Individual" (*EL* 3: 242). But in the years immediately preceding and following this "kernel of his message" (as William James called it),[13] self-reverence had assumed such absolutist proportions in his thought, had brought him so close to a relativistic view of the merely social order (as against "the infinitude of the private man"), that he seems actually to have entertained the possibility of a wholesale reordering of the state, *verging on* the redistribution of property and wealth. He was becoming increasingly angry with a "selfish commerce & government [which] have got possession of the masses"; and although he found "no instant prospect of a virtuous revolution; yet I confess I should not be pained at a change which threatened a loss of some of the luxuries or conveniences of society" (*JMN* 7: 282; *W* 1: 235). Accordingly, in two lectures

[13]William James, speech printed in the *Boston Evening Transcript*, May 25, 1903, p. 3.

at the start and end of 1841, "Man the Reformer" (January 25) and "Lecture on the Times" (December 2), he may be said to have come *to the edge* of class analysis; and in his journals and letters of 1840–1841 he sometimes ventures further still, *almost* beyond the bounds of liberalism:

> In every knot of laborers, the rich man does not feel himself among his friends,— and at the polls he finds them arrayed in a mass in distinct opposition to him. . . . [T]he people do not wish to be represented or ruled by the ignorant and base. They only vote for these, because they were asked with the voice and semblance of kindness. They will not vote for them long. . . . The state must consider the poor man, and all voices must speak for him. Every child that is born must have a just chance for his bread. Let the amelioration in our laws of property proceed from the concession of the rich, not from the grasping of the poor. Let us understand that the equitable rule is, that no one should take more than his share. (*W* 1: 253–54)
>
> . . . .
>
> The monastery[,] the convent did not quite fail. Many & many a stricken soul found peace & home & scope in those regimens[,] in those chapels & cells. The Society of Shakers did not quite fail, but has proved an agreeable asylum to many a lonesome farmer & matron. The College has been dear to many an old bachelor of learning. What hinders them that this age better advised should endeavor to sift out of these experiments the false & adopt & embody in a new form the advantage[?] (*JMN* 7: 394–95)

I italicize the qualifying terms—*almost, verging on, to the edge*—because we know that Emerson never really gave serious thought to social reorganization. Nor did he take seriously the "experiments" in collective living and common wealth. This is evident in the very playfulness of his language ("fanatics," "perhaps this . . . will content all," "amused . . . with my thrum," "did not quite fail"), as well as in his short-list of exemplary radicals (monks, nuns, Shakers, and the old bachelor professor). It is evident, too, considering the course of international Romanticism, in the conspicuous absence of any reference whatever to socialism in the utopian passages of *Essays: First Series*, and relatively few (most of them pejorative) to "individuality" anywhere in his writing. Even at the height of his heresy, Emerson's cultural roots were too deep for him to envision "a new form" in the "Art of Living" that would be anything other than a purified version of free enterprise (as in the 1842 journal) or a pastoral dream of agrarian laissez-faire. Even in his most quasi-antinomian pronouncements, as in his 1840 declaration that "the very idea of Government in the world is Interference," he defined individuality through liberal presuppositions. Emerson's own most daring venture in communalism was to invite the servants to dinner one day in 1841, an invitation which, once declined, was not renewed (*EL* 3: 260; *L* 2: 322; *EL* 3: 246; *L* 2: 389).

Still, he had to acknowledge the seriousness of the socialist challenge. All too many others were taking it up, including the admirable young people he names in the 1842 Journal (Channing, Brownson, Peabody, Greene, "and possibly Bancroft"); he was being solicited for support of Brook Farm; and he was "much thrust upon," he complained, by radical tracts and manifestoes, in which, astutely, he read the signs of impending revolution in Europe. The result was the social-rhetorical crisis I noted; its issue has already been suggested. Increasingly through the 1840's, Emerson drew out the liberal underpinnings of his dissent—i.e., the premises of his commitment to America in its full bi-polar implications, ideal *and* (not or) actual. And increasingly through the decade, in journals, lectures, *Dial* reviews, and Transcendentalist "Conversations," he engaged in a pointed, persistent, and eventually vehement polemic against socialism. Having discovered that he "could not reconcile the socialist principle with [his] own doctrine of the individual," he proceeded to situate individuality within culture as individualism.[14]

The 1842 lacuna marks Emerson's presentiment of that bond between ideology and utopia. The discovery itself is first recorded in "New England Reformers," an address delivered March 3, 1844, which Emerson considered important enough to publish later that year as the concluding section to *Essays: Second Series*. It is an eloquent summary of his ruminations from 1840 on about socialist theories and schemes, and perhaps a catalytic event was the restructuring that year of Brook Farm. The community had begun in a tension between the "individualists," such as Hawthorne, and the "associationists" (Brownson et al.) whom Emerson chides in the 1842 journal entry. But the leading individualists either left or else (as in the case of Emerson and Thoreau) refused to join altogether, and the associationists gradually gained control. In January 1844, under the direction of George Ripley and Albert Brisbane, Brook Farm effactually became "the center of Fourierism in the United States." In Hawthorne's words, the motley group of idealists he had joined three years before—"Persons of marked individuality . . . [whose] bond was not affirmative, but negative"—had "blundered into the very emptiest mockery [of an] . . . effort to establish the one true system."[15]

The blunder seems to have provoked Emerson to an unambiguous attack on the methods of socialism. He had written privately in 1842, as Brook Farm got underway, that the socialists had "skipped no fact but one, namely life" (*JMN* 8: 209). Now he recognized that he had to protect the ideal against their attempts at its realization. "New England Reformers" may be described as a more or less systematic application of that insight to the recent "progress of dissent" in Europe and America. To all varieties of "ultraists" Emerson offers a general rebuke concerning the primacy of the self:

> The criticism and attack on institutions which we have witnessed [against everything from "the system of agriculture . . . [to] the institution of marriage"], has

---

[14]*L* 3: 146; John C. Gerber, "Emerson and the Political Economists," *New England Quarterly*, 22 (1940), 352.

[15]John L. Brown, "The Life of Paradise Anew," in *France and North America: Utopias and Utopians*, ed. Mathé Allain (Lafayette, La., 1978), p. 79; Hawthorne, *The Blithedale Romance*, in *Novels*, ed. Millicent Bell (New York: Library of America, 1983), pp. 686, 830.

made one thing plain, that society gains nothing whilst a man, not himself renovated, attempts to renovate things around him. (W 3: 261)

Then he proceeds to his own visionary alternative. Lifting virtually verbatim the long journal passage of 1842, Emerson hails the current "spirit of protest" (a world "awaking to the idea of union") and repeats its many "magic" effects, from communication "by lightning" to "concert" without words. He omits only the separation of fact from ideal ("It is spiritual and must not be actualized"); and makes only one addition, as though to explain why that separation no longer obtains. What had been, amorphously, "union ideal,—in actual individualism, actual union" is rendered, apodictically, "The union must be ideal in actual individualism" (W 3: 251, 266–67).

Actual individualism, ideal union! The paradox is ultimately christic, the incarnation applied to a secular way of life. It is a rhetorical flourish adequate to the occasion, Emerson's first public use of the word individualism. He does not consciously acquiesce to ideology. By "actual" he means a version of the ideal, "individualism" as the intimation of an individuality lost and to be regained, as he makes plain in most subsequent references to individualism through the 1840's—though always, tellingly, by contrast with socialism. Thus in a Notebook addendum to the journal entry of 1842 he complained that

> The *a priori* convictions are there [in individualism]. The plans of Owen and Fourier are enforced by counting & arithmetic. All the fine *aperçus* are for individualism. The Spartan broth, the hermit's cell, the lonely farmer's life are poetic; the phalanstery [Fourier], the self-supporting Village [Owen], are culinary & mean[.] (*JMN* 10: 378)

Thus too he complained in 1847, in a journal passage he was to use a year later to lecture European revolutionaries:

> Individualism has never been tried. All history[,] all poetry deal with it only & because now it was in the minds of men to go alone and now before it was tried, now, when a few began to think of the celestial Enterprise, sounds this tin trumpet of a French Phalanstery and the newsboys throw up their caps & cry, Egotism is exploded; now for Communism! But all that is valuable in the Phalanstery comes of individualism. (*JMN* 10: 154)

And yet (to repeat) through this same decade the ideological tenets of Emersonian individualism become increasingly clear. To begin with, the invective against socialism grows sharper, more pointed. In 1846, contemplating how all "excellence is inflamed or exalted individualism," Emerson wondered if "Community" (or "communatism"), by contrast, were not simply "the dream of Bedlam"; by 1847 he concluded that "Fourier, St. Simon, . . . Leroux, and the Chartist leader, [were] all crazy men," and perhaps Fourier in particular ("a French mind, destitute of course of the moral element") (*JMN* 9: 424, 402, 100). More telling are his unabashed endorsements from 1842 to 1850 of what can only be called free enterprise ideology. The contours of the paradise that were shadowed forth in 1842 are detailed through the decade in the frequent and direct examples he finds of "the concept of laissez-faire [in] the natural world." Adam Smith, he decided, was the one "great man among the economists," and his doctrine of "Laissez faire [was] the only way"[16]:

> Meddle, & I see you snap the sinews with your sumptuary laws . . . the powers that make the capitalist are metaphysical; the force of method, & the force of will makes banks, & builds towns. . . . [We must therefore] leave the individual. . . to the rewards and penalties of his own constitution. . . . persons and property have their just sway. They exert their power, as steadily as matter its attraction. . . . Hence the less government we have the better, —the fewer laws and the less confided power. . . . And though tender people may object to an aristocracy of wealth, if you think what that means, opportunity, free trade, & bringing all the powers to the surface,—it is what all aim at. . . . (*JMN* 11: 45, 9; *W* 3: 219, 205, 215; *JMN* 9: 39)

Emerson did not willingly enlist on the Jacksonian side of the transatlantic debate on individualism. Indeed, I quote him here at such length precisely because it was his intention to de-ideologize the entire issue—to reconceive socialism and liberalism as different roads toward the same meta-systemic ideal, culminating in "the majestic Presence" itself. That reconception, however, was now grounded in a historical distinction. Socialism had the idea, but the reverse methods; liberalism too had the idea, and in addition it had the modern means and methods to realize it. Five years before his 1844 epiphany (if I may call it so)—the revelation in "New England Reformers" that "the union must be ideal in actual individualism"—Emerson had defined the modern period as "the age of the first person singular." In a justly-famous analysis of "The Present Age" (one that he would reiterate over and again, from 1848, in explaining his opposition to the French revolutionaries, to 1880, in his last appearance before the Concord Lyceum), Emerson proclaimed:

> The modern mind teaches that the nation exists for the Individual. . . . This is the Age of Severance, of Dissociation, of Freedom, of Analysis, of Detachment. It is the age of the first person singular. . . . The association [i.e., socialism] is for power merely, for means; the end is the enlargement and independency of the individual. Anciently society was in the course of things: there was a Sacred Band, a Theban Phalanx [prototype of the Fourierist community]. There can be none now. . . . But two parties endure, the party of the Past and the party of the Future. (*EL* 3: 189; *W* 10: 326–27)

In 1839, and through 1842, the party of the Future was ambiguously American and/*or* transcendent. By the Spring of 1844, it had found a local habitation, the Northern United States, and an ideological name, individualism. As an idea, individualism had been the subject of "all history, all poetry" (*JMN* 10: 154). But all history, Emerson had come to understand, was not the

---

[16]Gerber, "Emerson and the Political Economists," pp. 355, 338.

same. The modern period made a difference, as had Plato's Athens, the gospel of Christ, and the discovery of America. As an idea, individualism was a universal a priori, prefigured in Spartan broth and the hermit's cell. Now, in this "age of the first person singular," history was bringing those types to fulfilment. Hitherto "shining social prosperity was the beautitude of man," so that "the ancients thought the citizen existed for the government" and "former generations . . . sacrificed uniformly the citizen to the State" (W 10: 326). But those "primitive" habits of thought and behavior—together with the "warm negro ages of sentiment and vegetation—[were] all gone; another hour had struck" (W 10: 329), and a new principle of "actual union" had been set loose on the world, a moral credo comparable to Newton's *principia*: "Gravity is the Laissez faire principle, or Destiny, or Optimism, than which nothing is wiser or stronger" (*JMN* 11: 77). So perceived, history unfolded in a three-fold spiral from East to West, Athens to Jerusalem and Rome, towards the New World:

1. *the Greek*; when men deified nature . . .
2. *the Christian*; when the Soul became pronounced, and craved a heaven out of nature & above it. . . .
3. *the Modern*; when the too idealistic tendencies of the Christian period running into the diseases of cant, monarchism, and a church, demonstrating the impossibility of Christianity, have forced men to retrace their steps, & rally again on Nature; but now the tendency is to marry mind to nature, to put nature under the mind, convert the world into the instrument of Right Reason. Man goes forth to the dominion of the world by commerce, by science, & by philosophy. (*JMN* 11: 201)

To appreciate the import of this movement toward synthesis and domination we should recall Emerson's 1836 essay on "The Individual":

Not in time is the race progressive. Phocius, Socrates, Anaxagoras, Diogenes are great men, but . . . all theory, all hope are defeated when applied to society. . . . Progress belongs [only] to the Individual. . . . By myself, for myself, I can have faith, Ideas, Progress, God; but if I must apply all these to Society as we see it they become Philistery. (*EL* 2: 175, 176; *JMN* 5: 190)

By 1846, a decade later, Emerson had found the *social* context for progress, faith, and the individual—and it turned out to be the story of America.[17] Here, in this land of "the Modern," where "commerce . . . science, [and] philosophy" were at last keeping pace—so that "our economics in house & barn rapidly show their relation to the laws of geometry, of morals, & of natural history" (*JMN* 11: 313–14)—a new idea had come to light, an "idea roughly written in revolutions and national movements" of the past, but at last articulated with "precision" (W 10: 326):

the individual is the world. (W 10: 326)

17Emerson's use of individualism varies somewhat after the mid-1840s but its meanings always keep within the bounds established by that act of appropriation. Characteristically, it implies the reciprocity between self-interest and the general good.

This perception is a sword such as was never drawn before. Now, "for the first time" in history, the dream of self-reliance was organic to a certain society, in a certain place, as a tendency towards perfect union inherent in its laws, customs, assumptions, and institutions. Despite and *through* "this rude stripping" and "granulation," "actual individualism" was the "celestial Enterprise" in process (*JMN* 10: 154):

> Everybody knows these exaggerating schemers, maniacs who go about in marts. . . . This is the madness of a few, for the gain of the world. The projectors are hurt, but the public is immensely a gainer. . . .
>
> If we could be directly rich, namely, by insight . . . by grandeur of thought; by imagination . . . of course, we should not then need to be indirectly rich by farms, mills, goods, & money. . . . But now the habit of alluding to our wealth, or the wealth of our blood-relations shows the invincible belief, betrays an inveterate persuasion[,] that wealth is the natural fruit of nobility of soul.
>
> America is the idea of emancipation[:]
>
> abolish kingcraft, Slavery, feudalism . . . explode priestcraft. . . . Extemporize government, California, Texas, Lynch Law. All this covers selfgovernment. All proceeds on the belief that as the people have made a gov.t they can make . . . their Union & law. . . .
>
> The American Idea [:]
>
> Emancipation[,] selfreliance[,] selfhelp[,] advance[.] (*JMN* 11: 392, 267, 406, 407)

Union, self-reliance, mills and money, self-government, the nobility of soul, the gain of the world: it amounts to a breathtaking work of culture—a wholesale appropriation of utopia, all the hopes of reform and revolution nourished on both sides of the Atlantic by the turmoil of modernization, for the American Way.

I spoke of "New England Reformers" as our first record of that act of appropriation, and strictly speaking that address rounds out Emerson's 1842 meditation on means and ends, process and telos. But to complete the record it should be supplemented in this regard by its companion-piece, an address delivered a month before (on February 7, 1844) in the wake of the Brook Farm debacle, "The Young American" is a landmark in the development of American symbology, the New England jeremiad recast as a State of the Ideal Union Message. Where the Puritans spoke of a wilderness to be planted, Emerson hails the "sanative and Americanizing influence" of "the *land*"—this "bountiful continent that is ours, state on state, and territory on territory, to the waves of the Pacific" (W 1: 370, 364). Where the Puritans invoked the unfolding of scripture prophecy, he points to "the new and anti-feudal power of Commerce," including the railroad, open markets, and free trade, whose "history" is the "sublime and friendly Destiny by which the human race is guided" (W 1: 370, 371). All this was standard fare in 1844. But then, taking what appears to be a radical shift in direction, Emerson turns for his proof of national destiny to "the appearance of new moral causes which are to modify the state" (W 1: 391). "Government," he observes, "has other offices than those of banker and executioner"; "the true offices of the State" require us "to instruct the ignorant, [and] to supply the poor with work and with good guidance." Hence

> the new movements in the civilized world, the Communism of France, Germany, and Switzerland; the Trades' Unions; the English League against the Corn Laws; and the whole *Industrial Statistics*, so called. In Paris, the blouse, the badge of the operative, has begun to make its appearance in the saloons. Witness too, the spectacle of three Communities [Brook Farm, Fruitland, and Hopedale] which have within a very short time sprung up within this Commonwealth, besides several others undertaken by citizens of Massachusetts within the territory of other States. (W 1: 380)

This daring integration of national mission with international socialism is a dramatic moment in the history of American dissent. Emerson might have presented us with a fundamental clash of modern ideologies, or else with a confrontation of alternative Americas, liberal or collectivist, or perhaps with an Olympian assessment of socialism and individualism under the aspect of utopia. Instead, he subsumes the goals of socialism under the actualities of the developing northern United States. The "value of the Communities," he argues, is "not what they have done, but the revolution which they indicate as on the way" (W 1: 384); and the way, it turns out, together with the revolution it indicates, is that of liberal individualism. On those grounds, Emerson embraces the "moral causes" of socialism in order to absorb these into the "beneficient tendenc[ies]" of the "laws and institutions" which have already made New England the country's "leader," and which are "destined" to make America the "leading nation" of the world:

> We cannot look on the freedom of this country, in connexion with its youth, without a presentiment that here shall laws and institutions exist on some scale of proportion to majesty of nature. . . . Which should be [the "leading nation" of the world, therefore,] but these States? Which should lead that movement, if not New England? Who should lead the leaders, but the Young American? . . . [Our present system] converts Government into an Intelligence-Office, where every man may find what he wishes to buy, and expose what he has to sell. . . . This is the good and this the evil of trade, that it would put every man into market. . . .
>   By this means, however, it has done its work . . . trade was the principle of Liberty . . . trade planted America and destroyed Feudalism . . . it makes peace and keeps peace. . . . Trade is an instrument in the hands of that friendly Power which works for us in our own despite. . . . This beneficent tendency . . . exists and works. . . . One thing is plain for all men of common sense and common conscience, that here, here in America, is the home of man. (W 1: 370, 387–88, 377–79, 391)

In this spirit of conscience and common sense, Emerson confronted the outbreak of revolution in Europe four years later. The European Forty-Eight presented itself to many Americans as a test of modern collectivist theories—a sort of preview of the utopia to be reached by Old World methods—and Emerson, along with other leading intellectuals, crossed the Atlantic to see the results first-hand. His antipathy, and that of most other American observers, may be simply explained. The European radicals did not believe in individualism. It was not so much the violence that troubled Emerson (though he lamented that "in France 'fraternity' [and] 'equality' . . . are names for assassination"), nor was it the burdens of political engagement (though he noted in London concerning talk of "a Chartist revolution on Monday next, and an Irish revolution the following week," that the scholar's "kingdom is at once over & under these perturbed regions") (W 5: 64; 10: 64; JMN 10: 310). As a utopianist, Emerson could accommodate ideas of all kinds, could even support insurrection under extreme circumstances. He demanded only that insurrection serve the cause of utopia, as he defined it. And in 1848 he discovered experientially what he had worked out half a decade before in his journals and lectures, that cause, means, and method were inseparable from actual individualism. This accounts for the generosity of his response. His sympathy for the "masses" of Paris and London, "dragged in their ignorance by furious chiefs to the Red Revolution," was grounded in his now-firm belief that all hope for change, reformist or revolutionary, peaceful or violent, belonged to individualism:

> For the matter of Socialism, there are no oracles. The oracle is dumb. When we would pronounce anything truly of man, we retreat instantly on the individual. . . . [T]ruly [however] I honor the generous ideas of the socialists. . . . We are authorized to say much on the destinies of one, nothing on those of many. . . . [They are] the effects of the age in which [they] live. They [are] not the creators they believe themselves; but they [are] the unconscious prophets of a true state of society; one which the tendencies of nature lead unto, one which always establishes itself for the sane soul, though not in that manner in which they paint it. . . . (JMN 10: 310; W 10: 357)
>
> In the question of socialism, which now proposes the confiscation of France[,] one has only this guidance. You shall not so arrange property as to remove the motive to industry. If you refuse rent & interest, you make all men idle & immoral. As to the poor a vast proportion have made themselves so, and in any new arrangement will only prove a burden on the state. . . . Revolutions of violence then are scrambles merely. . . . (JMN 10: 312, 318) There will be no [true] revolution until there are revolutionists [which is to say, true individualists]. . . .
>
> To America, therefore, monarchs look with apprehension & the people with hope.[18]

Emerson tells us that just before he left England he was asked if there was "an American idea?" and that he spoke in reply of "monsters hard by the setting sun, who believed in a future such as was never a past, but if I should

---

[18]"Politics and Socialism," Houghton Library ms. 200 (8), leaves 95, 101, quoted in Larry J. Reynolds, *European Revolutions and the American Literary Renaissance* (New Haven: Yale Univ. Press, 1988), p. 42; *JMN* 2: 115.

show it to them [his English hosts], they would think French communism solid and practicable by comparison" (*W* 5: 397–98). Soon after his return, he recalled further (in *English Traits*) that at this farewell dinner he had identified the Americans who held "the idea . . . of the right future" as "fanatics of a dream which I should hardly care to relate to . . . English ears, to which it might be only ridiculous,—and yet it is the only true" (*W* 5: 287). No doubt he had in mind something analogous to the "perfect union" he envisioned in 1842. He clarified its relation to actual individualism in his journals and lectures from 1848 through 1851:

> [A] pure reverence for character, a new respect for the sacred quality of the individual man, is that antidote which must correct [the vices of the age]. . . . From the folly of . . . association we must come back to the repose of self-reverence. . . . Now I believe in the closest affinity between moral and material power. Virtue and genius are always on the direct way to the control of society in which they are found. It is in the interest of society that good men should govern, and [in America] there is always a tendency so to place them. . . .
>
> The tools of our time, namely steam, ships, printing, money and popular education, belong to those who can handle them; and their effect has been that advantages once confined to men of family are now open to the whole middle class. (*W* 10: 36, 65; 5: 196)

This passage comes from "Natural Aristocracy," an 1848 address which recasts Jefferson's agrarian concept in terms appropriate to the dawning age of Social Darwinism. Emerson delivered "Natural Aristocracy," on several occasions during the next decade and reprinted part of it in *English Traits* (1856)—fittingly, for *English Traits* is a sustained apologia for modern liberal culture. Indeed, its particular focus on the superiority of the Anglo-Saxon race and the Westering progress of civilization may be said to begin the last phase of Emerson's journey into ideology: his more or less outright identification of individuality with industrial-capitalist "Wealth" (1851) and "Power" (1860), with "American Civilization" (1862), and summarily with "The Fortune of the Republic" (1864):

> One hundred years ago the American people attempted to carry out the bill of political rights to an almost ideal perfection. They have made great strides in that direction since. They are now proceeding, instructed by their success and by their many failures, to carry out, not the bill of rights, but the bill of human duties.
>
> And look what revolution that attempt involves[:] . . . we are a nation of individuals. . . . Faults in the working . . . in our system . . . suggest their own remedies. . . . Here is practical democracy; here is the human race poured out over the continent to do itself justice. . . . The people are loyal and law-abiding. They . . . have no taste for misrule or uproar. . . . As the globe keeps its identity by perpetual change, so our civil system, by perpetual appeal to the people.
>
> The revolution is the work of no man, but the external effervescence of nature. It never did not work. . . . Never country had such a fortune . . . as this, in its geography, its history, and in its majestic possibilities. . . . They [who] complain of

the flatness of American life . . . have no perception of its destiny. They are not Americans. Let us realize that this country, the last found, is the great charity of God to the human race. (*W* 11: 517–18, 529, 525, 526, 528, 530, 536)

Behind this vision lies Emerson's paradoxical credo of 1842–1844: "actual individualism"/"union ideal." But it is paradox now devoid of volatility or tension: "revolution" without conflict, personal agency identified with "civil system," America's "majestic possibilities" grounded in local "history," perfectionism reconceived as the progress of "a nation of individuals" from an "almost ideal" bill of rights to a universal "bill of human duties." The sense of *repose* this conveys is contextualized for us by Emerson during the late 1860's, in a long glance backwards over the revolutionary decades 1820–1840—a time, as he now saw it, when

young men were born with knives in their brain . . . [and] a certain sharpness of criticism, an eagerness for reform . . . showed itself in every quarter. . . . I please myself with the thought that our American mind is not now eccentric or rude in its strength. . . . If I have owed much to the special influences I have indicated, I am not less aware of that excellent and increasing circle of masters in arts and . . . science, who cheer the intellect of our cities in this country to-day,—whose genius is not a lucky accident, but normal, and with broad foundation of culture, and so inspires the hope of steady strength advancing on itself, and a day without night. (*W* 10: 329, 337, 369–70)

That millennial day clearly differs from the perfect union that Emerson envisioned in 1842. Then the process of fulfillment ("culmination of science, useful art, fine art") depended on the self. Now it has its "broad foundation" in a certain culture, "this country to-day," and in an "increasing circle of masters in arts and science . . . whose genius is not a lucky accident, but normal." But the two utopias are not discontinuous. The ideological word, "individualism," that joins them both is inscribed from the beginning. It may be said to have its first public dawnings in *Nature* (1836), in the distinctly American features of Emerson's Orphic poet, singing a "revolution in things [which] will attend the [coming] influx of the spirit" (*W* 1: 76), and a year later, in his first Phi Beta Kappa address, as the promise of individuality embodied in "The American Scholar." At mid-century, the same "hope of steady strength advancing on itself"—fusing historical progress and inward apocalypse—finds its grounding in Emerson's overview of the modern options for radical change: "revolutions . . . in the interest of feudalism and barbarism," such as those he had just witnessed in Europe, versus "revolutions . . . in the interest of society," a procession of "triumphs of humanity" culminating in "the planting of America" (*W* 11: 514, 515). "The Atlantic," he wrote in his journals, recalling his 1848 ocean-crossing from the Old World back to the New, "is a sieve through which only or chiefly the liberal adventurous sensitive *America-loving* part of each city, clan, family, are brought . . . [and] the Europe of Europe is left" (*JMN* 11: 397–98).

The journal entries of November/December 1842 may be said to have launched Emerson, fresh from his "heretical" *Essays: First Series*, on a journey from utopia to ideology; but as I hope I have made clear, the relation between those two sites is dynamic rather than linear. The journey from one to the other is not so much a progression (or regression) as it is an oscillation between center and circumference. The European Forty-Eight marks the return of Emerson's utopia to its ideological home. His early *and abiding* utopianism demonstrates the radical energies potential in American liberal ideology. The same convictions which led Emerson to reject socialism also impelled him a decade earlier outward to the revolutionary concepts of European individuality. It was not then, or ever, a matter of transcending his culture, but (on the contrary) of plumbing its depths. Effectually, it was an effort to carry the basic premises of his culture as far as they would go, to the hither verge (the boundaries and/or frontiers) of what was ideologically conceivable, and thereby to challenge society in the act of drawing out (amplifying, heightening, naturalizing) its grounds of consensus. To universalize, in this sense, was to subvert. Emerson discovered in his culture's symbols, values, and beliefs the agencies of change, reform, and "the new" that expressed the utopian dimensions not only of his own society but of modern liberal culture at large. The later essays collapse the ambiguities this entails; but they also indicate by contrast the enabling source of ambiguity. Emersonian dissent reminds us that ideology in America works not by repressing radical energies but by redirecting them—characteristically, as "America"— into a constant conflict between self and society: the self in itself, a separate, single, resistant individuality, and society en masse, individualism systematized. And it reminds us that that utopian imperative to conflict defines individuality within the ideological parameters of actual individualism.

So defined, the terms of conflict express the basis of liberal cohesion. Modern "civil society," writes Jürgen Habermas, is

> conceived as a principle of marketlike . . . association. For [in Hegel's words,] "the principle of modern states has prodigious strength and depth because it allows the principle of subjectivity to progress to its culmination in the extreme of self-subsistent personal particularity, and yet at the same time brings it back to the substantive unity and so maintains this unity in the principle of subjectivity itself."[19]

Habermas offers this as the "solution" to "the problem of the mediation of state and society." But it is a solution whose strength and depth rest on an ambiguous "and yet"; a solution, that is, which not only allows but calls for a continuing dissonance between fusion and fragmentation, unity and subjectivity. Roberto Ungar describes this as the self-generating friction between public and private spheres which underlies the dynamics of group pluralism. Translated into the terms of Emersonian dissent, these dynamics issue in a

[19]Habermas, *The Philosophical Discourse of Modernity: Twelve Lectures*, trans. Frederick Lawrence (Cambridge, Mass., 1987), p. 39.

vision of autonomy preserved, precariously but decisively, and all the more decisively for its precariousness, within the bounds of community; a form of protest that is bound to challenge (subvert, defy, resist) the consensus it represents—*bound* to challenge and by that act authorized to sustain the polarity of self and society upon which consensus depends. This is essentially the process that authorizes the contradictory-reconciliatory symbol of America: contradictory, in that it *compels* the opposition between the actual and the ideal; reconciliatory, in that it defines that oppositionalism as the gap-to-be-bridged between individual and society. In a sense, these categories are archetypal, universal (as are virtually all other ideological categories, including those of slave and feudal societies), but here as elsewhere they gather substance from their specific historical content.

I am not arguing that Emersonian individualism is a form of liberal co-optation. It is a form of utopian consciousness developed within the premises of liberal culture. It carries with it the profoundly unsettling energies released by that culture in its formative phase—well designated "the era of boundlessness"[20]—and it sustains that profoundly energizing, destabilizing, centrifugal thrust by an appeal to subjectivity as the sine qua non of union, an appeal grounded (as Emerson's 1842 journal demonstrates) in the combined sacred and secular authority of Protestant non-conformity and the theory of natural rights. These liberal premises provided an effective framework for social cohesion before the Civil War and, after it, a triumphant rhetoric of regional and continental incorporation. They also generated the enormous volatility that on the one hand fuelled civil war and on the other hand allowed for the subversive infusion of individuality into the very concept of nationhood. So circumscribed and so empowered, Emersonian individualism comes down to us as a distinctive type of radical thought, at once opposed to systemic individualism and dependent on it—a radicalism as compelling (and in its way as comprehensive) as the competing, socialist types of radical consciousness then emerging in Europe.

The distinction I would make here requires a word of explanation. Recently, the subversive in literature has been raised to the status once reserved for the noble, the tragic, and the complex. The result is a familiar allegory with a new twist: a Manichean struggle between the One and the Many (as between good and evil), where the One takes the antagonist guise of Heterogeneity. Every hegemony, we are told, is hegemonic in its own way, but all forms of subversion, like all happy families, are essentially alike. My assumption is that oppositional forms, like those of cohesion, co-optation, and incorporation, are fundamentally and variously forms of culture. "Emergent," "residual," "anti-hegemonic," "utopian"—all such definitions of the subversive are useful insofar as we demystify their claims to transcendence, universality,

[20]Habermas, *Philosophical Discourse*, p. 39; John Higham, *From Boundlessness to Consolidation: The Transformation of American Culture, 1848–1860* (Ann Arbor, 1969).

and the Real. This applies to the many anti-individualistic movements of the 1840's—collectivism in all its varieties ("the Phalanx, Owenism, Simonism, the Communities") from Leroux to Marx. It applies as well to Emersonian individualism, a liberal mode of resistance which is susceptible equally to liberal strategies of socialization and to the volatility of liberal thought. What makes it independent also makes it counter-dependent and vice-versa: what binds it to the culture in symbiotic antagonism also infuses it with a destabilizing, energizing, centrifugal vision of its own. The very terms that predicate social continuity posit the necessity for change.

The difference here between Emerson and what I termed the Jacksonian ideologues recalls Victor Turner's distinction between the central and final phases of the liminal process. The ideologues, from the manifest destinarian John O'Sullivan to the Loco Foco Robert Rantoul, apologist for minimal government, make process synonymous with cultural expansion and consolidation. Emerson's radical appropriation of individuality (1836–1841) expresses the anti-structures of that process: it turns all the power of hope, mind, and imagination unleashed by free enterprise capitalism in an apparently open, empty, and endlessly malleable New World *against* the tendency towards reaggregation. The result is a standing invitation to resist that has all the energy of pure utopia—of an ideal (to recall the phrase that Emerson deleted in 1844) which "must not be actualized"—but with a modern difference. According to Hans Blumenberg, utopia at its most intense is "a sum of negations"; it avoids "contamination by what currently exists" by banning all definition whatever, placing "a prohibition against saying anything positively imagined . . . about the new land as it will be."[21] That prohibition applies in this case as well, except that here it also expresses, ambiguously, something already imagined: the new land as America; ideal union potential in actual individualism.

I have called that form of radical imagining *dissent* because the term seems best to convey its distinctive emphasis on negation and transition, its resistance on principle to institutional controls, its open-ended, *self*-enclosed tropism for reform and change. It is a form of protest conceived at the interstices of free enterprise theory, and developed within the gaps or lacunae in the principle of subjectivity itself between the actual and the ideal, selfhood and union; between substantive unity on the one hand and, on the other, a self-subsistent personal peculiarity with a consecration of its own. . . .

The appeal of Emersonian dissent lies in an extraordinary conjunction of forces: its capacity to absorb the radical communitarian visions it renounces, and its capacity to be nourished by the liberal structures it resists. It demonstrates the capacities of culture to shape the subversive in its own

---

21Blumenberg, *Work on Myth*, trans. Robert Wallace (Cambridge, Mass., 1985), p. 221. Cf Raymond Williams, *Marxism and Literature* (Oxford, 1977), pp. 121–28; Fredric Jameson, *The Political Unconscious: Narrative as a Socially Symbolic Act* (Ithaca, 1981).

image, and *thereby*, within limits, to be shaped in turn by the radicalism it seeks to contain. Theodore Adorno claims (as the summa of "negative dialectics") that to be radical is not to "bow to *any* alternatives," since "freedom means to criticize and change situations, not to confirm by deciding within their coercive structure."[22] Emersonian dissent testifies against that dream of autonomy. Or to put it in positive terms, it testifies to the oppositional forms generated within the structures of society—in Emerson's terms, somewhere at the margins of culture, at some transitional moving point, perpetually inchoate because transitional on principle, between center and circumference.

This implies a somewhat different model of the liminal process from the one I just mentioned. Turner, following Van Gennep, speaks of anti-structure and reaggregation as a logical sequence of phases (central and final) leading to ritual closure. The example of Emerson suggests that the expressive forms of anti-structure may so influence the ritual forms of socialization as to make closure an office of anti-structural process. The *radical* complementarity this entails is defined by neither harmony nor synthesis nor compromise, although Emerson's career shows how it may be reduced (or returned to) such vehicles of reaggregation. Rather, it builds on a necessary friction between the various agents of reciprocity—necessary, because the friction sustains the *movement between* actual individualism and perfect union. In "Self-Reliance" this inbetweenness takes the form of the symbiosis between the ritual of cultural continuity (Independence Day) and an antagonist rhetoric of discarding (good and bad, father and mother, "this bountiful cause of Abolition" together with "the coat of philanthropy"). It finds an apt symbol in the *A*'s for self-reliance which Emerson devised sometime between 1837 and 1839:

Selfreliance[:]

A greater respect for Man indicated by the movements
of   Antigovernment [i.e., laissez-faire]

AntiAssociation [i.e., anti-socialism]	their pursuits
AntiMonopoly	politics
AntiChurch [i.e, multi-denominationalism]	education
	religion
	(*JMN* 12: 153)

—and to which he added this legend or motto: "The antidote to [social] abuse is the growth of the Individual. . . . We think our civilization near its meridian, but we are yet only at the cock-crowing and the morning star" (*W* 3: 215, 216–17).

In that volatile conjunction of ends and means lies the importance of "America" in Emerson's early thought. So long as he did not have to confront ideological alternatives, he could extend the circle of self-reliance to the point where individuality was turned against individualism. From that liminal

<hr />

[22]Adorno, *Negative Dialectics*, trans. E. B. Ashton (New York, 1973), p. 226.

position at mid-century, circling from *"movement"* to *"pursuit"* (away from government, association, and church, towards some ever-imminent, ever-receding "meridian" of political, educational, and religious "growth")—a dynamic, to repeat, resistant to the brink of abandonment—all of our classic writers distinguished American dissent from the tradition which they dismissed as Old World revolution. All of them, with Emerson, repudiated the European Forty-Eight, and each of them, partly through that act of repudiation, forged a subversive mode of his own. Probably the most fortifying examples of subversion, so conceived, are *Walden* and *Leaves of Grass*. Emerson said of Thoreau that he "was in his own person a practical answer, *almost* a refutation, to the theories of the socialists" (my italics) (*W* 10: 356). We might say much the same of Whitman, from an opposite perspective: he offers a theory of the Self-En Masse which is a personal answer, almost a refutation, to the abuses of industrial capitalism. The limitations of that theory appear most dramatically in the examples of political protest I mentioned earlier: Thoreau's defence of John Brown (in spite of Brown's armed revolt) as a son of Puritan New England and "the most American of us all"; Garrison's allegiance (against the Constitution) to personal renovation and the Declaration of Independence; Fuller's jeremiadic invocation (as it were beyond Italian socialism) to "my America," "the land of the future," and "the spirit of our fathers." Considered from either a literary or a political angle, the major discourse on this mode of radical containment—in the double sense of the term, as confining and nurturing radicalism—comes in Melville's work: in *Pierre; or, The Ambiguities* (1852), for instance, a story of individuality born in the euphoria of Young America, nourished by an antipathy to systemic individualism, trapped in the ideology of the self, and destroyed by an absolute faith in process, potential, and negation; or of "Bartleby the Scrivener: A Tale of Wall Street" (1853), where "actual individualism" signifies *both* resistance on principle *and* liberal society as defined by its radical critics ("a system of isolation, or isolated selves"; "the exclusive domination of capital"), and whose adversarial/representative protagonist mocks both sides of the equation.[23]

To paraphrase the great July Fourth declaration of "Self-Reliance," Emerson wrote on the lintels of the doorpost to the future, *Individualism*. In doing so, he expanded the meaning of the term to accommodate the utopian powers of individuality—among these, the appeal to subjectivity as the sine qua non of union, an appeal sustained (as in the 1842 journals) by the combined sacred and secular authority of Protestant non-conformity and the theory of natural

[23]Henry David Thoreau, "A Plea for Captain John Brown," in *Reform Papers*, ed. Wendell Glick (Princeton, 1972), p. 125; Margaret Fuller Ossoli, *At Home and Abroad, or Things and Thoughts in America and Europe*, ed. A. B. Fuller (1856; rpt. Port Washington, New York, 1971), pp. 326–27; William Lloyd Garrison, "Fourth of July Address, 1829," and "No Union with Slaveholders" (1832), in *William Lloyd Garrison*, ed. George M. Fredrickson (Englewood Cliffs, N.J., 1968), pp. 11–22, 52–56, 141–42.

rights. And at the same time he confined the prospects of utopia, like some Avenging Angel, within the rhetorical magic circle of the resisting representative self. "In dealing with the State," he wrote in "Politics"—an address he kept revising from 1836–1837, the volatile years of *Nature* and "The American Scholar" to the Fall of 1842—"we ought to remember that its institutions are not aboriginal, though they existed before we were born. . . .[E]very one of them was once the act of a single man" (*W* 3: 199). William James rightly heard in such lines the "bugle blast" of a new philosophy, or as he put it in *Pragmatism* (1907), "a program for more work, and more particularly . . . an indication of the ways in which existing realities may be *changed*."[24] Our own view, almost a century later, need not be less sanguine for recognizing the limitations inherent in this concept of radicalism. Indeed, I have been arguing throughout that the radicalism is inseparable from those limitations, which function simultaneously as boundary and as frontier. But we would do well also to recognize the mixed blessings of the cultural symbology this represents.

That critical imperative is also part of the Emersonian legacy. Our century has been witness to an extraordinary course of change: in Europe and the United States, a remarkable series of conflicts of all kinds (economic, racial, ethnic, ideational); and in the United States, a still more remarkable process of expansion, consolidation, and incorporation. We should remember in this regard that Emerson's recourse to the "single man," as to the summits of individuality, bespeaks the pervasive reach of the liberal state, even unto the realm of the protean imagination. And in dealing with the state, we should remember further, as Emerson advised, that our pluralist "traditions of individualism," linking William James, Irving Howe, E. L. Doctorow, and Francis Fukuyama, are neither aboriginal nor post-millennial, neither modern reflections of Central Man nor "the end point of mankind's ideological development," but institutional. Emerson hoped that they would eventuate in somewhat more than "actual individualism" at last; and they have: the ambiguities they have spawned, concerning subversion and/or co-optation, subjectivity as agency of change and/or agent of social control, protest as counter-culture and/or as cultural counter-dependence, remain the central problematic of American literary and political dissent.

---

[24]William James, speech printed in the *Boston Evening Transcript*, May 25, 1903, p. 3, and *Pragmatism* (1907), quoted in Poirier, *The Renewal of Literature*, p. 178.

Is There an I for an Eye?

Richard Poirier

Henry Nash Smith points, I think, to one of the most interesting aspects of Emerson when he refers to "Emerson's problem of vocation."[1] Implicit in his rejection of "society" was a rejection of the roles which it honored and rewarded. Having abandoned the ministry in 1832, having found no satisfactory substitute for it either in the strongly acquisitive business society of Boston during that decade or in the groups of reformers in the next who, like those at Brook Farm, surrendered to yet another kind of institutionalized action, Emerson invented the ideal type of self-expressive man who supplies the titles of some of his essays—The Scholar, Representative Men, The Poet. Being a poet in the sense that he defines one, being, that is, a man who can relinquish the accouterments of society and civilization in order to possess a purer and larger sense of the self—this represents a touching solution to his "problem of vocation." The "transparent eyeball" (*CW* 1: 10) is itself an imaginary role, a version of "the poet," to which he attempts to give a greater reality than that belonging to the roles he rejects. Obviously, the eyeball as possessor is an imaginative analogue to the great American enterprise of the period. To a man of the early nineteenth century in America, possessing landscape was necessarily more than a romantic commonplace of descriptive-reflective poetry. Possession was also a national goal entrusted to enterprising men who faced an opportunity for profit unique in history.

The position in which Emerson found himself should engage the same appreciation given nowadays to the situation of artists at a time closer in spirit to our own, of the *fin de siècle* as represented in, say, Pater, or in Joyce's "portrait" of a Pateresque artist. What was left to Emerson was the task of imagining a role for himself not merely as a writer. He had literally to enact the role *in* his writing. Only here could he be the "poet" he imagines. Rejecting as explicitly as he does all institutionalized allegiances, he is forced to claim a place and function for himself almost wholly through his style. His function could not come to life outside his pages since he is explicitly

[1]Henry Nash Smith, "Emerson's Problem of Vocation." *New England Quarterly* 12 (1939), 52–67.—ED.

disdainful of the idea that absorbs the attention of Fitzgerald and James: that the idealized self can function in terms of the world of social and economic systems.

To put such a burden on style is not uncharacteristic of American writers, especially of Melville, James, or Faulkner. To do so while writing in the polite forms and styles of Emerson's essays, however, is sometimes to miscalculate the burden. He had a distaste for fiction and thus for a form in which he could have had a multitude of voices strengthening his own by manipulated contrasts. Such a technique is obviously indispensable to the novelists just mentioned, to James, say, in convincing us of the virtues of Isabel or Strether, to Melville in revealing the heroism of Ahab. Emerson was primarily an essayist and lecturer, seldom choosing to argue alternative positions within a given piece, and he writes the same way, uses the same style for all aspects of experience. His personal letters are in this respect no different from his public speeches. His unalterable consistency of tone, except in rare instances like the essay "Experience," is perhaps one reason why he *sounds* rather simple to modern readers. But evidence that he was theoretically aware of the difficulties of his situation and of the literary problems it involved is abundant, as in "The Transcendentalist," where he gives his account of our "double consciousness" (*CW* 1: 213), or in his characterization of the only momentary successes of the poet who seems to "be free" and to "make free" only in his tropes, or in his lamentation in "Experience" that grief itself has no reality for him (*CW* 3: 18, 29). The latter essay is nearly an admission that Emerson's renowned indifference to evil might be charged as much to emotional shallowness as to philosophical conviction.

Emerson's theories and recognitions must not, however, be confused with his performances. In his performances, his structuring of sentences and paragraphs, especially in so early an effort as "Nature," he often unwittingly evades the struggle with language to which those causes would seem necessarily to commit him. His style, by which I mean his projected presence in the rhythms and vocabularies of his prose, often reveals a subjection, even an allegiance to the very forms and conventions which are at the same time being attacked. The pictorialized elements in the opening of "Nature," for example, are not wholly coherent with the audible ones. There is no speaking "I" for the seeing "eye." Or to put it another way, the romantic images of relinquishment and possession get entrapped within the social environment created in the speaker's address to his readers.

Of course, if we forget about voice, and consider the passage rather mechanically only as an extended metaphor about sight, then the opening of "Nature" would be demonstrably coherent. In this respect, the passage shows every evidence of Emerson's metaphoric power exerting itself to authenticate an incredible moment of self-transformation. The moment occurs when, "Standing on the bare ground,—my head bathed by the blithe air and uplifted into infinite space,—all mean egotism vanishes. I become a transparent eyeball; I am nothing; I see all; the currents of the Universal Being circulate through me; I am part or parcel of God. The name of the nearest friend sounds then foreign and accidental: to be brothers, to be acquaintances, master or servant, is then a trifle and a disturbance" (*CW* 1: 10). The many variations on ideas of seeing and transparency in the preceding paragraphs of "Nature" do indeed condition us to welcome the "transparent eyeball" when it appears. The narrator's transformation is further anticipated by his curious changes and expansions of identity throughout the opening of the essay, especially in his use of pronouns. The opening sentence is general and aphoristic ("a man needs to retire"), the next is more emphatically personal ("I am not solitary whilst I read and write"). The shifts continue: from "a man" to "I" to "one" simply to "man" as subjects of the verbs, and throughout the remainder of the passage there are similar shifts—to "we" back to "I" to "most persons" to "man" to "I" and so forth, even though he is usually talking about his own uniquely quasi-mystical relation to things. Thus, even in the grammar we experience the speaker's capacity to relinquish his particular identity and assume an ever more inclusively general one. In addition, he shifts into tones of voice and into vocabularies reserved for the different vocations that deal professionally with the relation between men and landscape—terms that belong to the surveyor, the farmer, the philosopher, the aesthetician. He mixes these voices and vocabularies with a self-confident ease, thereby sounding like a composite man before he explicitly claims to be one. The reader comes to accept a man so multiple, so general, so inclusive as to be in effect a "transparent eyeball," seeing everything and letting us see everything in him, long before he actually claims to be one. So that there is plenty of evidence in the passage of Emerson trying to transport us from the society of "joint stock companies"—where the landscape belongs to Miller, Locke, and Manning, who own its farms—to the world of Emerson's imagining, where such ownership is relinquished so that the Self may be possessed by and come into possession of the cosmos.

The writing is, in the manipulation of metaphors, a stunning example of Emerson's genius. But if we listen to the passage rather than merely work out patterns of metaphor, if we ask ourselves not what is revealed by analysis of images but what is experienced by our being alert to the sound of the voice addressing us, we cannot then say that Emerson as "transparent eyeball" has managed to displace Miller, Locke, and Manning as owners of the landscape or as proprietors of reality. Emerson's opposition to conventional systems prevents his appealing for support to any realities constituted outside his own language. And yet Emerson's tone in the opening of "Nature" seldom manages to be more than compliantly evocative of the social forms it wants us to disown. Even in the few passages already quoted, the reader is made to feel in a relation less to a revolutionary than to an urbane, highly literary, even rather clubbable man. To speak of withdrawal with the elegant presumptuousness of the opening sentence—"To go into solitude, a man needs to retire as much from his chamber as from society"—may invite all of us into the woods but will it offend anyone who stays in the drawing room? He sounds as if he were planning a trip to the country not with Wordsworth but with Addison and Steele. A man who says that the stars "light the Universe with their admonishing smile" and who refers to "the charming landscape which I saw this morning" is using phrases that domesticate both himself and nature, phrases of a genteel good taste that necessarily moderates our response to the later hyperbolic definition of his relation, as a "transparent eyeball," to nature, to society, and to the reader. Even the direct criticisms made in the passage, such as the remark that "to speak truly few adults can see nature," defers to polite sentimentalities about *really* seeing things, and leaves to speculation the meaning of "nature" itself. The energy expended here, and the corresponding energy elicited from the reader are conspicuously insufficient to Emerson's intentions. Indeed we recognize the ambitions of this passage only by sensing that there is something askew in its style. By contrast we might recall Thoreau's very vigorous activity in sentences where he wants the reader's active assent to his claims that "I retained the landscape and . . . annually carted off what it yielded without a wheel barrow." Emerson in this and many other instances is victim of what Santayana calls the "kindly infidelities of language," its tendency to "vitiate the experience it expresses."

Emerson in many respects *is* American literature, both by virtue of the themes and images of which he is its storehouse and because of the exciting ways in which the impossible ambitions he has for his writing often fail, but only just barely, of being realized. Thus his style in this passage, admittedly an early one, tends to make his ideas of relinquishment and possession seem safe and respectable—an anticipation of what happens to Mark Twain in *Huckleberry Finn*—despite the necessities of his personal position. "Emerson had his message," James the novelist wisely observed, "but he was a good while looking for his form." And in this difficulty he is the exemplum of those American writers, to me the most interesting, who cannot hide their dissatisfaction and their resultant struggle with the forms and styles they are using.

Again, though by now it should be apparent, my interest is not in tracing in American literature images of the poetic eye and attendant images of relinquishment and possession. I am concerned rather with the condition of these images within the environments created by particular works or passages. Obviously the only possible environment for them is in a context invented by the writer, the initial proposition being that they are only antagonistically received, if indeed they aren't obliterated, in the real world, or in literature which allows itself to be merely a mirror of that world. The results of my emphasis will, I hope, reveal something about history as well as about literature: it should let us measure the degree of conflict between assumptions of reality embedded in the conventions of literary expression, as against the often antagonistic assumptions implicit in certain images of American romantic idealism. American writers show a noticeable difficulty both in escaping those conventions of expression and in creating a stylistic environment that will be hospitable to the "poet" enacting the drama of relinquishment and possession. When Emerson remarks in his *Journals* that the two barriers to literary and intellectual accomplishment in America are "our devotion to property" and the "influence of Europe," he reveals an intuitive grasp of how efforts to dispel the first are inseparable from the literary problems posed by the second. In trying to modify "our devotion to property" it was necessary profoundly to modify the literary conventions, especially of prose, that constrain or even direct our consciousness of the self and of reality.

Tone

Jonathan Bishop

As rhythm is the literary expression of the organic faculty, and metaphor the characteristic literary mode of action of the Soul as intellect, so the moral sentiment, when it moves over into words, becomes tone. The meanings that metaphor embodies exist in the eternity of the impersonal intellect. Tone, though, is always personal; with tone one enters a world where people exist. To speak is to put yourself in a world containing at least you and your listener, a world of moral behavior. By tone Emerson re-enters the world from which the habits of his intellect might tend to exclude him, engaging the moral agency of the Soul for himself and his reader. His letters show how alert he was to the waver and touch of human intercourse, how acutely he cultivated the anxious joys of friendship, how perpetually the interests of his interlocutors, imagined or present, were scrupulously uppermost. The presence of tone is a kind of social test of truth, a sign that one's perceptions ring true emotionally, that they resonate within a self and not in some philosophic void. By tone one shows one's "presence of mind"—a useful phrase, for in one sense it means one's personal note; in another, the amount of impersonal mind, of the Oversoul, that one has at command. In this phrase the two senses are momentarily one, and they manifest one distinct and multiple Soul. One hears in a man's tone the amount of truth that is in him, his capacity for experience, the life he is ready to bring to bear on the human predicament within which you encounter him, the size and range of the Soul in him.

For Emerson it is a characteristic fault of a man like Disraeli that "he makes at last no impression, because the hearer asks Who are you? What is dear to you? What do you stand for? and the speech & the speaker are silent, & silence is confession" (J 7: 503). For the reverse of the same reason Emerson admires the seventeenth-century writers who "jumped into their book bodily themselves" so entirely that "not a pinch of dust" remains behind (J 8: 503). "It makes a great difference to the force of any sentence whether there be a man behind it or no. In the learned journal, in the influential newspaper, I discern no form; only some irresponsible shadow; oftener some moneyed corporation, or some dangler who hopes, in the mask and robes of his paragraph, to pass for somebody. But through every clause and part of speech of a right book I meet the eyes of the most determined of men; his force and terror inundate every word; the commas and dashes are alive so that the writing is athletic and humble—can go far and live long" (W 4: 282).

Almost surely Emerson is thinking of Carlyle here, and his words may explain to a twentieth-century reader the otherwise not very comprehensible service Carlyle performed for his fellow Victorian writers. Carlyle could mean a realized if crude success at the task of becoming a man in words, of having power enough to dominate the verbal world, to reduce the school rules to chaos and yet be able to remake a newly relevant individual order. Ruskin and Dickens and Melville learned from Carlyle, in all three cases more imitatively than Emerson. Carlyle's formula for the artist's tone is an aggressive one, and Emerson was not an aggressive man, in or out of language; but he was attracted to power in writing as he was attracted to wealth and bodily strength and even fanatic determination when he saw these qualities in other people. The tendency to derive vicarious satisfaction from the contemplation of such burly identities as Webster, John Brown, or the British nation grew as Emerson himself became more benignly yielding in manner.

There is a certain distance, though, between the true, secret Emerson and the tones he envies and occasionally adopts: it is an experimental rather than an inevitable self that he throws "bodily" into his books. This is more obvious in the poetry than in the prose, for the poems often present speakers who are held at a distance from the mind that composed them. Frequently these semifictionalized identities grow to have a separate name, the better to figure as mock-mythical representatives for the different impulses in their author. So we encounter Uriel, Methuselah, Cupid, Saadi—even a bumblebee and a titmouse. In the verse such projected identities are playful, even capricious. They are not recommended as responsibly as the abstract roles of the prose—the scholar, the preacher, the poet—or as the various representative heroes of intellectual, moral, artistic, or practical action. And the different unnamed voices in the prose are more subtle and responsible still, since they are less obviously detached for separate contemplation, more nearly taken for granted as expressions of his self. The equivalent in prose of the self-mythologizing we find in the poetry is irony; and for Emerson, irony is more serious than myth.

Tone is therefore never entirely straightforward for Emerson. The preacher of self-reliance was also the critic of egotism, and both to an extreme degree. The apparent contradiction may readily be elucidated in general moral terms, but what consistent sense is a *writer* to make of an admonition to "communicate himself, and not his vanity" (W 8: 229)? In the world of words, how do you tell the difference? Emerson's own answer would appear to be, by adding self-knowledge to self-expression. "A poem, a sentence causes us to see ourselves. I be & I see my being, at the same time" (J 4: 180). The implication is, I see and approve: I calmly am what I clearly see. Here Emerson has gone beyond Carlyle, whose assertions are all blind and from within. Emerson's tone is himself, yet it is also at a distance; he is and he knows who he is. Always he exhibits the Soul as intellect as well as the Soul as self.

Such tonal emphasis plus self-consciousness would apply, of course, only to the interesting moments of tone; one makes a drastic selection to arrive at these. There is no point in elaborately analyzing the dull tones, the preacherly commonplaces, the high-minded vapid identity behind so much of what we cannot, except by force, attend to. Emerson would be the first to encourage us to neglect any presences we cannot respect and be surprised by. The tones that interest are those that genuinely present the Soul impersonated before us, those that involve us in a confrontation with an identity testing itself in words.

One's identity, false or true, blindly committed or self-consciously tentative, is found by distinguishing a self from those who are not oneself. The set of others against whom the early Emerson chiefly defines himself is the world of philistines and traditionalists. His tone is sharpest and most conscious of enemy values in "Self-Reliance." There he swings out unqualifiedly against the world of the wicked dollar and comes forward uncompromisingly as the adviser of rebel youth. There are many quotable sentences that demonstrate the tone that follows from and embodies this stance: "I would write on the lintels of the door-post, *Whim*. I hope it is somewhat better than whim at last, but we cannot spend the day in explanation" (W 2: 51–52). There is a tart consciousness in such remarks that "we" are being overheard by a world that will call our ideas "whims," a world whose judgment we are, indeed, in some danger of sharing: to write the word on the door-post defies our own fears as well as the prejudices of the enemy. Tone can be a sign of a war within the self, as well as between the self and the world.

Emerson is as capable of a complementary rigor at the expense of his own, the reformer's, party; "we" as well as "they" come under attack. To be sure, this is more private. It is in the journal that we read of the "exaggerating people" who "talk of moments when their brains seemed bursting with the multitude of thoughts" but who had better rest easy: "I believe they were mistaken; there was no danger" (J 8: 542). A still better instance of the tone to be heard here, with its sharpening of the nostrils and chill set of the upper lip, is a reply he records himself as having made to Ellery Channing. His friend had objected (one can imagine with what willfully capricious cleverness of his own) to the usurpation of fame by Homer and Shakespeare, which kept out the talented men of the present: "Oh certainly, I assure him, that oaks & horse-chestnuts are entirely obsolete, that the horticultural society are about to recommend the introduction of cabbages as a shade tree, so much more convenient and every way comprehensible; all grown from the seed upward to its most generous crumpled extremity within one's own short memory; past contradiction the ornament of the world, & then so good to eat, as acorns & horsechestnuts are not. Shade trees for breakfast!" (J 6: 422).

Perhaps this raillery goes on too long, even for a journal entry; it is possible to pursue such a line of fanciful teasing of petulantly unappreciated talent only from a conservative position, which Emerson occupies at some spiritual peril to himself. He cannot afford to identify permanently with the system of values that would sneer consistently at Ellery Channing. Irony invariably involves some doubt as to who one is, and, when this combines with uncertainty about one's standards, it can become equivocal or spiteful. Emerson by nature is on both sides, and the ability, or the fate, to be on both sides of an issue is probably involved with the whole possibility of tone. Single-minded men need not have any special "presence of mind." But there is bound to be doubleness in the allegiances of a writer who can express some single identity sharply enough to be aware that he has created a self in words, for the awareness places him at a distance from his own self-creation. In irony, a writer invites his reader to share that distance.

What one prefers to find is a certain hovering evaluation, a refusal to come down too firmly on either side of the question, a willingness to let a reader find his own way to the judgment that ought to be stressed. At Oxford on his second English visit in 1848, Emerson had a chance to meet "several faithful, highminded young men, some of them in the mood of making sacrifices for peace of mind,—a topic, of course, on which I had no counsel to offer" (W 5: 199). The tone of this observation from *English Traits* has something in common with the journal entry on Channing, but it is less simply conservative and morally more interesting. It is tempting to say that the last sentence is simply ironic: Emerson had plenty to say on just this topic, had in fact been saying it all his life. But in all irony the straight meaning survives as an understatement, and especially so here. Why might he "of course" have no counsel to offer? For one thing, because he is not English himself, the issues of religious conformity that face these young men do not take a form of which he has an intuitive comprehension. There is an instinctive scrupulosity in the withdrawal here, very typical of Emerson; there is also emotional reserve. This may amount to a cool self-detachment from the spiritual cowardice these Englishmen are ready to yield to, but it may also express a profounder identification with exactly this weakness: has he too not made some sacrifices for peace of mind, now that he is famous, a traveling sage in request by worshipful foreigners? How then can he speak, except obliquely, on behalf of courage? He is either too free from the particulars of these English problems of conscience or too involved in a universal failure of nerve either to blame or to help. The range of possibilities is implicit in the tone: tart and tender, reserved, precise, and melancholy. Such doublings of tone enlarge the self that tone presents, and hence give and provoke more of the Soul.

English Traits is relatively late Emerson; here is a sentence from *Nature*: "The advantage of the ideal theory over the popular faith is this, that it presents the world in precisely that view which is most desirable to the mind" (W 1: 59). This is effrontery, cool and calculated. A voice assumes with casually innocent authority just the point that his reader would (if this were not Emerson he was reading) be settling down to hear argued out. But *this* tone says: you, reader, are not to judge me; I pass by that illusion with which you are accustomed to flatter yourself when you read philosophic books; I am possessed by a perception that need not beg for your acceptance. It is even conceivable that seeing me take my authority for granted will induce in you the shock of surprise that will put you in possession of what I know. What is "desirable to the mind" is, from the ordinary sensible point of view, some illusion, a fantasy that obscures the facts sane men must face. This of course is to misunderstand the point of idealism, a point that Emerson is not putting discursively but leaving to the tone. For "mind" here is not merely the defensive self, which may indeed conceal reality behind a haze of fantasy, but those faculties to which the facts themselves are "presented." If the word "mind" must change its definition, so too must "desire." "Desirable to the mind" is going to mean something like "consistent with the nature of the mind."

Like metaphor, then, tone can be a way to miniaturize doctrine, to preach in words, artfully. I believe the pleasures of the Emersonian tone are at their best when the speaker fronts the enemy and borrows one or another of his idioms to make his point. This is the tonal equivalent of taking over some part of the businessman's or farmer's world to make a metaphor of it; it is a characteristic part of Emerson's most healthy strategy, for it helps to guarantee that the whole world is being assimilated by a man of many parts, a true hero of the Soul. The strategy need not be anything ambitiously or deliberately philosophical. Listen to his description of telegraphy:

> We had letters to send; couriers could not go fast enough nor far enough; broke their wagons, foundered their horses; bad roads in spring, snowdrifts in winter, heats in summer; could not get the horses out of a walk. But we found out that the air and earth were full of Electricity, and always going our way,—just the way we wanted to send. *Would he take a message?* Just as lief as not; had nothing else to do; would carry it in no time. Only one doubt occurred, one staggering objection,— he had no carpet-bag, no visible pockets, no hands, not so much as a mouth, to carry a letter. But after much thought and many experiments we managed to meet the conditions, and to fold up the letter in such invisible compact form as he could carry in those invisible pockets of his, never wrought by needle and thread,—and it went like a charm. (W 7: 27–28)

This passage from "Civilization" is as fanciful as the attack on Channing, but nobody is getting hurt. The occasion provides a lazy opportunity for spinning out an agreeable metaphor, a way of keeping the parts of the argument casually together. This tone asks us to sit loose in the world, know as much as we can of it and use what falls handy, like any gossip at the depot. Such a strategy is more regularly transcendental when it hints at a range of meanings beyond those we would consider within such a practical man's field of vision. "By drainage we went down to a subsoil we did not know, and have found there is a Concord under old Concord, which we are now getting the best crops from; a Middlesex under Middlesex; and, in fine, that Massachusetts has a basement story more valuable and that promises to pay better rent than all the superstructure" (W 7: 150). One may hear a moral or imaginative meaning here; the tone leaves it up to the reader, who may if he pleases think of more than drainage. Drainage is still quite definitely the subject and loses none of its dignity in this reference. "We" are farmers of Concord, and the speaker means to go on talking like a farmer, as suits an essay on "Farming," though willing enough to let a reader overhear him saying more than farmers generally intend.

Conservatism as a social judgment is a simplification of self for Emerson; as a grip on facts it is the necessary condition of clear insight. When Emerson has an observation to make about the nature of things, one that has grown out of his relation to life rather than irritability with his liberal acquaintances, this grip on facts, and the plain man's tone that goes with it, can validate the free play of the mind that constitutes his permanent radical base. "There is a crack in everything God has made. It would seem there is always this vindictive circumstance stealing in at unawares even in the wild poesy in which the human fancy attempted to make bold holiday and to shake itself free of the old laws,—this back-stroke, this kick of the gun, certifying that the law is fatal; that in nature nothing can be given, all things are sold" (W 2: 107). The sad observation is firmed by the country images, which solidly underlie the philosophic generality, adding a touch of wryness to the tone; what else, the farmer from whose world these images are drawn might say, did you expect. One borrows a tone in such circumstances not to assert or disguise one's real identity as a moral philosopher or as a human being, but to place it among familiar facts, and so confess a fate common to those among whom one actually lives. Tone can unite as well as separate.

"No article so rare in New England as Tone" (J 5: 307),[1] he complains more than once in the journal. To the attentive ear of that time this tone, the practical man's voice, must have been common enough in New England, available to a literary man capable of hearing and isolating the identity and set of attitudes it expressed. We know from the writers of the Saturday Club how the plain man's voice could be reproduced accurately enough as a piece of comic theater. Emerson's use of it is more serious because it becomes one of his own modes of approaching the world and himself, and not merely a scarecrow held at a distance for the amusement and edification of readers who, in social intercourse, would look down on the speaker who used it naturally without necessarily having an expressible identity of their own to back up their condescension. The word "article" in Emerson's complaint here itself attests the presence of what neither he nor New England was really without. In its pure form, without special additions and ironic qualifications, this voice can be found in such nasal remarks as "He can't make any paint

---

[1]Bishop's general point is well-taken, but *JMN* 7: 284, which appeared after Bishop's book, shows that "Tone" was a misprint for "Tom," probably Tom Wyman, the potter-squatter mentioned in the "Former Inhabitants" chapter of Thoreau's *Walden*.

stick but his own" (W 12: 53), or "We say the cows laid out Boston. Well, there are worse surveyors" (W 6: 122). Here is the tone Thoreau based his irony upon, the tone that first identifies Melville's Ishmael. Both of Emerson's literary descendants made far more of it than he did.

But in complaining of the absence of tone in New England he more probably had in mind the absence of a civilized presence, a courteous manner—what the plain man would call "high-toned" behavior. Here Emerson himself is to my ear unique. There was no one then in New England who quite caught the tone that is to be heard here and there in Emerson: "Now then we hear rarely a true tone, a single strain of the right ode" (J 7: 207–208). This longed-for superior note can appear on the modest level of talk where one becomes aware of Emerson's most private voice, a voice not borrowed half-mockingly from the village but, as far as we can judge, intrinsic, a manifestation of an uncombative identity, which speaks from a position nearer silence than the countryman's voice and infinitely farther from the public habits of an alien world. We can hear, in the passages where this higher voice speaks, a virtually unspecifiable distinction, precise, low-keyed, intimate, unconsciously alert to the weight of words. A passage from *Representative Men* on the uses of a great man manifests it well: "He must be related to us, and our life receive from him some promise of explanation. I cannot tell what I would know; but I have observed there are persons who, in their character and actions, answer questions which I have not skill to put. One man answers some question which none of his contemporaries put, and is isolated" (W 4: 6–7). There is something special here, but so undramatic it is hard to catch. In the last sentence, it may finally be noticed that we do not get the ending we surely expect: if a great man answers a question his contemporaries have not asked, the consequence should be something like ". . . and is made a public hero." Instead we get, "and is isolated." The new phrase means both made separate from the mass and made solitary or lonely. The copresence of the idea of isolation enlarges the idea of heroism. So too the phrase "persons . . . answer questions which I have not skill to *put*" rather than "skill to *answer*." And can "life" receive a "promise of explanation"? In what sense? To read such sentences is to be placed, by slight touches, on the alert. This speaker is not, to be sure, saying anything of the first importance; at present he is not going out of his way, nor does he expect that you should go out of yours, but he does ask that you take notice that his argument is a degree more informative and carefully worked than you had supposed. "The most fugitive deed and word, the mere air of doing a thing, the intimated purpose, expresses character" (W 2: 156), he says in another context, and when such a tone occurs prose is character. "Character" is *habitual* moral stance, and its reflection in words marks the habitual respect of a practiced man of letters for his medium.

I hear this tone again in "We do not quite forgive a giver. The hand that feeds us is in some danger of being bitten" (W 3: 162). Is it to be found in the exactness with which "quite" and "some" are placed to do their qualifying work? Or in the imperturbability with which the half-rhyme of "forgive" and "give" is allowed us to do as we wish with? Something is due to the air of disinterestedness with which these literary gestures are made. Nothing is apologized for, and everything that is said is meant, but nothing is explained. Whatever the reader may do to pursue sense while preserving syntax is allowed to be part of the point made. Another remark of the same sort is a characterization of proverbs as "always the literature of reason, or the statements of an absolute truth without qualification" (W 2: 108–109). There is nobody standing on the sidelines here to react to the gasp of an innocent reader who objects that this assertion, under the guise of casual synonymy, is going a great distance from the first member of the series to the last. Surely it is not good logic to identify proverbs with reason, or reason with absolute affirmations. But the sentence means what it assumes. The canny, or noninnocent, reader is willing to risk the gap and see what the sentence may mean if taken literally. The redefinition of "reason" that is bound to follow will be instructive." "In good society,—say among the angels in heaven,—is not everything spoken by indirection & nothing quite straight as it bifel?" (J 6: 77). Apparently so.

Again, as with the other dimensions of literary action, we are in the presence of some form of doubleness: a doubleness of position and voice, an indication of a willingness to engage a matter on two sides at once. Tone comes in with the evocation of a double judgment upon a situation. A person—the creation of tone—is somebody who doubts the sufficiency of a single statement, who reserves himself, withdrawing as he speaks from his words. You cannot *hear* a man saying something entirely straight, that is, like a telephone book or a street sign. Tone is a way of reminding a reader that he is reading words; like metaphor, like rhythm, this rudimentary rhetorical resource is peculiarly adapted to Emerson's interest in what is radical in the use of language. To notice tone is to notice the independent existence of language, which can bring a phantom person into our imaginative presence. We are necessarily aware that we meet a person, and that we do not meet him—that we are in the act of using language for literary purposes. Tone is to the mind's ear what metaphor is to the mind's eye, but it is more radical than metaphor. We believe what we hear more thoroughly than what we see; the eye is accustomed to be deceived by illusions. A person whom we hear speak, though, exists irreducibly for us, and since the identity of the speaker depends on our own identity as a member of the world in which we and the speaker jointly live, we are deeply involved in the discovery of tone. Persons are more intimately challenging portions of the Soul than the bare mind.

Let me come back to the matter of doubleness. When Emerson asks himself, "shall the young man aim at a leading part in law, in politics, in trade?" he answers: "It will not be pretended that a success in either of these kinds is quite coincident with what is best and inmost in his mind" (W 4: 158).

A person speaks here because the sentence splits in two. It voices at one and the same time a deep sympathy with the young man's scorn for the world and a certain awareness, hovering over the word "quite," that the high-mindedness of young men is not necessarily to be taken at their own valuation. This does not mean it is the world's valuation of this quality that should be accepted. The ultimate judge is the person capable of saying, or feeling, the truth expressed in this very sentence; the state of mind here doubly exemplified has the authority to adjudicate the respective claims of youthful impatience and worldly fact. "There is much," he goes on, "to say on both sides." Such tonal puns mark the distinction of many by-remarks like "Such as you are, the gods themselves could not help you" (W 6: 239). One can hear a voice that says this insultingly and another voice, intimate and quiet, that says it encouragingly.

There are many examples of this sort of thing: the more detachable and aphoristic remarks are the easiest to split into their component voices. "I desire not to disgrace the soul" (W 2: 163), for instance. One voice, modest and low, makes "not" modify the infinitive "to disgrace"—not to disgrace the soul is all this speaker asks for. Another voice proudly attaches the "not" to the main verb "desire," and pauses oratorically before continuing with the predicate infinitive. The whole sentence then becomes a lofty understatement, flung out magnanimously: I have no intention of disgracing the soul, and you, my audience, know how little likely I am to do so. The proud voice seems a function of the modest one, which the reader hears first with the other just after it, a relation that implies an argument: ask for the least quantity of genuine Soul (or clarity, or insight, or vigor), and you will get enough to be proud of.

This activity of mind is not rare in Emerson—the pleasure of reading the essays is kept up for us by the frequency with which tones redouble and sentences open upon the ear as a chord of voices. As with Swift or any other worthy ironist, nothing extra is said that is not intended as a contribution to the education of the reader, whose power to hear and know is constantly tested: are you alive or not?

Tone selects an inner audience within the whole group apparently addressed. The chosen audience hears two voices, where the larger group hears one only; though finally, as the full sense sinks in, the inner audience will have one sense again. One does not *stay* with doubleness, though one has to go through it to get at a proper view of the straight meaning. Look at "I suppose no man can violate his nature" (W 2: 58). The chord of voices here generated about "suppose" creates an affectation of blandness that the chosen ear will detect: an inner voice may be heard to say, "Given my notion of 'nature,' you will surely allow me to presume that no man can violate his nature."

The speaker of a good, noticeable sentence typically pretends to mean less than he does. Is not this the essence of transcendentalism once again? Here too, as with metaphor or rhythm, Emerson can show us the chances all writers who wish to do anything with words are obliged to take, and may as well take joyfully. To mean even one simple thing is extraordinary enough; to mean something besides is literature. But "literature," as we have seen, is only the way we have of doing in special verbal situations something we do anyway in life without noticing it and without pleasure: that is, to create meanings and assume dramatic situations. Literature teaches us to return to ordinary sayings and hear them as what they were all the time, statements standing out with the solidity of voices, the distinctness of a limited meaning, the cadence of an assimilable rhythm. Doubleness is justified because it lets us reappropriate the singleness of "ordinary" experience.

One wants, in order to notice the final admirable note in Emerson's range of tones, a set of terms that are not readily available—terms to describe the key elements of good manners and of pathos. For frequently the best moments of tone seem to involve an underconfession of loss and limitation that complements and makes acceptable radical leaps of spirit. Finally, one wants terms to identify the verbal element in mystical exaltation. It would be worth a struggle to understand the causes of excellence in such a paragraph as the one in which Emerson records his try at explaining the American Idea to some English friends. They are all on an expedition to Stonehenge. Emerson had been a successful lecturer and man about London society, representing in many ways the American Idea himself, however oppressed he occasionally was by the expectations his audiences and disciples had of him. Just before leaving England, he wrote in his journal a comment incorporated in *English Traits*:

> On the way to Winchester, whither our host accompanied us in the afternoon, my friends asked many questions respecting American landscape, forests, houses,—my house, for example. It is not easy to answer these queries well. There, I thought, in America, lies nature sleeping, overgrowing, almost conscious, too much by half for man in the picture, and so giving a certain *tristesse*, like that rank vegetation of swamps and forests seen at night, steeped in dews and rains, which it loves; and on it man seems not able to make much impression. There, in that great sloven continent, in high Alleghany pastures, in the sea-wide sky-skirted prairie, still sleeps and murmurs and hides the great mother, long since driven away from the trim hedge-rows and over-cultivated gardens of England. And, in England, I am quite too sensible of this. Every one is on his good behavior and must be dressed for dinner at six. So I put off my friends with very inadequate details, as best I could. (W 5: 288)

What prevails and governs here is quiet, humorous, inward, able to hold in check occasional man-of-the-world slang ("too much by half . . . a certain *tristesse*") and poetical expansions ("the great mother"); able to shift from the report of an individual afternoon to hints of private reticences and hesitations ("my house, for example"); able, always, to preserve a level-headed communion with an imagined American reader who really understands, a reader, it is worth remembering, whom he could not expect to be reading his journal. The passage ends with a wry acknowledgment that he could not explain, not to these people, not in England. The catalogue heaped up by the commas is, to be sure, imperfect, and he knows it; the rhythm starts ("There, I thought, in America, lies nature sleeping, overgrowing, almost conscious, too much by half for man in the picture"), but it never does come to a climax; the second repetition of the meditative "There, in that great sloven continent" is a sign that he has not yet explained America to himself much more thoroughly than to these clever, not-really-interested gentlemen who have been so kind as to prepare a tour for him. The excellence that remains, the sense of a civilized spirit, lies perhaps in the fine acknowledgment of his own reserve. This reserve he was obliged to maintain by a hundred influences of temperament, situation, audience, and, most intimately, subject: how do you talk briefly about one man's experience of America, especially when you have devoted years to that very question?

There is a parallel note of necessary restraint, though more sharply put and without any implication of a withdrawal for social reasons, in a comment good enough to serve as a kind of master epigram for much—including the literary predicament just exhibited. It appears in "Circles": "But lest I should mislead any when I have my own head and obey my whims, let me remind the reader that I am only an experimenter. Do not set the least value on what I do, or the least discredit on what I do not, as if I pretended to settle anything as true or false. I unsettle all things" (W 2: 318). This warning is quite literally true, yet the tone also warns that what is said should itself be taken experimentally. Try, for instance, giving a different weight to the phrase, "have my own head," so as to let it mean something more sober than its rhetorical twin, "obey my whims"—something like, "be in cool possession of my full Soul." Then another voice will be heard that *does* settle something. The same applies to "only," in "I am only an experimenter." Unstressed, it intends modesty; accented, it makes the modesty itself ironic. The whole remark is "unsettling" in its bones.

Let me end this section on literary tone with a sure piece of eloquence from "New England Reformers," which brings together the wit of this last example and the elegiac note struck in the meditation on America. The previous context has established the naturalness and inevitability of each man's relation to an inner "spirit":

> This open channel to the highest life is the first and last reality, so subtle, so quiet, yet so tenacious, that although I have never expressed the truth, and although I have never heard the expression of it from any other, I know that the whole truth is here for me. What if I cannot answer your questions? I am not pained that I cannot frame a reply to the question, What is the operation we call Providence? There lies the unspoken thing, present, omnipresent. Every time we converse we seek to translate it into speech, but whether we hit or whether we miss, we have the fact. Every discourse is an approximate answer: but it is of small consequence that we do not get into verbs and nouns, whilst it abides for contemplation forever. (W 3: 282)

"New England Reformers" is peculiarly rich in examples of tone. This, though, is Emerson at his richest and subtlest. The mystical eloquence is due partly to the calm of assured possession, which is, paradoxically, elegiacally expressed. Can acceptance of "the whole truth" grow only by yielding, in the act, the power of literary expression? The voice is unassertive, on the verge of withdrawal into silence, like an old man so sure he is deaf to questions, and even ready to use conventional terms like "highest life" and "Providence" if these are handy. Yet awareness of the language used is not altogether lost; that degree of self-abandonment would come next, in the stage of pure "contemplation." "So subtle, so quiet, yet so tenacious" is a sequence that moves consciously to an emphasis upon its third word, whose connotations of muscular effort and stubborn retention abruptly oppose the easy image conveyed by the phrase "open channel" established at the beginning of the same sentence. The lofty exaggerations ("I have never expressed," "I have never heard") build authority for *their* rhythmic completion, in the understatedly unemphatic "I know that the whole truth is here for me." The repetition of "I cannot . . . I cannot" firmly removes the talkative ego, the answerer of specific questions, from the reader's presence, for the speaker wishes to make himself entirely empty of pretense before he says, "There lies the unspoken thing, present, ominpresent." One is, I am sure, not meant to hear any theological stress on that "omni-." There is no need of it. "Whoever said it, this is in the right key" (*W* 6: 248).

Emerson: Power at the Crossing

Harold Bloom

I

Emerson is an experiential critic and essayist, and not a Transcendental philosopher. This obvious truth always needs restating, perhaps now more than ever, when literary criticism is so overinfluenced by contemporary French heirs of the German tradition of Idealist or Transcendental philosophy. Emerson is the mind of our climate, the principal source of the American difference in poetry, criticism and pragmatic post-philosophy. That is a less obvious truth, and it also needs restating, now and always. Emerson, by no means the greatest American writer, perhaps more an interior orator than a writer, is the inescapable theorist of all subsequent American writing. From his moment to ours, American authors either are in his tradition, or else in a countertradition originating in opposition to him. This continues even in a time when he is not much read, such as the period from 1945 to 1965 or so. During the last twenty years, Emerson has returned, burying his undertakers. "The essays of Emerson," T. S. Eliot remarked, "are already an encumbrance," one of those judicial observations that governed the literary academy during the Age of Eliot, but that now have faded into an antique charm.

Other judicial critics, including Yvor Winters and Allen Tate, sensibly blamed Emerson for everything they disliked in American literature and even to some extent in American life. Our most distinguished living poet, Robert Penn Warren, culminated the counter-traditional polemic of Eliot and Tate in his lively sequence, "Homage to Emerson, on Night-Flight to New York." Reading Emerson's essays in the "pressurized gloom" of the airliner, Warren sees the glowing page declare: "There is / No sin. Not even error." Only at a transcendental altitude can Warren's heart be abstract enough to accept the Sage of Concord, "for / At 38,000 feet Emerson / Is dead right." At ground level, Emerson "had forgiven God everything" because "Emerson thought that significance shines through everything."

Sin, error, time, history, a God external to the self, the visiting of the crimes of the fathers upon the sons: these are the topoi of the literary cosmos of Eliot and his Southern followers, and these were precisely of no interest whatsoever to Ralph Waldo Emerson. Of Emerson I am moved to say what Borges said of Oscar Wilde: he was always right. But he himself always says it better:

> That is always best which gives me to myself. The sublime is excited in me by the great stoical doctrine, obey thyself. That which shows God in me, fortifies me. That which shows God out of me, makes me a wart and wen. There is no longer a necessary reason for my being. (W 1: 131–32)

One might say that the Bible, Shakespeare and Freud show us as caught in a psychic conflict, in which we need to be everything in ourselves while we go on fearing that we are nothing in ourselves. Emerson dismisses the fear, and insists upon the necessity of the single self achieving a total autonomy, of becoming a cosmos without first ingesting either nature or other selves. He wishes to give us to ourselves, although these days supposedly he preaches to the converted, since it is the fashion to assert that we live in a culture of narcissism, of which our smiling President is the indubitable epitome. Emerson, in this time of Reagan, should be cited upon the limitations of all American politics whatsoever:

> We might as wisely reprove the east wind, or the frost, as a political party, whose members, for the most part, could give no account of their position, but stand for the defense of those interests in which they find themselves. . . . A party is perpetually corrupted by personality. Whilst we absolve the association from dishonesty, we cannot extend the same charity to their leaders. They reap the rewards of the docility and zeal of the masses which they direct. . . . Of the two great parties, which, at this hour, almost share the nation between them, I should say, that, one has the best cause, and the other contains the best men. The philosopher, the poet, or the religious man, will, of course, wish to cast his vote with the democrat, for free trade, for wide suffrage, for the abolition of legal cruelties in the penal code, and for facilitating in every manner the access of the young and the poor to the sources of wealth and power. But he can rarely accept the persons whom the so-called popular party propose to him as representatives of these liberalities. (W 3: 208–10)

Emerson writes of the Democrats and of the Whigs (precursors of our modern Republicans) in the early 1840's, when he still believes that Daniel Webster (foremost of "the best men") will never come to advocate the worst cause of the slaveholders. Though his politics have been categorized as "transcendental anarchism," Emerson was at once a believer in pure power and a prophet of the moral law, an apparent self-contradiction that provoked Yvor Winters in an earlier time, and President Giamatti of Yale more recently. Yet this wise inconsistency led Emerson to welcome Whitman in poetry for the same reasons he had hailed Daniel Webster in politics, until Webster's Seventh of March speech in 1850 moved Emerson to the most violent rhetoric of his life. John Jay Chapman, in a great essay on Emerson, remarked that, in his polemic against Webster, Emerson "is savage, destructive, personal, bent on death." Certainly no other American politician has been so memorably denounced in public as Webster was by Emerson:

> Mr. Webster, perhaps, is only following the laws of his blood and constitution. I suppose his pledges were not quite natural to him. He is a man who lives by his memory; a man of the past, not a man of faith and of hope. All the drops of his blood have eyes that look downward, and his finely developed understanding only works truly and with all its force when it stands for animal good; that is, for property. (W 11: 203, 204, 203–04)

All the drops of his blood have eyes that look downward; that bitter figuration has outlived every phrase Webster himself ventured. Many modern historians defend Webster for his part in the compromise of 1850, by which California was admitted as a free state while the North pledged to honor the Fugitive Slave Law. This defense maintains that Webster helped preserve the Union for another decade, while strengthening the ideology of Union that culminated in Lincoln. But Emerson, who had given Webster every chance, was driven out of his study and into moral prophecy by Webster's support of the Fugitive Slave Law:

> We are glad at last to get a clear case, one on which no shadow of doubt can hang. This is not meddling with other people's affairs: this is hindering other people from meddling with us. This is not going crusading into Virginia and Georgia after slaves, who it is alleged, are very comfortable where they are:—that amiable argument falls to the ground: but this is befriending in our own State, on our own farms, a man who has taken the risk of being shot or burned alive, or cast into the sea, or starved to death, or suffocated in a wooden box, to get away from his driver: and this man who has run the gauntlet of a thousand miles for his freedom, the statute says, you men of Massachussetts shall hunt, and catch, and send back again to the dog-hutch he fled from. And this filthy enactment was made in the nineteenth century, by people who could read and write. I will not obey it, by God. (W 11: 187–88)

As late as 1843, Emerson's love of Webster as incarnate Power had prevailed: "He is no saint, but the wild olive wood, ungrafted yet by grace." After Webster's defense of the Fugitive Slave Law, even Emerson's decorum was abandoned: "The word *liberty* in the mouth of Mr. Webster sounds like the word *love* in the mouth of a courtezan." I suspect that Emerson's deep fury, so uncharacteristic of him, resulted partly from the violation of his own cheerfully amoral dialectics of power. The extraordinary essay on "Power" in *The Conduct of Life* appears at first to worship mere force or drive as such, but the Emersonian cunning always locates power in the place of crossing over, in the moment of transition:

> In history, the great moment is, when the savage is just ceasing to be a savage, with all his hairy Pelasgic strength directed on his opening sense of beauty;—and you

have Pericles and Phidias,—not yet passed over into the Corinthian civility. Everything good in nature and the world is in that moment of transition, when the swarthy juices still flow plentifully from nature, but their astringency or acridity is got out by ethics and humanity. (W 6: 70–71)

A decade or so before, in perhaps his central essay, "Self-Reliance," Emerson had formulated the same dialectic of power, but with even more exuberance:

Life only avails, not the having lived. Power ceases in the instant of repose; it resides in the moment of transition from a past to a new state, in the shooting of a gulf, in the darting to an aim. This one fact the world hates, that the soul *becomes;* for that for ever degrades the past, turns all riches to poverty, all reputation to shame, confounds the saint with the rogue, shoves Jesus and Judas equally aside. Why, then, do we prate of self-reliance? Inasmuch as the soul is present, there will be power not confident but agent. To talk of reliance is a poor external way of speaking. Speak rather of that which relies, because it works and is. (W 2: 69–70)

Magnificent, but surely even the Webster of 1850 retained his Pelasgic strength, surely even *that* Webster works and is? Emerson's cool answer would have been that Webster had failed the crossing. I think Emerson remains *the* American theoretician of power—be it political, literary, spiritual, economic—because he took the risk of exalting transition for its own sake. Admittedly, I am happier when the consequence is Whitman's "Crossing Brooklyn Ferry" than when the Emersonian product is the first Henry Ford, but Emerson is canny enough to prophesy both disciples. There is a great chill at the center of his cosmos, which remains ours, both the chill and the cosmos:

But Nature is no sentimentalist,—does not cosset or pamper us. We must see that the world is rough and surly, and will not mind drowning a man or a woman; but swallows your ship like a grain of dust. The cold, inconsiderate of persons, tingles your blood, benumbs your feet, freezes a man like an apple. (W 6: 6–7)

This is from the sublime essay "Fate," which leads off *The Conduct of Life,* and culminates in the outrageous question: "Why should we fear to be crushed by savage elements, we who are made up of the same elements?" (W 6: 49). Elsewhere in "Fate," Emerson observes: "The way of Providence is a little rude" (W 6: 7), while in "Power" he restates the law of Compensation as "nothing is got for nothing" (W 6: 54). Emerson is no sentimentalist, and it is something of a puzzle how he ever got to be regarded as anything other than a rather frightening theoretician of life or of letters. But then, his personality also remains a puzzle. He was the true American charismatic, and founded the actual American religion, which is Protestant without being Christian. Was the man one with the essayist, or was only the wisdom uncanny in our inescapable sage?

II

A biography of Emerson is necessarily somewhat redundant at best, because Emerson, like Montaigne, is almost always his own subject, though hardly in Montaigne's own mode. Emerson would not have said: "I am myself the matter of my book," yet Emerson on "History" is more Emerson than history. Though he is almost never overtly autobiographical, his best lesson nevertheless is that all true subjectivity is a difficult achievement, while supposed objectivity is merely the failure of having become an amalgam of other selves and their opinions. Though his is in the oral tradition, his true genre was no more the lecture than it had been the sermon, and certainly not the essay, though that is his only formal achievement, besides a double handful of strong poems. His journals are his authentic work, and seem to me poorly represented by all available selections. Perhaps the journals simply ought not to be condensed, because Emerson's reader needs to be immersed in their flow and ebb, their own experience of the influx of insight followed by the perpetual falling back into skepticism. They move endlessly between a possible ecstasy and a probable shrewdness, while knowing always that neither daemonic intensity nor worldly irony by itself can constitute wisdom.

The essential Emerson begins to emerge in the journals in the autumn of 1830, when he was twenty-seven, with his first entry on Self-Reliance, in which he refuses to be "a secondary man" imitating any other being. A year later (October 27, 1831) we hear the birth of Emerson's *reader's Sublime*, the notion that what moves us in the eloquence, written or oral, of another, must be what is oldest in oneself, which is not part of the Creation, and indeed is God in oneself:

> Were you ever instructed by a wise and eloquent man? Remember then, were not the words that made your blood run cold, that brought the blood to your cheeks, that made you tremble or delighted you,—did they not sound to you as old as yourself? Was it not truth that you knew before, or do you ever expect to be moved from the pulpit or from man by anything but plain truth? Never. It is God in you that responds to God without, or affirms his own words trembling on the lips of another. (J 2: 425)

On October 28, 1832, Emerson's resignation from the Unitarian ministry was accepted (very reluctantly) by the Second Church, Boston. The supposed issue was the proper way of celebrating the Lord's Supper, but the underlying issue, at least for Emerson himself, was celebrating the self as God. Stephen Whicher in his superb *Emerson: An Organic Anthology* (still the best one-volume Emerson) gathered together the relevant notebook texts of October 1832. We find Emerson, sustained by daemonic influx, asserting: "It is light. You don't get a candle to see the sun rise," where clearly Jesus is the candle and Emerson is the sunrise (prophetic, like so much else in early Emerson, of Nietzsche's *Zarathustra*). The most outrageous instance of an inrush of God in

Emerson is the notorious and still much derided Transparent Eyeball passage in *Nature* (1836), which is based upon a journal entry of March 19, 1835. But I give the final text from *Nature:*

> Crossing a bare common, in snow puddles, at twilight, under a clouded sky, without having in my thoughts any occurence of special good fortune, I have enjoyed a perfect exhileration. I am glad to the brink of fear. . . . There I feel that nothing can befall me in life,—no disgrace, no calamity, (leaving me my eyes,) which nature cannot repair. Standing on the bare ground,—my head bathed by the blithe air, and uplifted into infinite space,—all mean egotism vanishes. I become a transparent eyeball; I am nothing; I see all; the currents of the Universal Being circulate through me; I am part or particle of God. (W 1: 9–10)

Nature, in this passage as in the title of the little book, *Nature,* is rather perversely the wrong word, since Emerson does not mean "nature" in any accepted sense whatsoever. He means Man, and not a natural man or fallen Adam, but original man or unfallen Adam, which is to say America, in the transcendental sense, just as Blake's Albion is the unfallen form of Man. Emerson's primal Man, to whom Emerson is joined in this epiphany, is all eye, seeing earliest, precisely as though no European, and no ancient Greek or Hebrew, had seen before him. There is a personal pathos as well, which Emerson's contemporary readers could not have known. Emerson feared blindness more than death, although his family was tubercular and frequently died young. But there had been an episode of hysterical blindness during his college years, and its memory, however repressed, hovers throughout his work. Freud's difficult "frontier concept" of the bodily ego, which is formed partly by introjective fantasies, suggests that thinking can be associated with any of the senses or areas of the body. Emerson's fantastic introjection of the transparent eyeball as bodily ego seems to make thinking and seeing the same activity, one that culminated in self-deification.

Emerson's power as a kind of interior orator stems from this self-deification. Nothing is got for nothing, and perhaps the largest pragmatic consequence of being "part or particle of God" is that your need for other people necessarily is somewhat diminished. The transparent eyeball passage itself goes on to manifest an estrangement from the immediacy of other selves:

> The name of the nearest friend sounds then foreign and accidental: to be brothers, to be acquaintances, master or servant, is then a trifle and a disturbance. (W 1: 10)

This passage must have hurt Emerson himself, hardly a person for whom "to be brothers" ever was "a trifle and a disturbance." The early death of his brother Charles, just four months before *Nature* was published in 1836, was one of his three terrible losses, the others being the death of Ellen Tucker, his first wife, in 1831, after little more than a year of marriage, and the death of his first born child, Waldo, in January 1842, when the boy was only five years old. Emerson psychically was preternaturally strong, but it is difficult to interpret the famous passage in his great essay, "Experience," where he writes of Waldo's death:

> An innavigable sea washes with silent waves between us and the things we aim at and converse with. Grief too will make us idealists. In the death of my son, now more than two years ago, I seem to have lost a beautiful estate—no more. I cannot get it nearer to me. If tomorrow I should be informed of the bankruptcy of my principal debtors, the loss of my property would be a great inconvenience to me, perhaps, for many years; but it would leave me as it found me,—neither better nor worse. So is it with this calamity; it does not touch me; something which I fancied was a part of me, which could not be torn away without tearing me nor enlarged without enriching me, falls off from me and leaves no scar. (W 3: 48–49)

Perhaps Emerson should have written an essay entitled "The Economic Problem of Grief," but perhaps most of his essays carry that as a hidden subtitle. The enigma of grief in Emerson, after all, may be the secret cause of his strength, of his refusal to mourn for the past. Self-reliance, the American religion he founded, converts solitude into a firm stance against history, including personal history. That there is no history, only biography, is the Emersonian insistence, which may be why a valid biography of Emerson appears to be impossible. John McAleer's biography sets out shrewdly to evade the Emersonian entrapment, which is that Emerson knows only biography, a knowledge that makes personal history redundant.[1] What then is the biographer of Emerson to do?

Such worthy practitioners of the mode as Ralph Rusk and Gay Wilson Allen worked mightily to shape the facts into a life, but are evaded by Emerson. Where someone lives so massively *from within*, he cannot be caught by chroniclers of events, public and private. McAleer instead molds his facts as a series of encounters between Emerson and all his friends and associates. Unfortunately, Emerson's encounters with others—whether his brothers, wives, children, or Transcendental and other literary colleagues, are little more revelatory of his inner life than are his encounters with events, whether it be the death of Waldo or the Civil War. All McAleer's patience, skill and learning cannot overcome the sage's genius for solitude. A biography of Emerson becomes as baffling as a biography of Nietzsche, though the two lives have nothing in common, except of course for ideas. Nietzsche acknowledged Emerson, with affection and enthusiasm, but he probably did not realize how fully Emerson had anticipated him, particularly in unsettling the status of the self while proclaiming simultaneously a greater overself to come.

---

[1]For the Emerson biographies by McAleer, Rusk, and Allen referred to in this and the next paragraphs, see Suggestions for Further Reading (pages 213–214).—ED.

III

The critic of Emerson is little better off than the biographer, since Emerson, again like Nietzsche and remarkably also akin to Freud, anticipates his critics and does their work for them. Emerson resembles his own hero, Montaigne, in that you cannot combat him without being contaminated by him. T. S. Eliot, ruefully contemplating Pascal's hopeless agon with Montaigne, observed that fighting Montaigne was like throwing a hand grenade into a fog. Emerson, because he appropriated America, is more like a climate than an atmosphere, however misty. Attempting to write the order of the variable winds in the Emersonian climate is a hopeless task, and the best critics of Emerson, from John Jay Chapman and O. W. Firkins through Stephen Whicher to Barbara Packer and Richard Poirier, wisely decline to list his ideas of order. You track him best, as writer and as person, by learning the principle proclaimed everywhere in him: that which you can get from another is never instruction, but always provocation.

But what is provocation, in the life of the spirit? Emerson insisted that he called you forth only to your self, and not to any cause whatsoever. The will to power, in Emerson as afterwards in Nietzsche, is reactive rather than active, receptive rather than rapacious, which is to say that it is a will to interpretation. Emerson teaches interpretation, but not in any of the European modes fashionable either in his day or in our own, modes currently touching their nadir in a younger rabblement celebrating itself as having repudiated the very idea of an individual reader or an individual critic. Group criticism, like group sex, is not a new idea, but seems to revive whenever a sense of resentment dominates the aspiring clerisy. With resentment comes guilt, as though societal oppressions are caused by how we read, and so we get those academic covens akin to what Emerson, in his 1838 journal, called "philanthropic meetings and holy hurrahs," for which read now "Marxist literary groups" and "Lacanian theory circles":

> As far as I notice what passes in philanthropic meetings and holy hurrahs there is very little depth of interest. The speakers warm each other's skin and lubricate each other's tongue, and the words flow and the superlatives thicken and the lips quiver and the eyes moisten, and an observer new to such scenes would say, Here was true fire; the assembly were all ready to be martyred, and the effect of such a spirit on the community would be irresistible; but they separate and go to the shop, to a dance, to bed, and an hour afterwards they care so little for the matter that on slightest temptation each one would disclaim the meeting. (*J* 4: 431)

Emerson, according to President Giamatti of Yale, "was as sweet as barbed wire," a judgment recently achieved independently by John Updike. Yes, and doubtless Emerson gave our politics its particular view of power, as Giamatti laments, but a country deserves its sages, and we deserve Emerson. He has the peculiar dialectical gift of being precursor for both the perpetual New Left of student non-students and the perpetual New Right of preacher non-preachers. The American Religion of Self-Reliance is a superb *literary* religion, but its political, economic and social consequences, whether manifested Left or Right, have now helped place us in a country where literary satire of politics is impossible, since the real thing is far more outrageous than even a satirist of genius could invent. Nathanael West presumably was parodying Calvin Coolidge in *A Cool Million*'s Shagpoke Whipple, but is this Shagpoke Whipple or President Reagan speaking?

> America is the land of opportunity. She takes care of the honest and industrious and never fails them as long as they are both. This is not a matter of opinion, it is one of faith. On the day that Americans stop believing it, on that day will America be lost.[2]

Emerson unfortunately believed in Necessity, including "the offence of superiority in persons," and he was capable of writing passages that can help to justify Reagan's large share of the Yuppie vote, as here in "Self-Reliance":

> Then again, do not tell me, as a good man did today, of my obligation to put all poor men in good situations. Are they *my* poor? I tell thee, thou foolish philanthropist, that I grudge the dollar, the dime, the cent I give to such men as do not belong to me and to whom I do not belong. There is a class of persons to whom by all spiritual affinity I am bought and sold; for them I will go to prison if need be; but your miscellaneous popular charities; the education at college of fools; the building of meeting-houses to the vain end to which many now stand; alms to sots; and the thousand-fold Relief Societies;—though I confess with shame I sometimes succumb and give the dollar, it is a wicked dollar, which by and by I shall have the manhood to withhold. (W 2: 52)

True, Emerson meant by his "class of persons" men such as Henry Thoreau and Jones Very and the Reverend William Ellery Channing, which is not exactly Shagpoke Whipple, Ronald Reagan and the Reverend Jerry Falwell, but Self-Reliance translated out of the inner life and into the marketplace is difficult to distinguish from our current religion of selfishness, as set forth so sublimely in the recent grand epiphany at Dallas. Shrewd Yankee that he was, Emerson would have shrugged off his various and dubious paternities. His spiritual elitism could only be misunderstood, but he did not care much about being misread or misused. Though he has been so oddly called "the philosopher of democracy" by so many who wished to claim him for the Left, the political Emerson remains best expressed in one famous and remarkable sentence by John Jay Chapman: "If a soul be taken and crushed by democracy till it utter a cry, that cry will be Emerson."

2*The Complete Works of Nathanael West* (New York: Farrar Straus, 1957), 150.—ED.

IV

I return with some relief to Emerson as literary prophet, where Emerson's effect, *pace* Yvor Winters, seems to me again dialectical but in the end both benign and inevitable. Emerson's influence, from his day until ours, has helped to account for what I would call the American difference in literature, not only in our poetry and criticism, but even in our novels and stories— ironic since Emerson was at best uneasy about novels. What is truly surprising about this influence is its depth, extent and persistence, despite many concealments and even more evasions. Emerson does a lot more to explain most American writers than any of our writers; even Whitman or Thoreau or Dickinson or Hawthorne or Melville serve to explain *him*. The important question to ask is not "How?" but "Why?" Scholarship keeps showing the "how" (though there is a great deal more to be shown) but it ought to be a function of criticism to get at that scarcely explored "why."

Emerson was controversial in his own earlier years, and then became all but universally accepted (except, of course, in the South) during his later years. This ascendancy faded during the Age of Literary Modernism (*circa* 1915–1945) and virtually vanished, as I remarked earlier, in the heyday of academic New Criticism or Age of Eliot (*circa* 1945–1965). Despite the humanistic protests of President Giamatti, and the churchwardenly mewings of John Updike, the last two decades have witnessed an Emerson revival, and I prophesy that he, rather than Marx or Heidegger, will be the guiding spirit of our imaginative literature and our criticism for some time to come. In that prophecy, "Emerson" stands for not only the theoretical stance and wisdom of the historical Ralph Waldo, but for Nietzsche, Walter Pater and Oscar Wilde, and much of Freud as well, since Emerson's elitist vision of the higher individual is so consonant with theirs. Individualism, whatever damages its American ruggedness continues to inflict on our politics and social economy, is more than ever the only hope for our imaginative lives. Emerson, who knew that the only literary and critical method was oneself, is again a necessary resource in a time beginning to weary of Gallic scientism in what are still called the Humanities.

Lewis Mumford, in *The Golden Day* (1926), still is the best guide as to *why* Emerson was and is the central influence upon American letters: "With most of the resources of the past at his command, Emerson achieved nakedness." Wisely seeing that Emerson was a Darwinian before Darwin, a Freudian before Freud, because he possessed a "complete vision," Mumford was able to make the classic formulation as to Emerson's strength: "The past for Emerson was neither a prescription nor a burden: it was rather an esthetic experience." As a poem already written, the past was not a force for Emerson; it had lost power, because power for him resided only at the crossing, at the actual moment of transition.

The dangers of this repression of the past's force are evident enough, in American life as in its literature. In our political economy, we get the force of secondary repetition; Reagan as Coolidge out-Shagpoking Nathanael West's Whipple. We receive also the rhythm of ebb and flow that makes all our greater writers into crisis-poets. Each of them echoes, however involuntarily, Emerson's formula for dicontinuity in his weird, irrealistic essay, "Circles":

> Our moods do not believe in each other. Today I am full of thoughts and can write what I please. I see no reason why I should not have the same thought, the same power of expression, tomorrow. What I write, whilst I write it, seems the most natural thing in the world; but yesterday I saw a dreary vacuity in this direction in which now I see so much; and a month hence, I doubt not, I shall wonder who he was that wrote so many continuous pages. Alas for this infirm faith, this will not strenuous, this vast ebb of a vast flow! I am God in nature; I am a weed by the wall. (*W* 2: 306–07)

From God to weed and then back again; it is the cycle of Whitman from "Song of Myself" to "As I Ebb'd with the Ocean of Life," and of Emerson's and Whitman's descendants ever since. Place everything upon the nakedness of the American self, and you open every imaginative possibility from self-deification to absolute nihilism. But Emerson knew this, and saw no alternative for us if we were to avoid the predicament of arriving too late in the cultural history of the West. Nothing is got for nothing; Emerson is not less correct now than he was 150 years ago. On November 21, 1834, he wrote in his journal: "When we have lost our God of tradition and ceased from our God of rhetoric then may God fire the heart with his presence" (*J* 3: 369). Our God of tradition, then and now, is as dead as Emerson and Nietzsche declared him to be. He belongs, in life, to the political clerics and the clerical politicians and, in letters, to the secondary men and women. Our God of rhetoric belongs to the academies, where he is called by the name of the Gallic Demiurge, Language. That leaves the American imagination free as always to open itself to the third God of Emerson's prayer.

Aggressive Allegory

Julie Ellison

One of the refined forms of torture that Emerson used against Thoreau dramatizes the distinction between soul and body. Emerson casts himself as the representative of mind or spirit, the "mystical master," and Thoreau as his "practical disciple," to use Melville's terms in chapter 37 of *The Confidence Man*. One of Thoreau's journal entries suggests the extent to which this contrast governed the perceptions of their mutual acquaintances and the extent to which it galled Thoreau:

> Alcott spent the day with me yesterday. He spent the day before with Emerson. He observed that he had got his wine, and now he had come after his venison. Such was the compliment he paid me.

The irony of the last sentence is unmistakable. Alcott's distinction between Emerson's wine and Thoreau's venison repeats Emerson's own binary oppositions of abstract spirit and concrete embodiment, Idealist and Materialist, Nominalist and Realist, with Thoreau being relegated to what is obviously the less prestigious pole. The fact that Thoreau's writings strive to transform the body into a visionary faculty does not affect my point here, which is that, in the context of Thoreau's relationship to Emerson, the body was a negative term, aggressively imposed by a masterful mind. Melville, Alcott, Thoreau, and Emerson himself agree, though in varying tones, that Emerson stands for the aggressive intellect. It is also clear from their remarks that this quality lends itself to description through parables and allegories. Taking this one step further, we can say that Emerson's prose demonstrates the aggressive uses of allegory.

The body/spirit dichotomy is one version of Emerson's habitual definition of others according to their opposition to or difference from himself. Thoreau's "most adapted and serviceable body" figures prominently in Emerson's oration on the occasion of his death. In a journal entry composed a short time after Thoreau's death, the conflicting intent of Emerson's references to Thoreau's physique becomes more evident. Commenting on Thoreau's journal, Emerson notes "the vigor of his constitution," the "oaken strength which I noted whenever he walked, or worked, or surveyed wood-lots":

From *Raritan* 3, no. 3 (1984), 100–15. Reprinted by permission of Julie Ellison.

> The same unhesitating hand with which a field laborer accosts a piece of work, which I should shun as a waste of strength, Henry shows in his literary task. He has muscle and . . . performs feats which I am forced to decline. . . . I find . . . the same spirit that is in me, but he takes a step beyond, and illustrates by excellent images that which I should have conveyed in a sleepy generality. Tis as if I went into a gymnasium and saw youths leap, climb, and swing with a force unapproachable,—though their feats are only continuations of my initial grapplings and jumps.

The compliment to Thoreau's energetic specificity ironically conveys Emerson's sense of superiority. He half-apologetically considers such athletic displays of imagery to be "a waste of strength," mere "continuations" of his "initial grapplings." His admission that he has been "forced to decline" such feats and to rely on "sleepy generalities" expresses the superior complacency of the idealist vis-à-vis the activist. Emerson uses the contrasts between mind and body, wine and venison, generalization and gymnastics to represent a relationship of oppositional difference, difference which gratifies the desire for argument or conflict.

In one of his journal entries, Thoreau describes this antagonistic tendency precisely:

> Talked, or tried to talk, with R. W. E. . . . . He, assuming a false opposition where there was no difference of opinion, talked to the wind—told me what I knew—and I lost my time trying to imagine myself someone else to oppose him.

Thoreau perceives that Emerson cares more about opposition than about essence, more about difference than about the content of his position. It is indicative of how thoroughly the relationship between Emerson and Thoreau was governed by their mutual need for difference that Emerson attributes to Thoreau exactly the same mood of unprincipled opposition that Thoreau had ascribed to him: "he [Thoreau] did not feel himself except in opposition. He wanted a fallacy to expose, a blunder to pillory, I may say, required a little sense of victory, a roll of the drum, to call his powers into full exercise." The transitivity of these accusations becomes even clearer when we realize that Emerson had used very similar language in the Divinity School "Address." There Emerson's hero, like Napoleon, is "not himself until the battle [begins] to go against him"; he is one of those men "who rise refreshed on hearing a threat."

This oppositional tendency is one of the spiritual laws of Emerson's prose. It is most clearly manifest, perhaps, in his use of abstract words, especially philosophical terms—or, since Emerson hardly wishes to speak as a philosopher, terms evocative of philosophical discourse. In Emerson's journals and essays, idealism, mind, soul, intellect, Reason—terms which designate abstracting thought—appear in a setting of conflict aimed at their opposites: materialism, body, nature, Understanding. In order to represent conflict verbally, Emerson speaks of men and aspects of himself as personified abstractions. The reductions such namings entail can usefully be thought of as allegorical. Emerson does not write allegories, but uses allegory as a tactic in the composition of a stylistically and generically miscellaneous prose. Terms like idealism and materialism, soul and nature, poet and skeptic, behave like figures borrowed from allegory. They are images of virtues, vices, or other invisible attributes engaged in actions, primarily contests and conquests. The theme of these actions is often the antiauthoritarian pleasure of allegorizing itself. Emerson anticipates twentieth-century writers on allegory by revealing the aggressive tendencies of the mode. In so doing, he demonstrates that the link between abstraction and violence prevails not only in theories of allegory, but also in perceptions of theory generally, for the allegorist in Emerson's works is a theorist.

Emerson, then, would side with recent writers on allegory who approve of it for the same reason that Coleridge condemned it. Emerson is quite content to regard allegory in Coleridgean terms as "a translation of abstract notions into a picture-language which is itself nothing but an abstraction." However, he celebrates the radical breach "between *Literal* and *Metaphorical*" (including the allegorical) rather than regretting it. Indeed, Emerson likes the power to turn sense perceptions into a "picture language," which the mind then interprets as "a translation" of its own "abstract notions." Though Emerson elects it and Coleridge censors it, they agree about allegory's violent reductiveness. Like Romantic notions of the sublime and of critical philosophy more generally, allegory was considered by Emerson's contemporaries to be an aggressive manifestation of thought at the expense of living nature. The extent to which this view of allegory still prevails is an index of the continuities between nineteenth- and twentieth-century perceptions of theory. For if our theorists of allegory are any indication, we are still intensely preoccupied with figurative evidence of the mind's power.

Walter Benjamin, the most Romantic of moderns, insists on the destructiveness of allegory only to show how the image causes us to transcend the allegorical catastrophe. He associates allegory with time, death, and ruin. These themes inhere in allegorical form itself, he argues, for allegorical representation is a kind of death. The characters of the *Trauerspiel* die, Benjamin writes, "because it is only thus, as corpses, that they can enter the homeland of allegory." The corpse is not just a memento mori which heightens our consciousness of humanity's sorrowful history, but also the appropriate emblem of allegory's "cold technique." However, Benjamin regards allegory as a dialectical genre. The allegorist reduces or kills experience in order to call attention to his knowledge of what lies beyond it:

> If the object becomes allegorical under the gaze of melancholy, if melancholy causes life to flow out of it and remains behind dead, but eternally secure, then it is exposed to the allegorist, it is unconditionally in his power. That is to say it is now quite incapable of emanating any significance or meaning of its own; such signifi-

cance as it has, it acquires from the allegorist. . . . For him it becomes a key to the realm of hidden knowledge; and he reveres it as the emblem of this.

In Benjamin's thought, the murderous consequences of allegory for the object are mysteriously redeemed by a passionate criticism that points the mind "beyond" the dead image. Angus Fletcher, too, stresses the fixating tendencies of allegory. The mode "incites action" and represents it but is populated by unnaturally consistent and goal-directed "daemonic agents." These reduced protagonists, like Emerson's Idealist and Materialist, engage in actions determined by "polarities of strength and weakness, confidence and fear, certainty and doubt." Allegory's "real violence," Fletcher remarks, "is inherent in [its] well-ordered meanings." Overly organized reductive meaning is thus the source of the demonic agent's aggressiveness.

Like Benjamin, Paul de Man promotes allegory and irony as demystifications of the Romantic symbol. He denies their aggressiveness, however, distinguishing the will to difference from the will to power. When conflict is a textual, not a social phenomenon, he argues, it involves only difference, not force. De Man recommends the way irony and allegory make apparent a sophisticated knowledge of the difference between man and nature. But because he regards such figurative language as turning on the difference between sign and object, mind and nature, he regards it as curiously benign. He suppresses the Romantic association of the mind's allegory with violence toward nature or other men.

> Within the realm of intersubjectivity one would indeed speak of difference in terms of the superiority of one subject over another, with all the implications of will to power, of violence, and possession which come into play. . . . But, when the concept of "superiority" is still being used when the self is engaged in a relationship . . . to what is precisely not a self, then the so-called superiority merely designates the *distance* constitutive of all acts of reflection. Superiority and inferiority then become merely spatial metaphors to indicate a discontinuity . . . within a subject that comes to know itself by an increasing differentiation from what it is not.

By divorcing reflection and thus difference from questions of power, de Man attempts to sanitize Romantic allegory. However, since Romantic writers typically represent consciousness itself as implicated in the "will to power, . . . violence, and possession," he does not convincingly lay to rest the connection between allegory and aggression that he inherits. Allegory becomes an honorific term for de Man, but only because he manages to evade its simultaneously dehumanizing and liberating power.

Recently, Sharon Cameron appears to have done just the opposite by treating allegory as a mode of social violence. She argues that the allegorical representation of violence inflicted on the body in *Moby-Dick* and Hawthorne's tales is symptomatic of a conceptual violence in notions of personal identity and intersubjective relationships. Although she does not present a theory of allegory, she nevertheless implies that allegorical representations of violence arise from violent thinking. Cameron concludes that the philosophical themes of Hawthorne's and Melville's works, which invite us to read them as hermeneutic experiments, in fact are implicated in this conceptual brutalizing of the self. Epistemological anxieties result from disturbed ideas about the self which are more truly manifested in figures of dismemberment, mutilation, and petrifaction. Cameron's analysis suggests that allegorical technique is the vehicle of Hawthorne's and Melville's critiques of dehumanizing conceptions. The way she links disturbed ideas of identity with images of violence leads us back to the fundamental connection between the disturbing power of ideas and the antagonistic tactics of allegory. That is, Cameron's reading of Hawthorne and Melville, which ties certain ideas to certain allegorical images, can be read as a demonstration of a larger relationship in Romantic literature between aggressive philosophical thought and allegorical representation.

In Emerson's works, to return to our central example, the most familiar instance of theory-as-allegory is chapter 6 of *Nature*, entitled "Idealism." Emerson begins by announcing that "all parts of nature conspire" to discipline man, which means that they convey to him the "meaning of the world." Then Emerson introduces his famous qualification, expressing the anxiety induced by allegory: "A noble doubt perpetually suggests itself—whether this end be not the Final Cause of the Universe; and whether nature outwardly exists." This seems to me to be a contrived crisis. Emerson brings up the "noble doubt" only to dismiss doubt as irrelevant to his aggressive ends. He shifts into the first person to reply to his rhetorical question: "In my utter impotence to test the authenticity of the report of my senses . . . what difference does it make?" He has introduced the idea of doubt in order to create an occasion for his cavalier refusal to engage in philosophical debate. The breezy tone of this refusal indicates that his real goal is the exercise of power and that "Idealism" is its trope. "Idealism," while clearly a term derived from and validated by philosophy, is transformed into a figure for the speaker. Whether the world is substance or "apparition," as he has been calling it, he is clearly at the center of it; "it is alike useful and alike venerable *to me*" (emphasis added). Dismissing the "noble doubt" of idealism leads to the noble confidence of Emerson.

His topic in subsequent paragraphs is the usefulness of idealism, the kind of power it makes possible. Idealism and the Idealist are allegorical entities here, but these terms also refer to the allegorical reduction itself. For what does Emerson say idealism accomplishes? It relaxes the "despotism of the senses which binds us to nature . . . and shows us nature aloof, and, as it were, afloat. . . ." Reason (a synonym) makes "outlines and surfaces become transparent . . . causes and spirits are seen through them." Finally: "Idealism beholds the whole circle of persons and things, of actions and events, of country and religion . . . as *one vast picture which God paints on the instant eternity for the contemplation of the soul*" (emphasis added). Idealism, then, reveals or creates a coherent pattern of lawful relationships. Its point of view is above the earth, a point from which nature is spread out below as "one vast picture." Emerson expresses the power of abstraction through the image of visual mastery. His idealistic method forces us to subordinate real objects to pure meaning, "causes and spirits." This perceptual conversion turns the world into figurative language, allowing the poet to make "dust and stones" into "the words of the Reason." As Emerson concludes, "the use which the Reason makes of the material world" is "subordinating nature for the purposes of expression." We usually think of allegory as a technique which fixes ideas in the form of objects, rather than one which dissolves objects or makes them "float" or become "transparent." Emerson does rigidify ideas in this way. He hypostasizes consciousness by calling it "Idealism," but then, revealing the aggressive motives of allegory and of theory, he proposes that the consequence of this is the dissolution of nature.

The power of the idealist's allegory in chapter 6 of *Nature* is appalling. Emerson demonstrates that the "irrefragable analysis" of poet, philosopher, astronomer, or geometer "transfer[s] nature into the mind, and [leaves] matter like an outcast corpse." "The material is degraded before the spiritual," he announces. The purpose of reducing nature to an allegory of spirit, for Emerson, is to make the idealist or allegorist feel powerful by treating the world as an element of his own mind. "Possessed himself by a heroic passion, he uses matter as symbols of it," another version of consciousness speaking to itself through a "pantomimic scene." The use of matter as symbol expresses and further inflames the heroic passion: "Whilst we behold unveiled the nature of Justice and Truth . . . we apprehend the absolute. As it were, for the first time, *we exist*. We become immortal. . . ." This is allegory as wish fulfillment. Emerson frankly admits that the "advantage of the ideal theory is . . . that it presents the world in precisely that view which is most desirable to the mind." The desired view is that which offers alienated figurative evidence of the poet-philosopher's power.

At about this point in *Nature*, Emerson becomes aware that his gestures are transgressive and apologizes: "I have not hostility to nature, but a child's love to it. . . . I do not wish to fling stones at my beautiful mother, nor soil my gentle nest." The short-lived efficacy of Emerson's aggression is a consistent feature of his prose. An idea functions as a source of power for a few sentences, but then yields to self-doubt and self-correction. These pauses, however, only carry us forward once again to another notion that will temporarily serve as the figurative vehicle for Emerson's desire. Thus, characteristically, he repeats the aggressive sequence of chapter 6 in chapter 7 of *Nature*. Idealism gives way to "Spirit" in what looks like a developing argument but is, in fact, substitution. In order to substitute "Spirit" for "Idealism," Emerson conveniently forgets that he has not been treating idealism as a philosophical idea and criticizes it as mere philosophy: "Idealism is a hypothesis to account for nature by other principles than those of carpentry and chemistry. Yet," says Emerson's imaginative appetite, "if it only deny the existence of matter, it does not satisfy the demands of the spirit. It leaves God out of me." Of course, idealism *has* satisfied the demands of the spirit, which are for both denial and godliness, but these demands are never gratified by any one term for more than a paragraph or two in Emerson's works. Spirit repeats the accomplishment of idealism by similarly transforming both nature, which becomes "a projection of God in the unconscious," and persons, who become projections of God in consciousness.

Emerson does not always give names like Idealism, Spirit, or Mind to these aggressive thoughts. In "Fate," both of the principal terms, "Fate" (associated with nature's determinism) and "Power" (associated with mind), provide the same pleasure by exposing the skeleton of universal law. Ever since Stephen Whicher's *Freedom and Fate* appeared thirty years ago, "Fate" has been read as the manifesto of Emerson's grim later phase of self-revision and resignation. However, the rather gleeful tone of the essay suggests that contemplating fate gives Emerson considerable joy. The first part of the essay is devoted to presenting—one could say celebrating—the force of inescapable givens or "adamantine bandages," as he calls them: instinct, climate, heredity, temperament, statistical probability. The essay repeatedly stages David-and-Goliath encounters between infant man and a gigantic universe (hence the numerous references to babies). Emerson suggests that the formidable adversary, Fate, has a bracing effect on overcivilized humanity:

> The way of Providence is a little rude. The habit of snake and spider, the snap of the tiger and other leapers and bloody jumpers, the crackle of the bones of his prey in the coil of the anaconda—these are in the system, and our habits are like theirs. . . . The forms of the shark, the *labrus* [a predatory fish], the jaw of the sea-wolf paved with crushing teeth, the weapons of the grampus, and other warriors hidden in the sea, are hints of ferocity in the interiors of nature.

Fate (natural law) and energy are closely allied in Emerson's imagination, which accounts for the essay's demented cheerfulness. Insofar as law is freedom's limit, it provokes, like all other opponents or obstacles, Emerson's energetic response. The snap, crackle, and pop of his language when warning us about carnivorous nature indicate his excitement. This complex agitation is compounded of the thrill of reducing experience to law, the energy of pure confrontation, and, finally, the speaker's identification with the fierceness he perceives around him.

As in *Nature*, abstract terms, Fate and Power, are the agents of an invigorating contest of which the abstracting mind itself is the hero. In the second half of "Fate," power becomes, not the opposite of fate, but its conscious acceptance, knowledge of fate. The "revelation of Thought" which takes man "out of servitude into freedom" on "the great day of the feast of life," is none other than the moment when "the inward eye opens to the Unity of things, to the omnipresence of law. . . ." Emerson argues that the mind converts fate into power; it passes "facts" "under the fire of thought." He shows that the sensation of power arises not just from any thought, but from the thought of "Fate." Giving determinism a name, which he did at the beginning of the essay, is the conversion he calls for at the end of the essay. The mind's "Blessed Unity" had been proved at the start by its thought of "Beautiful Necessity."

Emerson's representation of the allegorizing or theoretical mind, particularly in "Fate," is strongly reminiscent of the Romantic sublime. From Longinus to Weiskel, the sublime has been defined as the inspiration caught by the author from his hero, the reader from a text, the observer from nature. But more specifically, it became associated with the power of consciousness over the sensory world. The similarity between Kant and Emerson does not suggest the direct influence of the one on the other so much as the existence of a rather widely held view of Reason as an aggressive faculty that masters nature by leaping from perception to thought. The victory of Kant's Reason in *The Critique of Judgment* is predicated on the defeat of sense perception and accompanied by pleasure in the "power of resistance . . . which gives us courage to be able to measure ourselves against the seeming omnipotence of nature." First, the mind's cognitive faculties collapse or are blocked, not so much from the force or magnitude of the perceived object, but from the desire of the imagination and the demands of the reason. "Precisely because there is a striving in our imagination towards progress *ad infinitum,* while reason demands absolute totality, as a real idea," the failure of apprehension marks "the awakening of a feeling of a supersensible faculty within us. . . ." While at times Kant wishes to argue that Reason wins by default after the failure of cognition, passages like this indicate that our need for "progress *ad infinitum,*" toward the idea of "absolute totality," can cause us willfully to sacrifice cognition to Reason. This pattern has been much discussed in psychoanalytic terms. Here I wish instead to point out its resemblance to Emerson's view of an idealizing Reason which masters the chaos of ordinary perceptions by turning nature into an allegory of the mind's freedom. If Emerson's allegories of allegorizing are, as I believe, representations of the theoretical mind at work, he was not alone in his fascination with the productive aggressiveness of philosophical analysis or of abstract thought in general.

Schiller's version of the sublime, far more dramatic than Kant's, from which it is derived, shows even more clearly the relationship between the sublime and the dynamics of Emerson's terms, "Power" and "Fate." Like Emerson, Schiller imagines the sublime as humanity's heroic last stand against determinism. "Surrounded by countless forces, all of which are superior to his own and wield mastery over him," Schiller writes, man "lays claim by his nature to suffer violence from none of them." Culture helps us to resist nature "idealistically" by voluntarily submitting to it. In Schiller's *On the Sublime,* the mind's knowledge of natural law makes possible assent to it, and thus moral freedom from it: "We are ravished by the terrifying because we are able to will that which our sensuous impulses are appalled by and can reject what they desire." The echo of this strain in "Fate" is unmistakable: "every jet of chaos which threatens to exterminate us is convertible by intellect into wholesome force." A vision of Promethean resistance charges the rhetoric of both writers. Emerson lauds the mind's "fatal courage," "savage in resistance" to the world's "savage atoms," while Schiller proclaims that "nature in her entire boundlessness cannot impinge upon the absolute greatness within ourselves."

Most importantly for our purposes, Schiller's sublime results in allegory. The "shock" of his leap from dependence to freedom has the Emersonian consequence of making nature figurative and therefore intelligible: "no sooner does he discover in the flood of appearances something abiding in his own being—then the savage bulk of nature about him begins to speak quite another language about his heart; and the relative grandeur outside him is the mirror in which he perceives the absolute grandeur within himself." The consciousness of Schiller's hero, like that of Emerson's Transcendentalist, is manifested in "a pantomimic scene." Mind treats nature as its mirror image, or as an allegory of its own processes: "The . . . absence of a purposive bond among this press of appearances . . . makes them an all the more striking image for pure reason, which finds in just this wild incoherence of nature the depiction of her own independence of natural conditions." In Emerson's lighter phrase, "Where [the Mind] shines, Nature is no longer intrusive, but all things make a musical or pictorial impression. . . ." In such writings as these, allegory is meaningful only as the product of thought. For this reason, allegory in Romantic texts is usually subordinate to the recurring theme of the aggressive idealistic or theoretical mind.

The reception of Emerson's works shows that this kind of mind was attacked as often as it was defended. The issue of intellectual violence was central to critical argument then, as it is now. Reviewing *Nature* in 1837, the Harvard philosophy tutor, Francis Bowen, knew that rhetoric in the service of a theory was characterized by aggression, even tactlessness. His review was couched almost entirely in terms of personal conflict between opposing temperaments, tones, and manners. Such a project as Emerson's, he lamented, "gives a dictatorial tone to the expression of opinion, and a harsh, imperious and sometimes flippant manner to argumentative discussion." The links between egotism, incomprehensibility, and un-American activity were as close then as they are in responses to recent critical writings. "The arrogant tone has been too quickly assumed, for the new philosophy wants even the first recommendation to notice," Bowen continues. "It is abstruse in its dogmas, fantastic in its dress, and foreign in its origin." The antisocial character of theorists, manifested in their verbal obscurity and alien affiliations, is their worst fault; it "injures the generous and catholic spirit of speculative philosophy by raising up a sect of such a marked and distinctive character that it can hold no fellowship either with former laborers in the cause; or with those who . . . are aiming at the same general object." Bowen's sense of the conflict between the "new philosophy" and the old does not differ appreciably from Emerson's. Both pretty much agree on seeing the newcomers as the aggressors. Bowen refuses to give up "the old tests" of "meek and gentle features without, as indications of truth and goodness dwelling within." He identifies established truth with a friendly manner, which suggests why he necessarily associates aggression with critical challenges. And Emerson accepts the violence attributed to him: "by this screen of porcupine quills, of bad manners & hatred, is the sacred germ of individual genius concealed & guarded in Secular darkness." Emerson's figures reflect his critical environment, for his allegories of forceful idealism embrace the conflicts that already had polarized intellectual argument in England and America.

Emerson, of course, was born into a conflict that had already begun in the preceding generation. The American opposition to "German metaphysics" repeated the hostility encountered during the 1790s by Coleridge and others in England. Germany, as the homeland of Kant, the higher critics, and Goethe, became a stereotype for everything wrong with intellectuals: incomprehensibility; religious skepticism; and loose morals. While one cannot discount the nationalistic impulse in English resistance to ideas associated with Germany in the 1790s and early 1800s, one has the feeling that foreign theory was only the clearest instance of the foreignness of theory itself.

More recent responses to Emerson show the extent to which we still operate within the structure of Romantic argument. We are still polarized by our acceptance or rejection of aggression. The relationship between critical theory and perceived aggression is perhaps more self-conscious among us than in the rituals of accusation typified by the exchange between Bowen and Emerson, though these rituals persist. Current theorists tend to be interested in connections between writing and authority, reading and power, without seeking to perpetuate authority and power. Antiauthoritarian theories (a category which includes Marxist, feminist, phenomenological, and deconstructive approaches) are negatively oriented to the forms of aggression that are their subject matter. Regardless of the critic's desire to avoid contamination from the subject of force, it is safe to say that the more "theoretical" the critic, the more interested he or she is in power. This, it seems to me, is a logical development from the critical tradition I have been outlining. The association between analysis and aggression leads directly to the intensive analysis of aggression. Inevitably, we find such discriminations operating in criticisms of Emerson. The most theoretical treatments, particularly those of Harold Bloom and, in response to him, Eric Cheyfitz, focus most sharply on Emerson's aggressiveness. Other books, by Joel Porte, Barbara Packer, and Gay Wilson Allen, present a more forceful and neurotic figure than the one encountered in the readings of ten or twenty years ago. Still, this group of commentators finds Emerson a less violent rhetorician than does Bloom. There is a link between a critic's theoretical motive and his characterization of Emerson as an aggressive writer

In his lack of ambivalence about interpretive ferocity, Bloom is, as he desires to be, truly Emersonian. He is less worried about Emerson's violence, of which he is always the vicarious beneficiary, than about our inability to recover it. Bloom has always described his own critical aggression in terms of Emerson's, which, as we have seen, gives genuine occasion for such identification. In his latest work, Emerson's negativity becomes more than ever a parable of Bloom's gnostic religion. *Agon* shifts, rhetorically, between the outright appropriation of Emersonian force and the wish for it. In either mood, Bloom's treatment of Emerson conforms to an Emersonian "aesthetic of *use.*" An account of Emerson's "litany of rejections" turns into Bloom's own polemical liturgy. Bloom defies deconstructive criticism by showing how Emerson was always already beyond deconstruction. In a different tone, when considering the historical and theoretical significance of "*the* American religion, Emersonianism," Bloom confesses that he "aspires to identify, to describe, to celebrate, to join" it. Bloom's desire is always pervaded by intimations of its own hopelessness, however. His account of Emerson's exemplary theoretical status—as inventor of "the American difference," founder of an American canon, and source of anxiety for all later American Romantics—is also a lament over our reduced powers. Tragic and assertive tones alternate in Bloom's prose, and his desire to be aggressive is repeatedly called into question by admissions of his inability actually to become so. Nevertheless, he is correctly perceived as the celebrant, if not the possessor, of antagonism in critical as well as "literary" discourse.

Bloom's case is particularly revealing because his unabashed depiction of the inherent violence of reading draws fire from all sides. He is criticized precisely because his dominant metaphors are those of conflict and overcoming. His willingness to treat intertextuality as a power struggle provokes other critics to differentiate between theory and aggression in order to distance themselves from the latter. The response of Eric Cheyfitz illuminates these dynamics more than most similar reactions because he takes the relationship between Bloom and Emerson seriously; he understands interpretive aggression as a Romantic tradition. Cheyfitz regards his own theoretical project as the exposure and critique by the feminist, deconstructive reader, of the violence implicit in Bloom's Emerson. Cheyfitz is typical of recent critics of both Bloom and Emerson insofar as his attraction to the subject of aggression coexists with his desire to disassociate himself from it. He argues that Emerson's systems of binary terms can be reduced to the primary duality of Father and Mother, then attacks Bloom for perpetuating Emerson's repression of the feminine terms by means of masculine ones. In other words, he acknowledges that idealism is aggressive in Emerson's allegories, but wishes to make his own critical allegorizing nonviolent. Thus he concludes that the texts of both Emerson and Bloom deconstructively reveal that the seizure of power by masculine idealism is unsuccessful. Cheyfitz tacitly presents the deconstructive tendency in these texts as proof of the ethical and political superiority of his reading over Bloom's. His theoretical position involves a complex stance towards metaphoric aggression, causing him to ascribe patriarchal violence to the authors he examines while reserving liberating instability to his own insight. This ambivalent strategy of investigating force without defending it is more typical of current critical practice than Bloom's more Emersonian tactics.

Nevertheless, the fact that Emerson's writings have entered our discussions as allegories of aggression is strong proof of the persistence of Romantic critical terms. His own representations of abstract thought and the way he has now become an emblem for certain critical orientations suggest that a recurring debate about interpretive ethics organizes criticism from the late eighteenth century to the present. Though writers in all periods respond variously to the issue of intellectual aggressiveness, that issue remains central. Romantic critical philosophy developed out of the long struggle to find ways of reading the Bible as a human document. All educated Christians, not just biblical scholars, had to confront the implications of their emerging freedom to create meaning. The argument about whether the critic maintains a reverent, self-abnegating relation to the text or whether criticism is necessarily a self-serving appropriation of meaning is one of the debates that governs the criticism of Herder, Schleiermacher, Coleridge, Friedrich Schlegel, and Nietzsche, as well as Emerson. Our own discussions of literary theory are rarely couched in explicitly moral or religious terms, but frequently address the related issue of whether or not theoretically informed interpretation abuses, exploits, or distorts the text. This takes us back, obliquely, to where we started, with the question of allegory. For one of the most frequent complaints about recent criticism is that literature is reduced when made to illustrate or otherwise serve theoretical argument, reduced to a figurative weapon in the theoretical arsenal. This quarrel surfaces in the long-standing resistance to allegory, which correctly identifies the aggressiveness of that mode and its relation to abstract thought. The close connection between analysis and allegory, whether regarded in a friendly or unfriendly light, is evidence of a persistent contagion that spreads from philosophy to rhetoric in all Romantic eras.

Emerson's Craft of Revision: The Composition of *Essays* (1841)

Glen M. Johnson

Over the past two decades, with the publication of Emerson's *Early Lectures* and *Journals* and of studies by such scholars as Jonathan Bishop, Lawrence Buell, and William Scheick, we have begun to approach adequate understanding of the artistry in Emerson's prose works.[1] A principal focus of attention in most recent studies of Emerson's art has been the process that he called "Composition": the construction of an essay as a "living chain," a "union of many parts each of which came solitary and slowly into the mind and did not at first attain its full expansion" (*EL* 1: 317–18). By reducing an essay into segments as they originally appeared in lectures and journals, we can describe the principles of selection and arrangement that constituted Composition, and thus understand better the "continuity" that Emerson sought in his prose, his "method" in "writ[ing] out the spirit of . . . life symmetrically" (*JMN* 8: 49). Although much work remains to be done, scholars have demonstrated that Emerson's motives in Composition were as much "artistic" as ideological; and it is no longer necessary to defend his essays against the old generalization that their organization is largely arbitrary.

But one aspect of Emerson's practice in Composition has received little attention: his habit of revising passages transferred from lectures or journals into essays. Rarely does any statement taken from an earlier context appear verbatim in an essay; more often the alterations are extensive. Examining these revisions is particularly useful for a student of Emerson's craft. While changes for ideological reasons are found, the largest numbers of revisions are devoted to presentation rather than to content. Ideological content— including that conveyed by imagery or what Scheick calls "hieroglyphs"— appears to be a primary consideration during the earlier stages of Composition, selection, and arrangement. The final stage of revision is more strictly rhetorical, designed to serve the *communication* of meaning between

From Joel Myerson, ed., *Studies in the American Renaissance 1980* (Boston: Twayne Publishers, 1980), 51–72. Copyright 1980 and reprinted with the permission of Twayne Publishers, a division of G. K. Hall & Co., Boston.

[1]Bishop, *Emerson on the Soul* (Cambridge: Harvard University Press, 1964); Buell, *Literary Transcendentalism* (Ithaca: Cornell University Press, 1973); Scheick, *The Slender Human Word* (Knoxville: University of Tennessee Press, 1978).

artist and reader. In many—indeed, most—cases, the qualities of artistry that we recognize as Emerson's most characteristic and best result from revision more than from selection or arrangement.

The generalizations in the following study result from a comprehensive examination of revisions involved in the making of Emerson's most highly "composed" book, the *Essays* of 1841. The published text, in the first edition,[2] has been collated with all identified sources in lectures or, when no lecture source is known, in journals. Section I of this study considers the extent to which Emerson generalized or depersonalized his own experience while transferring it from journals to essays. Section II examines the revisions designed to serve logic or to accommodate a shift in Emerson's thinking on a subject. Section III then focuses on more strictly "artistic" revisions, those responsible for the recognizable, "Emersonian" prose style of the essays.

I

A standard assertion about Emerson's revisions is that, in moving from private (journal) to public (essay) statement, he generalized his individual experience and disguised or cut references to specific persons. At times this is clearly the case:

Ellen was never alone. I could not imagine her poor & solitary. (*JMN* 7: 168)	The lover cannot paint his maiden to his fancy poor and solitary. ("Love," *E* pp. 146–47)
I need hardly to say to any one acquainted with my thoughts that I have no System. When I was quite young I fancied that by keeping a Manuscript Journal by me, . . . in the course of a few years I should be able to complete a sort of Encyclopaedia containing the net value of all the definitions at which the world had yet arrived. (*JMN* 7: 302)	The world refuses to be analyzed by addition and subtraction. When we are young, we spend much time and pains in filling our note-books, . . . in the hope that in the course of a few years, we shall have condensed into our encyclopedia, the net value of all the theories at which the world has yet arrived. ("Intellect," *E* p. 281)

Frequently, Emerson's private exhortations to himself become, in public, Olympian pronouncements. Take, for example, this entry from the time of the Divinity School Address:

[2]*Essays* (Boston: James Munroe, 1841); hereafter cited in the text as *E*. A facsimile of this edition was published by the Charles E. Merrill Publishing Company in 1969. I choose the text of the first edition rather than that of the more familiar version of 1847, known as *Essays: First Series*, because Emerson revised the text again before the 1847 edition appeared. This later revision has not been considered here, because it was not strictly speaking a part of the "Composition" of the book and because it has been studied previously; see Paul Lauter, "Emerson's Revisions of *Essays* (First Series)," *American Literature*, 33 (May 1961): 143–58.

| Forget the past. Be not the slave of your own past. In your prayer, in your teaching cumber not yourself with solicitude lest you contradict somewhat you have stated in this or that public place. So you worship the dull God Terminus & not the Lord of Lords. . . . Trust your emotion. (*JMN* 7: 25) | But why should you keep your head over your shoulder? Why drag about this monstrous corpse of your memory, lest you contradict somewhat you have stated in this or that public place? Suppose you should contradict yourself; what then? . . . Trust your emotion. ("Self-Reliance," *E* p. 47) |

In such a case, the generalizing effect comes less from specific alterations of language than from the loss of a personal context. But the rhetorical effect is marked: a passage that in Emerson's journal evidences personal anxiety becomes, in "Self-Reliance," supremely assured transcendental thunder.

In revising personal references and anecdotes, Emerson seems to have been guided by both his sense of decorum and his conception of his public voice. For the most part, he eliminated references by name to living persons; those that remain—to Carlyle, Wordsworth, Cousin, Schelling—are impersonal and generally complimentary (*E*, pp. 205, 284, 292). Emerson consistently cut references to living Americans, both public figures and personal acquaintances. Thus Daniel Webster becomes "Burke"; Washington Allston, "an eminent painter"; Elizabeth Hoar, "a lady"; and J. S. Dwight, "my companion" (*E* pp. 9, 37, 15, 16; *JMN*, 5: 403, 377, 7: 61, 5: 504). The result of such a process is inevitably to generalize certain passages—and to weaken them:

| And now Alcott with his hatred of labor & commanding contemplation, a haughty beneficiary, makes good to the 19th Century Simeon the Stylite. (*JMN* 7: 211) | More than once some individual has appeared to me with such negligence of labor and such commanding contemplation, a haughty beneficiary, begging in the name of God, as made good to the nineteenth century Simeon the Stylite. ("History," *E* p. 23) |

And the anecdotes of the journals tend to become generalized exempla in the essays.

On the other hand, the establishing of his characteristic public voice in *Essays* sometimes led Emerson to make a statement *more* personal or individual:

| Our will never gave the images in the mind the rank they now take there. The regular course of studies, the years of academical or professional education have not yielded the man so many grand facts as some idle books under the bench at school. (*EL* 3: 37) | My will never gave the images in my mind the rank they now take. The regular course of studies, the years of academical and professional education have not yielded me better facts than some idle books under the bench at the Latin School. ("Spiritual Laws," *E* pp. 108–9; cf. *JMN* 5: 94) |

Such alterations usually occur when Emerson is constructing the exemplary persona, touched with transcendental militancy, familiar in works of the period from *Nature* through *Essays*. In fact, in constructing this voice Emerson sometimes created anecdotes out of general comments in journals or lectures. Four well-known anecdotes in *Essays* seem to be of this created variety: (1) the "answer which when quite young I was prompted to make to a valued adviser. . . . 'If I am the devil's child, I will live then from the devil' "; (2) the "good man" who "to-day" told the self-reliant Emerson "of my obligation to put all poor men in good situations"; (3) the preacher who "lately" argued for compensation in the next life, and the congregation which accepted this "without remark"; and (4) the "person who always deferred to me" in "an academical club," thinking that "my experiences had somewhat superior; whilst I saw that his experiences were as good as mine" (*E* pp. 41–42, and *JMN* 5: 49; *E* p. 43, and *JMN* 7: 224; *E* p. 78, and *JMN* 7: 182–83; *E* pp. 275–76, and *JMN* 7: 490). Such examples indicate that Emerson's motives in revising journal or lecture passages for inclusion in essays were more complex than has generally been recognized. He did often depersonalize or generalize his experience, motivated by his sense of privacy or decorum or by his desire to present an exemplary persona. But the latter consideration—the literary motive—also led him to individualize and to personalize his statements when such changes added rhetorical impact to the expression.

II

Given the nature of "Composition" and the diversity of Emerson's sources, one expects to find in the essays revisions devoted to transitions or other kinds of connections and to alterations of meaning. In fact, revisions of either kind are relatively infrequent. Standard logical connections were of little interest to Emerson; indeed, he frequently cut subordinating conjunctions and conjunctive adverbs in revising lecture passages for essays. Consequently, signposts like the following italicized words (all added in revision) are rare: "The lesson is forcibly taught *by these observations*"; "*Thus* is the soul the perceiver"; "*For this reason*, an index or mercury of intellectual proficiency is the perception of identity" (*E* pp. 110, 235, 281; cf. *EL* 3: 312, 18; *JMN* 7: 181). More to Emerson's liking is the witty or paradoxical assertion which leads from one topic to another. This revision, from the lecture "Duty" to "Self-Reliance," shows the greater freedom provided by the written form: "But beside pledges and the overgood religionist there is still another mechanical aid that is thrust upon the soul, namely creeds and classifications" (*EL* 3: 140–41) becomes "As men's prayers are a disease of the will, so are their creeds a disease of the intellect" (*E* p. 64).

While eschewing formal transitions and other logical connectives, Emerson worked for coherence by setting up, within individual essays and *Essays* as a whole, patterns of ideas, images, and language. The thematic relationship of

"History" and "Self-Reliance," the first two chapters in the book, is reinforced by these additions to the original sources: "The obscure consciousness of this fact is the light of all our day, the claim of claims; . . . the foundation of friendship and love, and of the heroism and grandeur which belongs to acts of self-reliance" ("History," *E* pp. 5–6; "Friendship," "Love," and "Heroism" are also in *Essays*) and "Let us . . . hurl in the face of custom, and trade, and office, the fact which is the upshot of all history, that there is a great responsible Thinker and Actor moving wherever moves a man ("Self-Reliance," *E* p. 50). Revisions also serve the internal coherence of "Self-Reliance" by helping to set up patterns of imagery involving childhood, imprisonment, and standing upright. The italicized images were all added in revision: "Great men have always . . . confided themselves *childlike* to the genius of their age"; "Of such an *immortal youth* the force would be felt"; "Meantime nature is not slow to equip us in the *prison-uniform* of the party to which we adhere"; and "He *walks abreast* with his days, and feels no shame" (*E* pp. 39, 41, 45, 62; cf. *EL* 3: 139; *JMN* 7: 50; *EL* 3: 309, 265). "Spiritual Laws" provides the most obvious example in *Essays* of a verbal pattern added in revision. Five sentences, all of which head paragraphs in the essay, pick up the syntactic pattern established by an excerpt taken from the lecture "Religion": "What a man does, that he has"; "He may have his own"; "He may see what he maketh"; "He may read what he writeth"; "He shall have his own society"; "He may set his own rate" (*E* pp. 117, 121, 122, 123). The echoes among essays and the imagistic and syntactic patterns within essays show that Emerson, despite his rejection of traditional connectives, nevertheless saw coherence as a goal of composition. In revising for *Essays* he provided fewer and more subtle, but effective, links of thought and language.

Despite Emerson's heavy revision, *Essays* provides few examples of *pentimento*. Taking his own advice to "speak what you think to-day in words as hard as cannon balls, and to-morrow speak what to-morrow thinks," Emerson rarely made revisions that were primarily motivated by a change of opinion on a topic. Since one purpose of *Essays* was to provide a record of his own "genesis" or growth, he generally let his earlier expressions stand, even when this led to inconsistencies. Besides, he made no pretense of having arrived at the truth; he was as much a seeker in 1841 as he had been in 1832, and he sought to record in his book the dialectical play of his mind. His method of composition aided him in doing so, since it allowed him to draw together his thoughts, public and private, sanguine and dejected, from a period of nearly a decade. He seems consciously to have decided not to impose ideological unity on his sources: "When I have my own head, and obey my whims, let me remind the reader that I am only an experimenter" (*E* p. 262).

Still, no alteration in a passage can be completely neutral ideologically, and many of Emerson's revisions do affect meaning. For example, the sentence from "Self-Reliance" quoted above—"Of such an immortal youth the force would be felt"—originally read: "If the scholar would be true, instantly his natural & formidable position would appear" (*E* p. 41; *JMN* 7: 50). Questions of clarity and cadence aside, the revision was obviously motivated by the placement of the excerpt at the end of a paragraph which develops the metaphor of uncompromising "boys who are sure of a dinner." But the youth is also a more democratic figure than the scholar, and the change reinforces the democratic promise of greatness through self-reliance. It also documents Emerson's movement away from the scholar as an ideal; the scholar's successor, the poet, is mentioned one sentence before the immortal youth.[3]

Sometimes context alone alters meaning. For example, take this rather conventional preacherly passage, written in 1834, when Emerson was temporarily weary of ideological battle: "How dear how soothing to man arises the Idea of God peopling the lonely place, effacing the scars of our mistakes & disappointments. When we have lost our God of tradition & ceased from our God of rhetoric then may God fire the heart with his presence" (JMN 4: 342). It is surprising to find this rather wistful and doctrinally inoffensive passage transferred almost verbatim into one of the most assertive and least orthodox paragraphs of "The Over-Soul." Emerson made two significant alterations in the excerpt: he put an exclamation point at the end of the first sentence, and he changed "have lost our God" to "have broken our god." But the most important difference is in the context. In "The Over-Soul," the excerpt is preceded by this sentence: "The simplest person, who in his integrity worships God, becomes God." It is followed by this: "It ['God's presence'] is the doubling of the heart itself" (E pp. 241–42). Largely through force of context, a prayer to God has become a claim to be God.

Other changes in emphasis, if not in meaning, result from simple elimination of elements in the sources. In such cases, one often sees the emergence of a motive in addition to that of providing a record of Emerson's mental and spiritual growth. Essays is also a hortatory book, and it is arranged for maximum impact on the reader. In the following cases, the cuts seem to have been made with the reader in mind. The text is that of Essays; brackets enclose material eliminated in revision.

Every soul must know the whole lesson for itself—must go over the whole ground. What it does not see, what it does not live, it will not know. . . . Somewhere or other, some time or other, it will demand and find compensation for that loss by doing the work itself. [How, then, since each must go over every line of the ground can there be any progress of the Species?] ("History," E pp. 8–9; JMN 5: 384)

But in all unbalanced minds [(and whose is not so?)], the classification is idolized, passes for the end, and not for a speedily exhaustible means. ("Self-Reliance," E p. 65; EL 3: 141)

Thus revering the soul, . . . man will come to see that the world is the perennial miracle which the soul worketh. . . . He will . . . be content with all places and

3See Henry Nash Smith, "Emerson's Problem of Vocation," New England Quarterly, 12 (March 1939): 52–67; and Stephen E. Whicher, Freedom and Fate: An Inner Life of Ralph Waldo Emerson (Philadelphia: University of Pennsylvania Press, 1953), especially chapter 7.

any service he can render. [A man should stand among his fellow men as a coal lies in the fire it has kindled, radiating heat but lost in the general flame.] ("The Over-Soul," *E* p. 245; *EL* 2: 356)

Although a denial of the idea of progress is implicit in Emerson's historical theory, as noted in the original (1837) version of the first passage, he obviously did not want to make this explicit in "History." He realized, one may conjecture, that to question the cherished notion of progress so early in the book would divert attention from the grandly positive point he wished to make. And so he cut the question from "History," delaying his confrontation with the idea of progress until the end of "Self-Reliance"; by that point, the reader is prepared to see that Emerson denies progress only that he may offer a more splendid alternative. The second passage above eliminates a statement that, while consistent with the themes of *Essays*, is nevertheless not strategically advisable: in this section of "Self-Reliance" the reader is being led to *separate* himself from classifiers and other idolators. And in the third passage Emerson's original metaphor, though understandable in terms of the mysticism of "The Over-Soul," is nevertheless inexact in its reference, therefore potentially misleading and best eliminated.

For another example of revision primarily by exclusion, made with an eye to a specific impression on the reader, consider these passages from "Manners" and "History":

'What is the foundation of that enduring interest which all men feel in the form of life and manners of the old Greeks and Romans? . . . A very large part of our youth and especially of such as receive a learned education is devoted exclusively to the language and history of these nations. . . .

What is the foundation of that interest all men feel in Greek history, letters, art and poetry? . . .

This period keeps a permanent interest for us because it describes a perfectly natural state of society and one through which in some sort every man passes. The Greeks and the Romans were but noble savages. Their greatness is the era of the bodily nature; the perfection of the senses; and of the spiritual nature unfolded in subordination to the body. The Christian era is the reverse of this; it is the period of philosophy; the era of the spiritual nature manifested in the subjugation of the body. (*EL* 2: 132–33)

This period draws us because we are Greeks. It is a state through which every man in some sort passes.

The Grecian state is the era of the bodily nature, the perfection of the senses,—of the spiritual nature unfolded in strict unity with the body. (*E* p. 20)

The revision here shows a movement away from a notion of historical cycles and toward a genuinely subjective, ontogenetic history. But the change seems motivated less by ideology—Emerson had certainly not abandoned cyclical history—than by the specific impression he desired to make in "History." Thus the facile contrast is eliminated and the Greek era becomes a metaphor for man's youth—fitting the dominant image pattern of the essay as well as the myth of a golden age of integrity—rather than for the nonspiritual extreme of human nature.

Finally, certain substantive revisions in *Essays* fall into patterns, and thus are particularly revealing about Emerson's changing ideas and his artistic motives. For example, there are his revisions of passages concerning the role of the understanding:

Facts encumber them, tyrannize over them, and make the men of routine, the men of understanding, the men of sense. (*EL* 3: 48)	Facts encumber them, tyrannize over them, and make the men of routine, the men of *sense*. ("History," *E* p. 27)
And we distinguish this primary wisdom as *Intuition*, whilst all subordinate teachings are *tuitions*. (*EL* 3: 35)	We denote this primary wisdom as Intuition, whilst all later teachings are tuitions. ("Self-Reliance," *E* p. 52)
But culture, . . . imperiously demands that conveniences of every sort, even health and bodily life, shall not be sought for themselves, but in a rigid subordination to the higher nature. It uses and requires Prudence as an ally and a means to serve the ends of wisdom and virtue. (*EL* 2: 312)	But culture, . . . degrades every thing else, as health and bodily life, into means. It sees prudence not to be a several faculty, but a name for wisdom and virtue conversing with the body and its wants. ("Prudence," *E* p. 185)

In the late 1830s, Emerson was moving away from an untenable position championing Reason in opposition to understanding;[4] the examples above, clearly exceptions to the generalization that Emerson did not revise primarily to indicate a change of opinion, verify the movement. The first revision breaks the identification of understanding and sensuality on which Emerson's opposition to the former was based. The second revision shows Emerson no longer willing to characterize knowledge gained through the understanding as inherently inferior, except in time, to that gained through intuition. And he now makes prudence an integral part of "culture," rather than "imperiously" degrading it to the role of a vaguely unpleasant ally.

The most extensive pattern of substantive revisions in *Essays* involves the gradual secularization of Emerson's thought and language. *Essays* remains, of course, a profoundly religious book, and Emerson makes extensive use of

[4]See Leonard Neufeldt, "The Vital Mind: Emerson's Epistemology," *Philological Quarterly*, 50 (April 1971): 253–70.

religious terms, images, and allusions. Some of his revisions, indeed, increase or make explicit the religious connotations of certain passages:

. . . he sees the reality and divine splendor of the inmost nature bursting through each chink and cranny. (*EL* 2: 312)	. . . reverencing the splendor of the God which he sees bursting through each chink and cranny. ("Prudence," *E* p. 185)
Yet I desire, . . . to indicate the domain of this great light. (*EL* 3: 280)	Yet I desire, . . . to indicate the heaven of this deity. ("The Over-Soul," *E* p. 223)

As these two examples indicate, such changes generally come in passages in which the religious emphasis is overt or in which Emerson is concerned to identify "God" with either nature or the self-reliant individual.

Usually, however, Emerson's revisions move in the opposite direction, away from traditional religious language. For example, "God" becomes "the internal ocean" in "Self-Reliance," and "Nature" in "Intellect"; "the creator" becomes, in "Love," either "the heart" or "Eternal Power" (*E* pp. 58, 270, 152, 154; cf. *JMN* 7: 174; *EL* 2: 249; *EL* 3: 65, 66). There is a tendency to transfer active powers away from "God":

What a man does that he has. . . . With God is no paltering or double dealing and all Hope and Fear may in front of his attributes be left behind. (*EL* 2: 95)	What a man does, that he has. What has he to do with hope or fear? In himself is his might. ("Spiritual Laws," *E* p. 117)
To those who have crimes to conceal, . . . fire, water, snow, wind, gravitation become penalties & the sun & the moon are the frowns of God & lanthorns of his police. (*JMN* 7: 197)	The laws and substances of nature, water, snow, wind, gravitation, become penalties to the thief. ("Compensation," *E* p. 96)
We do not determine what we will think; we only open our senses, . . . and let God think through us. (*EL* 2: 250)	We do not determine what we will think. We only open our senses, . . . and suffer the intellect to see. ("Intellect," *E* p. 272)

Essays shows a general secularization of Emerson's language, sometimes quite subtle. In the first example below, "life" is changed from a passive to an active subject; in the second, the words "sacred" and "shames" are replaced by the more secular "mysterious" and "laws":

Life is constituted with inevitable conditions which the unwise seek to dodge. . . . He has resisted the Spirit there and fled from himself and the deep retribution makes the conditions good by banishing his soul this very hour from life. (*EL* 3: 148)	Life invests itself with inevitable conditions, which the unwise seek to dodge. . . . He has resisted his life, and fled from himself, and the retribution is so much death. ("Compensation," *E* p. 87)

| Human life . . . seems to us a sacred and inviolable thing and we hedge it round with penalties and shames. (*EL* 3: 21) | Human life . . . is mysterious and inviolable, and we hedge it round with penalties and laws. ("History," *E* p. 5) |

Often the decrease in religious reference is accompanied by an increased emphasis on individuality and self-reliance:

| He that perceives that the Moral Sentiment is the highest in God's order, rights himself. . . . (*JMN* 5: 362) | He who knows that power is in the soul, that he is weak only because he has looked for good out of him and elsewhere, and so perceiving, throws himself unhesitatingly on his thought, instantly rights himself. . . . ("Self-Reliance," *E* p. 73) |

And the decline in religious language is matched by a greater use of legal or scientific vocabulary and images:

| He will learn . . . that all history is sacred; he will come to know that where he is, God is; where he listeneth, God speaketh. (*EL* 2: 356) | He will learn . . . that all history is sacred; that the universe is represented in an atom, in a moment of time. ("The Over-Soul," *E* p. 245) |

These revisions show that Emerson, who throughout his life had thought and spoken in traditional religious terms—even, as in *Nature*, where his message was anything but traditional—was in the late 1830s attempting to break the habit. His dominant vocabulary continued to be that of his Unitarian forebears, but he now used religious terminology more sparingly, consciously, and strategically. When Emerson added biblical or traditional religious language to *Essays*, it was likely to be calculated to produce a specific effect—and the message was likely not to be traditional: "Speak your latent conviction and it shall be the universal sense; for always the inmost becomes the outmost,—and our first thought is rendered back to us by the trumpets of the Last Judgment" ("Self-Reliance," *E* p. 37). Or: "Friend, client, child, sickness, fear, want, charity, all knock at once at thy closet door and say, 'Come out unto us.'—Do not spill thy soul; do not all descend; keep thy state; stay at home in thine own heaven" ("Self-Reliance," *E* p. 59).

III

Most of the revisions involved in the making of *Essays* were devoted primarily to the presentation of ideas rather than to the ideas *per se*. Having cast himself as the "teacher of the coming age" (*JMN* 4: 93), Emerson worked to make his message as clear, as fresh sounding, as provocative, as memorable as possible. So he revised thinking of himself as a communicator as much as a thinker; what he was communicating was, finally, less a set of propositions than an attitude and style of thinking. His own literary style and attitude, his tone, were all important. He had spent years on the podium, polishing his style; with the *Essays* of 1841 he began adapting it to the written medium.

He seems to have been incapable of simply copying his earlier expressions verbatim; he changed almost every passage in some way. Indeed, he seems sometimes to have made changes simply for the sake of change. There are, for example, passages in which words or phrases are inverted, for no apparent reason: "worms & frogs" becomes "frogs and worms"; "tormentable or convulsible" becomes "convulsible or tormentable"; "sometime or other, somewhere or other" becomes "somewhere or other, some time or other" (*E* pp. 180, 265, 9, and *JMN* 7: 325, 387; 5: 384). Rarely was a list or catalogue copied verbatim, and some such revisions seem arbitrary: "courage, strength, beauty, address, self-command, swiftness" becomes "courage, address, self-command, justice, strength, swiftness"; "Adam, then Guy, then Richard" becomes "John, then Adam, then Richard" (*E* pp. 20, 227, and *EL* 2: 133, 3: 312).

Such revisions, if they are indeed arbitrary, reflect both force of habit and Emerson's self-reliant aversion to merely repeating himself. Even if only in the change of a word or two, a passage would be the product of today's working, therefore "alive in a new day." And, especially for changes in lists, there was the impulse of catalogue rhetoric. Believing in a cosmic unity underlying worldly diversity, Emerson and his followers used lists, infinitely expandable and with interchangeable elements, as expressions of their vision of unity in plenitude.[5] Tinkering with lists, as Emerson almost always did, was a literary way of demonstrating the ontological democracy he preached. Of course, his lists were rarely arbitrary; his revisions of them usually reflect a literary purpose. Some set up a logical (here, historical) progression: "empire, kingdom, camp, republic, and democracy" (*EL* 2: 14) becomes "camp, kingdom, empire, republic, democracy" ("History," *E* p. 4). Others provide alliteration or assonance: "The cloud, the tree, the sod, the cat" (*JMN* 7: 181) becomes "The cloud, the tree, the turf, the bird" ("Intellect," *E* p. 281). And others do both: "Egypt, Greece, Rome, England, riches, poverty, learning, labor, pain & death" (*JMN* 7: 138–39) becomes "Egypt, Greece, Gaul, England, War, Colonization, Church, Court, and Commerce" ("History," *E* p. 8).

The main purpose of Emerson's presentational revisions in *Essays* was the development of his characteristic written style, a style which differs considerably from that of the early lectures. The lectures, as befits works prepared for oral delivery, and as might be expected from a man trained as a sermonizer, develop slowly. There are frequent repetitions and redundancies in both thought and language, as each point is explained, illustrated, and amplified. Emerson's cadences tend to be oratorical, his periods balanced and hypotactic. His essays, on the other hand, move rapidly; he could, in fact, condense an entire lecture into a few paragraphs of a printed piece. (He compressed the

[5]See Buell, *Literary Transcendentalism*, chapter 6.

first two-thirds of his "Introductory" lecture on "The Philosophy of History" into about three pages of the essay "History.") Discussions or elaborations in essays are concise, sparing, often elliptical. Cadences tend toward the conversational; periods are loose, aphoristic, and paratactic. These are tendencies rather than absolutes; to generalize is to make the differences seem greater than they are. But Emerson's revisions unquestionably show him working consistently toward maximum conciseness and sharpness in his printed presentations.

In order to assure understanding in his lecture audiences, Emerson often made the same point twice in consecutive sentences or clauses. In *Essays* such repetitions are frequently eliminated, either by telescoping the sentences or clauses or by simple excision:

Of this one mind, History is the record. Of this mind the events of history are the work. (*EL* 2: 13)	Of the works of this mind history is the record. ("History," *E* p. 3)
Men even dream that they find in the inspired Scriptures and men, answers to these questions; that Jesus has left replies to precisely these interrogatories. (*EL* 3: 277)	They even dream that Jesus has left replies to precisely these interrogatories. ("The Over-Soul," *E* p. 234)
The consideration of time and place, of you and me, of profit and hurt, tyrannize over most men's minds. Whatever they look at, they look at under those aspects. (*EL* 2: 249)	The consideration of time and place, of you and me, of profit and hurt, tyrannize over most men's minds. ("Intellect," *E* p. 270)

Throughout his career, Emerson was fond of rhetorical doubles—pairs, compound constructions, verbal echoes, and incremental repetition.[6] Such redundancies serve a purpose in oral delivery, but can be irritating when read; although Emerson employed "iteration" for effect in *Essays*, he did eliminate many doubles found in the original sources. These examples show revised doubles of various kinds:

The preternatural stength and success of the hero. (*EL* 1: 260)	The preternatural prowess of the hero. ("History," *E* p. 28)
For that sentiment of essential life, the sense of being which in calm hours rises. . . . (*EL* 3: 35)	For the sense of being which in calm hours rises. . . . ("Self-Reliance," *E* p. 52)
A making it the subject of thought—the glance of the intellect raises it. (*EL* 2: 58)	The making a fact the subject of thought, raises it. ("Intellect," *E* p. 270)

6See Sheldon W. Liebman, "The Development of Emerson's Theory of Rhetoric, 1821–1836," *American Literature*, 41 (May 1969): 185–86.

Let him subdue the rebellious muscles, let him subdue the palpitations of fear and face the object of apprehension. . . . (*EL* 2: 319)	Let him front the object of his worst apprehension. . . . ("Prudence," *E* p. 196)

Since Emerson's doubles and redundancies are a principal cause of the rolling oratorical style of the lectures, his revisions help to produce the simpler style of the essays:

Do I not know beforehand that not possibly can he say a new or spontaneous word? Do I not know that with all this affectation of examining the grounds of the institution,—of the creed, of the law, he will do no such thing—that the establishment is to him sacred? Do I not know that he is pledged to himself beforehand not to look but at one side; the permitted side, not as a man but as a parish minister, a sworn partisan, a paid vote? (*EL* 3: 309)	Do I not know beforehand that not possibly can he say a new and spontaneous word? Do I not know that with all this ostentation of examining the grounds of the institution, he will do no such thing? Do I not know that he is pledged to himself not to look but at one side; the permitted side, not as a man, but as a parish minister? ("Self-Reliance," *E* p. 45)

Another kind of redundancy involves using elaborations, examples, or metaphors to amplify or illustrate an assertion. His years on the platform had given Emerson a sure sense of the needs of an audience in this respect; frequently, in *Essays*, one finds him adding explanations or elaborations of points not altogether clear in lectures:

Men descend to meet. They seem to me to resemble those Arabian sheikhs who dwell in mean houses and affect an external poverty. . . . (*EL* 3: 19)	Men descend to meet. In their habitual and mean service to the world, for which they forsake their native nobleness, they resemble those Arabian Sheikhs. . . . ("The Over-Soul," *E* p. 230)
Heraclitus said, "Dry light makes the best souls," looking upon the affections as moist and colored mists. (*EL* 2: 249)	Heraclitus looked upon the affections as dense and colored mists. In the fog of good and evil affections, it is hard for man to walk forward in a straight line. ("Intellect," *E* p. 270)

The more frequent tendency, however, was to cut or to shorten elaborations and explanations:

A man is to know that they all are his; suing his notice, petitioners to his faculties that they will come out and take possession; born thralls to	Yet they all are his, suitors for his notice, petitioners to his faculties that they will come out and take possession. ("Self-Reliance," *E* p. 51)

his sovereignty; conundrums he alone
can guess; chaos until he come like a
creator and give them light and
order. (*EL* 2: 223)

Consider who is the first drawing-master,—only in humble aid of whom our earthly drawing-master comes. Whence had you those primary lessons in drawing,—the elements on which all practical skill must be based?—Without instruction we know very well the ideal of the human form. (*EL* 3: 74)	Who is the first drawing-master? Without instruction we know very well the ideal of the human form. ("Intellect," *E* p. 278)

Through such revisions, Emerson developed a written style which combines clarity of thought with maximum economy in presentation. The essays consistently improve upon the lectures in both respects.

The economy of Emerson's prose in *Essays* derives from a rigorous pruning of words and constructions not carrying full weight in sentences. Common victims were adjectives, adverbs, and function words of various sorts; but Emerson was especially severe with circumlocutions and gratuitous subordinate constructions. Often cuts alone make a marked difference; this is a passage from the lecture "The School," with Emerson's excisions for *Essays* indicated by brackets: "[Yet is it easy to see and maturer years are always showing us that] persons are [only] supplementary to this primary teaching of the Soul. [It is] in youth [that] we are mad for persons. Childhood and youth [do] see [, as I have said,] all the world in them" (*EL* 3: 42–43; "The Over-Soul," *E* p. 229). More often, however, a passage is rewritten to achieve maximum sharpness:

As the signs of the zodiac—crabs, goats, scorpions, the balance, the waterpot—lose all their meanness when hung in the blue spaces of the empyrean from an unrecorded age so I can see the familiar and sordid attributes of human nature as objects of pure science when removed into this distant firmament of time. My appetites, my weaknesses, my vices, I can see in Solomon, Alcibiades, and Cataline, without heat, and study their laws without personal pique. (*EL* 2: 16)	As crabs, goats, scorpions, the balance and the waterpot, lose all their meanness when hung as signs in the zodiack, so I can see my own vices without heat in the distant persons of Solomon, Alcibiades, and Cataline. ("History," *E* p. 5)

Emerson's revisions for economy sharpen the focus and increase the impact of his prose. They also show his concern to take maximum advantage of the freedom provided by the printed medium. In his lectures—less so in the orations, for which he had virtually ideal audiences—he was confined by the limitations of his auditors, by their ability to absorb and coordinate abstract ideas presented orally. Thus the early lectures are characteristically leisurely in movement, wordy and redundant in development. It took the transfer to the written form to call out the strength of Emerson's art. In the revisions for *Essays* one can see Emerson developing a prose style with the qualities and strengths of poetry, especially the combination of clarity with economy. Like the great poetry to which they are often compared, Emerson's essays make considerable demands upon the reader; despite the rapid movement of thought, the prose cannot be read rapidly or understood without concentration. One of the strengths of Emerson's prose is its ability to make this demand of the reader. And this strength is something Emerson consciously worked for in revising.

In working on *Essays*, Emerson strove for a diction with freshness and vigor. This meant substituting strong terms for neutral ones, and specifics for generalities: "We see plainly how it lies all around us" (*EL* 2: 85) becomes "We know that it pervades and contains us" ("The Over-Soul," *E* p. 225); "The terrors of the storm are known only to those within the house" (*EL* 2: 320) becomes "The terrors of the storm are chiefly confined to the parlor and the cabin" ("Prudence," *E* p. 196). It meant removing clichés and language verging on the hackneyed:

It is evident that his constant strife with the iron soil and the blinding snows makes the inhabitant of the northern temperate zone so much wiser and abler man than his fellow who enjoys the perpetual smile of the tropics. (*EL* 2: 313)	The hard soil and four months of snow make the inhabitant of the northern temperate zone wiser and abler than his fellow who enjoys the fixed smile of the tropics. ("Prudence," *E* p. 187)
A man must consider what a rich realm he abdicates when he becomes a conformist. (*EL* 3: 309)	A man must consider what a blind-man's-buff is this game of conformity. ("Self-Reliance," *E* p. 45)

And it meant substituting images for denotative language, while improving images already present in lectures: "The affections are subordinated to the soul" (*EL* 3: 67) becomes "Our affections are but tents of a night" ("Love," *E* p. 155); "Paganini will draw celestial beauty out of a fiddle" (*EL* 3: 138) becomes "Paganini can extract rapture from a catgut" ("Spiritual Laws," *E* p. 116).

Emerson also sought to exploit the musical qualities of language. He made frequent use of alliteration and assonance, particularly in catalogues: "Hear the rats in the wall, see the lizard on the fence, the fungus under foot, the lichen on the log" (*E* p. 32). But his principal resource was rhythm. The cadences of Emerson's sentences are subtle and varied, and generalizations are difficult. He carefully avoided sentences that were too obviously metrical or jingling. He found, for example, this sentence in the lecture "Private Life": "By persisting in your path, by holding your peace, though you forfeit the little you gain the great" (*EL* 3: 255). This became, in "Friendship": "By persisting in your path, though you forfeit the little, you gain the great" (*E* p. 177). The sentence retains its cadence of two-stress phrases, along with the alliteration and parallel structure; but it has lost the singsong effect of the original, which fits too easily the rhythmical pattern of doggerel verse.

Emerson's prose has a strong, rhythmical forward momentum, influenced largely by two factors: the linguistic density of his sentences, which provides a rapid-moving pattern of stresses; and the frequent paralleling of syntactic patterns. In his oratorical manner—more characteristic of lectures than of essays—the effect is that of a rhetorical snowball, or avalanche: "If we consider what happens in conversation, in reveries, in remorse, in times of passion, in surprises, in the instructions of dreams wherein often we see ourselves in masquerade,—the droll disguises only magnifying and enhancing a real element, and forcing it on our distant notice,—we shall catch many hints that will broaden and lighten into knowledge of the secret of nature" ("The Over-Soul," *E* p. 224). This sentence seems overdone, with its self-conscious absolute construction and the long delay of the main clause. But it does show, in extreme form, Emerson's exploitation of prose rhythm. The key to this passage is the fact that readers of prose perceive equivalent syntactic units as somehow equivalent rhythmically, whatever the actual numbers of words they contain.[7] Thus the series of short, unqualified prepositional phrases establishes a rapid rhythm that, when it reaches the long sixth phrase and the absolute construction that accompanies it, creates a strong urge forward, a rhythmical urge that reinforces the syntactic urge toward the main clause. In the lecture version, from "Doctrine of the Soul," the urge is less strong; the rhythm is lost when the parallel structure of "in" phrases is broken at "the instructions of dreams": "If we consider what happens in conversation, in reveries, in remorse, in times of passion, in times when any affecting incident surprises us from our habits of prudence and inaction, the instructions of dreams wherein often we see ourselves in masquerade, in wild masquerade and yet ourselves, the droll disguises only magnifying and enhancing a real element and forcing it on our distinct notice—we shall catch many hints . . ." (*EL* 3: 15). The lecture version degenerates rhythmically and ends in a jumble. In revision, Emerson cut excess verbiage and added a crucial "in" to enforce parallelism; the result is to make the syntactic pattern clear throughout. Despite its density, the sentence unfolds coherently and rhythmically.

More characteristic of Emerson's prose rhythm is the sentence of "The Over-Soul" immediately following the one just discussed. This passage derives its rhythm from both repetition and balance—as one sees clearly when the sentence is printed as if it were verse:

7See Bishop, *Emerson on the Soul*, p. 115.

All goes to show that the soul in man is not an organ,
but animates and exercises all the organs;

is not a function, like the power of memory, of calculation, of comparison,—
but uses these as hands and feet;

is not a faculty,
but a light;

is not the intellect or the will,
but the master of the intellect and the will;—

is the vast back-ground of our being, in which they lie,—
an immensity not possessed and that cannot be possessed.

(E p. 224)

Taking punctuation as guide, the sentence divides into a series of five "couplets," syntactically parallel in that each provides a predicate for "the soul in man." The repetitions of "is" and "but" reinforce the parallels among couplets and "verses," with the lack of negative "not" and "but" signaling resolution in the final couplet. Most important to the rhythmical feeling of the sentence is the fact that the couplets are balanced internally. With one exception, each couplet breaks neatly into two verses; count stresses, syllables, or words, and the two lines balance rhythmically. Yet, with all these repetitions and balances, the sentence contains sufficient variation, in "line length" and in one unbalanced couplet, to prevent its developing the kind of lilt that would interfere with attention to the content.

The basic rhythmical structure of this sentence from "The Over-Soul" is already present in the lecture version (*EL* 3: 15), but in revising Emerson shortened the sentence by twenty-one words. The result is a passage that is long but lean, with an unusually high proportion of nouns and finite verbs— forty percent of total words. This density of words carrying strong natural stress, combined with the high proportion—three-quarters—of monosyllables, gives the passage the emphatic but rapid cadence that is characteristic of Emerson's prose. Indeed, Emerson's revisions, stripping down sentences to essentials, consistently produce the close, rapid, emphatic tread that gives his writing its ongoing momentum. Note, for example, this revision from the lecture "Genius" to the essay "Art":

In landscape, the painter's aim is not surely to give us the enjoyment of a real landscape; for, air, light, motion, life, heat, dampness, and actual infinite space, he cannot give us—but the suggestion of a better, fairer creation than we know. He collects a greater number of beautiful effects into his picture than coexist in any real landscape: the details—the prose of nature, he omits, and gives us	In landscapes, the painter should give the suggestion of a fairer creation than we know. The details, the prose of nature he should omit, and give us only the spirit and splendor. (*E* p. 289)

only the spirit and splendor, so that
we should find his landscape more
exalting to the inner man, than any
actual lake or hill-side. (*EL* 3: 73–74)

The rhythm of the finished passage is less a matter of shape, of recurring
patterns or balances, than of density in meaning and, consequently, in verbal
emphasis and stress. The sentence must march because, in cutting adjectives,
adverbs, and subordinate constructions, Emerson has left no room for relaxa-
tion. Terseness is characteristic of *Essays*, and this verbal density, as much as
balanced phrases and recurring syntactic patterns, produces the emphatic
forward impetus of Emerson's prose.

Inevitably, the momentum of Emerson's prose carries it toward rhetorical
climaxes—his aphorisms, the especially emphatic sentences that provide
summation, resolution, or momentary pause in forward movement. Aphorisms are probably the most frequently noticed characteristic of Emerson's
writing, and they provide a point at which to conclude this discussion of his
revisions. Occasionally an aphorism sprang from Emerson's head fully formed;
one of his most quoted lines—"All mankind love a lover"—appears in the
essay "Love" but not in an earlier lecture or journal (*E* p. 142). Usually,
however, an aphorism is the product of careful honing and polishing, a
rhetorical dart tempered and sharpened on the lecture platform. Indeed, the
same stripping-down process that gives Emerson's prose its characteristic
rhythm also produces the self-assured, direct, and unqualified tone of
aphorism:

Another virtue of the intellect, flowing also from its nature, is an entire self-reliance. That property of the Ideal, which I indicated in my first Lecture makes one soul a counterpoise of all souls, just as a capillary column of water is a balance for the sea, is never to be lost sight by the mind. (*EL* 2: 260)	Entire self-reliance belongs to the intellect. One soul is a counterpoise of all souls, as a capillary column of water is a balance for the sea. ("Intellect," *E* p. 284)
A religion that stands on *authority*,—what degradation in the word! What a gulf between the supple soul and its well-being! (*EL* 3: 282)	The faith that stands on authority is not faith. ("The Over-Soul," *E* p. 244)

Emerson had, by the time of *Essays*, developed an acute feeling for pointed,
quotable lines, and his revisions show the varied skills with which he could
create them:

Prudence is that science; the virtue of the senses, the regard to the right order of external events. (*EL* 2: 311)	Prudence is the virtue of the senses. ("Prudence," *E* p. 184)

And there is no man who hath left all, but he receives more. (*EL* 2: 258)	Who leaves all, receives more. ("Intellect," *E* p. 283)
Men see the institution and worship it. It is only the lengthened shadow of one man. (*EL* 3: 243)	An institution is the lengthened shadow of one man. ("Self-Reliance," *E* p. 50)
The soul's emphasis is the true one. (*EL* 3: 38)	The soul's emphasis is always right. ("Spiritual Laws," *E* p. 118)

In the first example, condensation alone does the work. The second, with its biblical echo, adds assonance and rhythmical balance to the lecture version. The third example shows a kind of revision common in *Essays*—the telescoping of two sentences into one—and reflects Emerson's awareness that a point is most memorable when encompassed in a single clause. The substituted words in the fourth example are, of course, more forceful than the originals; but they also give the sentence a measured, four-stress rhythm which is missing in the original version. All four passages share a general characteristic of Emerson's revisions: stylistically the changes are all for the better, and reveal Emerson in assured control of his medium.

As the examples above show, *Essays* is the product of exhaustive revision, primarily of materials that were already public as lectures. The qualities for which the essays are praised—clarity, economy, vivid diction and forceful aphorisms, subtle music of language—are products of this painstaking work. The results attest to Emerson's skill; and the working belies the claim which he sometimes made and which critics have sometimes turned against him, that it was all inspired overflow. The making of his *Essays* shows that Emerson revised with readers in mind. He wanted not to embalm his ideas in words, but to communicate his set of thought in such a way as to move a reader to mental and moral action. John Holloway's comment about the Victorian sage applies to Emerson: "What he has to say is not a matter of just 'content' or narrow paraphrasable meaning, but is transfused by the whole texture of his writing as it constitutes an experience for the reader."[8] In Emerson's essays, the texture of the writing is, to an extent not yet adequately appreciated, the product of his art in revision.

---

[8] *The Victorian Sage* (New York: St. Martin's, 1953), pp. 10–11.

Thinking of Emerson

Stanley Cavell

Thinking of Emerson, I can understand my book on *Walden* as something of an embarrassment, but something of an encouragement as well, since if what it suggests about the lack of a tradition of thinking in America is right, e.g., about how Emerson and Thoreau deaden one another's words, then my concentration on understanding Thoreau was bound to leave Emerson out. He kept sounding to me like secondhand Thoreau.

The most significant shortcoming among the places my book mentions Emerson is its accusing him of "misconceiving" Kant's critical enterprise, comparing Emerson unfavorably in this regard with Thoreau. I had been impressed by Thoreau's sentence running "The universe constantly and obediently answers to our conceptions" as in effect an elegant summary of the *Critique of Pure Reason*. When I requote that sentence later in the book, I take it beyond its Kantian precincts, adding that the universe answers whether our conceptions are mean or magnanimous, scientific or magical, faithful or treacherous, thus suggesting that there are more ways of making a habitable world—or more layers to it—than Kant's twelve concepts of the understanding accommodate. But I make no effort to justify this idea of a "world" beyond claiming implicitly that as I used the word I was making sense. The idea is roughly that moods must be taken as having at least as sound a role in advising us of reality as sense-experience has; that, for example, coloring the world, attributing to it the qualities "mean" or "magnanimous," may be no less objective or subjective than coloring an apple, attributing to it the colors red or green. Or perhaps we should say: sense-experience is to objects what moods are to the world. The only philosopher I knew who had made an effort to formulate a kind of epistemology of moods, to find their revelations of what we call the world as sure as the revelations of what we call understanding, was the Heidegger of *Being and Time*. But it was hard to claim support there without committing oneself to more machinery than one had any business for.

Now I see that I might, even ought to, have seen Emerson ahead of me, since, for example, his essay on "Experience" is about the epistemology, or say the logic, of moods. I understand the moral of that essay as contained in its

From *The Senses of Walden*, revised edition (San Francisco: North Point Press, 1981), 124–38. Reprinted by permission of Stanley Cavell.

late prayerful remark, "But far be from me the despair which prejudges the law by a paltry empiricism." That is, what is wrong with empiricism is not its reliance on experience but its paltry idea of experience. (This is the kind of criticism of classical empiricism leveled by John Dewey—for example, in "An Empirical Survey of Empiricisms"—who praised Emerson but so far as I know never took him up philosophically.) But I hear Kant working throughout Emerson's essay on "Experience," with his formulation of the question, "Is metaphysics possible?" and his line of answer: Genuine knowledge of (what we call) the world is for us, but it cannot extend beyond (what we call) experience. To which I take Emerson to be replying: Well and good, but then you had better be very careful what it is you understand by experience, for that might be limited in advance by the conceptual limitations you impose upon it, limited by what we know of human existence, i.e., by our limited experience of it. When, for example, you get around to telling us what we may hope for, I must know that you have experienced hope, or else I will surmise that you have not, which is to say precisely that your experience is of despair.

Emerson's "Experience" even contains a little argument, a little more explicitly with Kant, about the nature of experience in its relation to, or revelation of, the natural world. "The secret of the illusoriness [of life] is in the necessity of a succession of moods or objects. Gladly we would anchor, but the anchorage is quicksand. This onward trick of nature is too strong for us: *Pero si muove.*" In the section of the *Critique of Pure Reason* entitled "Analogies of Experience," one of the last before turning to an investigation of transcendental illusion, Kant is at pains to distinguish within experience the "*subjective succession* of apprehension from the *objective succession* of appearances." The anchor he uses to keep subjectivity and objectivity from sinking one another is, as you would expect, gripped in transcendental ground, which is always, for Kant, a question of locating necessity properly, in this case the necessity, or rules, of succession in experience. (It is curious, speaking of anchoring, that one of Kant's two examples in this specific regard is that of seeing a ship move downstream.) The acceptance of Galileo's—and Western science's—chilling crisis with the Church over the motion of the earth recalls Kant's claim to have accomplished a Copernican Revolution in metaphysics; that is, understanding the configurations of the world as a function of the configurations of our own nature. Now I construe Emerson's implicit argument in the passage cited as follows. The succession of moods is not tractable by the distinction between subjectivity and objectivity Kant proposes for experience. *This* onward trick of nature is too much for us; the given bases of the self are quicksand. The fact that we are taken over by this succession, this onwardness, means that you can think of it as at once a succession of moods (inner matters) and a succession of objects (outer matters). This very evanescence of the world proves its existence to me; it *is* what vanishes from me. I guess this is not realism exactly; but it is not solipsism either.

I believe Emerson may encourage the idea of himself as a solipsist or subjectivist, for example, in such a remark, late in the same essay, as "Thus inevitably does the universe wear our color." But whether you take this to be subjective or objective depends upon whether you take the successive colors or moods of the universe to be subjective or objective. My claim is that Emerson is out to destroy the ground on which such a problem takes itself seriously, I mean interprets itself as a metaphysical fixture. The universe is as separate from me, but as intimately part of me, as one on whose behalf I contest, and who therefore wears my color. We are in a state of "romance" with the universe (to use a word from the last sentence of the essay); we do not possess it, but our life is to return to it, in ever-widening circles, "onward and onward," but with as directed a goal as any quest can have; in the present case, until "the soul attains her due sphericity." Until then, encircled, straitened, you can say the soul is solipsistic; surely it is, to use another critical term of Emerson's, partial. This no doubt implies that we do not have a universe as it is in itself. But this implication is nothing: we do not have selves in themselves either. The universe *is* what constantly and obediently answers to our conceptions. It is what *can* be all the ways we know it to be, which is to say, all the ways we can be. In "Circles" we are told: "Whilst the eternal generation of circles proceeds, the eternal generator abides. That central life . . . contains all its circles." The universe contains all the colors it wears. That it has no more than I can give it is a fact of what Emerson calls my poverty. (Other philosophers may speak of the emptiness of the self.)

The Kantian ring of the idea of the universe as inevitably wearing our color is, notwithstanding, pertinent. Its implication is that the way specifically Kant understands the generation of the universe keeps it solipsistic, still something partial, something of our, of my, making. Emerson's most explicit reversal of Kant lies in his picturing the intellectual hemisphere of knowledge as passive or receptive and the intuitive or instinctual hemisphere as active or spontaneous. Whereas for Kant the basis of the *Critique of Pure Reason* is that "concepts are based on the spontaneity of thought, sensible intuitions on the receptivity of impressions." Briefly, there is no intellectual intuition. I will come back to this.

But immediately, to imagine that Emerson could challenge the basis of the argument of the *Critique of Pure Reason*, I would have to imagine him to be a philosopher—would I not? I would have, that is to say, to imagine his writing—to take it—in such a way that it does not misconceive Kant but undertakes to engage him in dispute. I like what Matthew Arnold has to say about Emerson, but we ought no longer to be as sure as Arnold was that the great philosophical writer is one who builds a system; hence that Emerson is not such a writer on the ground that he was not such a builder. We are by now too aware of the philosophical *attacks* on system or theory to place the emphasis in defining philosophy on a product of philosophy rather than on the process of philosophizing. We are more prepared to understand as philosophy a mode of thought that undertakes to bring philosophy to an end, as, say,

Nietzsche and Wittgenstein attempt to do, not to mention, in their various ways, Bacon, Montaigne, Descartes, Pascal, Marx, Kierkegaard, Carnap, Heidegger, or Austin, and in certain respects Kant and Hegel. Ending philosophy looks to be a commitment of each of the major modern philosophers; so it is hardly to be wondered at that some of them do not quite know whether what they are writing is philosophy. Wittgenstein said that what he did replaced philosophy. Heidegger said in his later period that what he was doing was thinking, or learning thinking, and that philosophy is the greatest enemy of true thinking. But to understand the attack on philosophy as itself philosophy, or undertaken in the name, or rather in the place, of philosophy, we must of course understand the attack as nevertheless internal to the act of philosophizing, accepting that autonomy. Church and State and the Academy of Poetry and the City may each suppress philosophy, but they cannot, without its complicity, replace it.

Can Emerson be understood as wishing to replace philosophy? But isn't that wish really what accounts for the poignancy, or dialectic, of Emerson's call, the year Thoreau graduated college, not for a thinker but for Man Thinking? The American Scholar is to think no longer partially, as a man following a task delegated by a society of which he is a victim, but as leading a life in which thinking is of the essence, as a man whose wholeness, say whose autonomy, is in command of the autonomy of thinking. The hitch of course is that there is no such human being. "Man in history, men in the world today are bugs, spawn" ("The American Scholar"). But the catch is that we aspire to this man, to the metamorphosis, to the human—hence that we can be guided and raised by the cheer of thinking. In claiming the office of the scholar "to cheer, to raise, and to guide men" as well as demanding that "whatsoever new verdict Reason from her inviolable seat pronounces on the passing men and events of today—this [the scholar] shall hear and promulgate," Emerson evidently requires the replacing of theology as well as of philosophy in his kind of building, his edification. We might think of this as internalizing the unended quarrel between philosophy and theology.

Whatever ways I go on to develop such thoughts are bound to be affected by the coincidence that during the months in which I was trying to get Emerson's tune into my ear, free of Thoreau's, I was also beginning to study the writing of the later Heidegger. This study was precipitated at last by a footnote of the editor of a collection of Heidegger essays, in which *The Senses of Walden* is described as in part forming an explication of Heidegger's notion of poetic dwelling (James G. Hart, in *The Piety of Thinking*). Having now read such an essay of Heidegger's as "Building Dwelling Thinking," I am sufficiently startled by the similarities to find the differences of interest and to start wondering about an account of both. I am thinking not so much of my similarities with Heidegger (I had after all profited from *Being and Time*, and it may be that that book leads more naturally to Heidegger's later work than is, I gather, sometimes supposed) but of Heidegger's with Thoreau, at least with my picture of Thoreau. The relation to Emerson was still unexpected, and hence even more startling. The title of the Heidegger collection I referred to is from a sentence of his that says: "For questioning is the piety of thinking." In the right mood, if you lay beside this a sentence of Emerson's from "Intellect" that says, "Always our thinking is a pious reception," you might well pause a moment. And if one starts digging to test how deep the connection might run, I find that one can become quite alarmed.

The principal text of Heidegger's to test here is translated as *What Is Called Thinking?* Here is a work that can be said to internalize the quarrel between philosophy and theology; that calls for a new existence from the human in relation to Being in order that its task of thinking be accomplished; a work based on the poignancy, or dialectic, of thinking about our having not yet learned true thinking, thinking as the receiving or letting be of something, as opposed to the positing or putting together of something, as this is pictured most systematically in Kant's ideas of representation and synthesis, and most radically in Nietzsche's will to power; that attempts to draw clear of Kant's subjectivity, and of the revenge upon time that Nietzsche understood us as taking. A climactic moment in Heidegger's descent into the origins of words is his understanding of the etymological entwining of thinking with the word for thanking, leading for example to an unfolding of ideas in which a certain progress of thinking is understood as a form of thanking, and originally a thanking for the gift of thinking, which means for the reception of being human. Here, if one can consider this to be something like philosophy, is something like a philosophical site within which to explore the crux in our relation to Emerson of his power of affirmation, or of his weakness for it.

We have surely known, since at least Newton Arvin (in "The House of Pain") collected the chorus of charges against Emerson to the effect that he lacked a knowledge of evil or of the sense of the tragic, that this missed Emerson's drift, that his task was elsewhere. Arvin insists, appropriately, that what Emerson gives us, what inspires us in him, "when we have cleared our minds of the cant of pessimism, is perhaps the fullest and most authentic expression in modern literature of the more-than-tragic emotion of thankfulness" (*Emerson: A Collection of Critical Essays*, ed. Konvitz and Whicher). But we might have surmised from Nietzsche's love of Emerson that no sane or mere man could have convincingly conceived "all things [to be] friendly and sacred, all events holy, all men divine" who was not aware that we may be undone by the pain of the world we make and may not make again. The more recent cant of pleasure or playfulness is no less hard to put up with. Yet a more-than-tragic emotion of thankfulness is still not the drift, or not the point. The point is the achievement not of affirmation but of what Emerson calls "the sacred affirmative" ("The Preacher"), the thing Nietzsche calls "the sacred Yes" ("Three Metamorphoses" in *Zarathustra*), the heart for a new creation. This is not an effort to move beyond tragedy—this has taken care of itself; but to move beyond nihilism, or beyond the curse of the charge of human depravity and its consequent condemnation of us to despair; a charge which is itself, Emerson in effect declares, the only depravity ("New England Reformers").

consequent condemnation of us to despair; a charge which is itself, Emerson in effect declares, the only depravity ("New England Reformers").

(I may interject here that the idea of thinking as reception, which began this path of reasoning, seems to me to be a sound intuition, specifically to forward the correct answer to skepticism [which Emerson meant it to do]. The answer does not consist in denying the conclusion of skepticism but in reconceiving its truth. It is true that we do not know the existence of the world with certainty; our relation to its existence is deeper—one in which it is accepted, that is to say, received. My favorite way of putting this is to say that existence is to be acknowledged.)

So the similarity of Emerson with Heidegger can be seen as mediated by Nietzsche; and this will raise more questions than it can answer. As to the question of what may look like the direction of influence, I am not claiming that Heidegger authenticates the thinking of Emerson and Thoreau; the contrary is, for me, fully as true, that Emerson and Thoreau may authorize our interest in Heidegger. Then further questions will concern the relation of the thinking of each of these writers to their respective traditions of poetry. To the figure of Hölderlin, Heidegger is indebted not alone for lessons of thought but for lessons in reading, and I suppose for the lesson that these are not different, or rather that there is ground upon which thinking and reading and philosophy and poetry meet and part. Emerson's implication in the history of the major line of American poetry is something that Harold Bloom has most concretely and I dare say unforgettably given to us to think through. Emerson's and Thoreau's relation to poetry is inherently their interest in their own writing; they are their own Hölderlins. I do not mean their interest in what we may call their poems, but their interest in the fact that what they are building is writing, that the writing is, as it realizes itself daily under their hands, sentence by shunning sentence, the accomplishment of inhabitation, the making of it happen, the poetry of it. Their prose is a battle, using a remark of Nietzsche's, not to become poetry; a battle specifically to remain in conversation with itself, answerable to itself. (So they do write dialogues, and not monologues, after all.)

Such writing takes the same mode of relating to itself as reading and thinking do, the mode of the self's relation to itself, call it self-reliance. Then whatever is required in possessing a self will be required in thinking and reading and writing. This possessing is not—it is the reverse of—possessive; I have implied that in being an act of creation, it is the exercise not of power but of reception. Then the question is: On what terms is the self received?

The answer I give for Emerson here is a theme of his thinking that further stands it with the later Heidegger's, the thing Emerson calls "onward thinking," the thing Heidegger means in taking thinking as a matter essentially of getting ourselves "on the way."

At the beginning of "Circles" Emerson tells us he means (having already deduced one moral in considering the circular or compensatory character of every human action) to trace a further analogy (or, read a further sense; or, deduce a further moral) from the emblem of the form of a circle. Since the time of "The American Scholar" he has told us that "science is nothing but the finding of analogy" (W 1: 86) and this seems a fair enough idea of thinking. In "Circles" he invites us to think about the fact, or what the fact symbolizes, that every action admits of being outdone, that around every circle another circle can take its place. I should like to extend the invitation to think about how he pictures us as moving from one circle to another, something he sometimes thinks of as expanding, sometimes as rising. I note that there is an ambiguity in his thoughts here as between what he calls the *generating* and what he calls the *drawing* of the new circle, an ambiguity between the picturing of new circles as forming continuously or discontinuously. I will not try to resolve this ambiguity now but I will take it that the essential way of envisioning our growth, from the inside, is as discontinuous. Then my questions are: How does Emerson picture us as crossing, or rather leaping, the span from one circumference to another? What is the motive, the means of motion, of this movement? How do we go on? (In Wittgenstein's *Philosophical Investigations*, knowing how to go on, as well as knowing when to stop, is exactly the measure of our knowing, or learning, in certain of its main regions or modes—for example, in the knowledge we have of our words. Onward thinking, on the way, knowing how to go on, are of course inflections or images of the religious idea of The Way, inflections which specifically deny that there is a place at which our ways end. Were philosophy to concede such a place, one knowable in advance of its setting out, philosophy would cede its own autonomy.)

You may imagine the answer to the question how we move as having to do with power. But power seems to be the result of rising, not the cause. ("Every new prospect is power" ["Circles"].) I take Emerson's answer to be what he means by "abandonment" (ibid.). The idea of abandonment contains what the preacher in Emerson calls "enthusiasm" or the New Englander in him calls "forgetting ourselves" (ibid.) (W 2: 321–22), together with what he calls leaving or relief or quitting or release or shunning or allowing or deliverance, which is freedom (as in "Leave your theory as Joseph his coat in the hand of the harlot, and flee" ["Self-Reliance"] [W 2: 57]), together further with something he means by trusting or suffering (as in the image of the traveler— the conscious intellect, the intellect alone—"who has lost his way, [throwing] his reins on the horse's neck, and [trusting] to the instinct of the animal to find his road" ["The Poet"] (W 3: 27)). (Perhaps it helps if you think, as he goes on to say, that what carries us through this world is a divine animal. To spell it out, the human is the rational divine animal. It's a thought—one, by the way, which Heidegger would deny.)

This idea of abandonment gives us a way to grasp the act Emerson pictures as "[writing] on the lintels of the door-post, Whim" ("Self-Reliance") (W 2: 51). He says he would do this after he has said that he shuns father and mother and wife and brother when his genius calls him; and he follows it by expressing the hope that it is somewhat better than whim at last. (Something has happened; it us up to us to name it, or not to. Something is wrestling us for our blessing.) Whether his writing on the lintels—his writing as such, I gather—is thought of as having the constancy of the contents of a mezuzah or the emergency of the passover blood, either way he is taking upon himself the mark of God, and of departure. His perception of the moment is taken in hope, as something to be proven only on the way, *by* the way. This departure, such setting out, is, in our poverty, what hope consists in, all there is to hope for; it is the abandoning of despair, which is otherwise our condition. (Quiet desperation Thoreau will call it; Emerson had said, silent melancholy.) Hence he may speak of perception as "not Whimsical, but fatal" (ibid.) (W 2: 65), preeminently, here, the perception of what we may call whim. Our fatality, the determination of our fate, of whether we may hope, goes by our marking the path of whim. We hope it is better than whim at last, as we hope we may at last seem something better than blasphemers; but it is our poverty not to be final but always to be leaving (abandoning whatever we have and have known): to be initial, medial, American. What the ground of the fixated conflict between solipsism and realism should give way to—or between subjectivity and objectivity, or the private and the public, or the inner and the outer—is the task of onwardness. In Heidegger: "The *thanc* means man's inmost mind, the heart, the heart's core, the innermost essence of man which reaches outward most fully and to the outermost limits" (*What Is Called Thinking?*). In Emerson: "To believe your own thought, to believe that what is true for you in your private heart, is true for all men—that is genius. Speak your latent conviction and it shall be the universal sense; for always the inmost becomes the outmost" ("Self-Reliance") (W 2: 45). The substantive disagreement with Heidegger, shared by Emerson and Thoreau, is that the achievement of the human requires not inhabitation and settlement but abandonment, leaving. Then everything depends upon your realization of abandonment. For the significance of leaving lies in its discovery that you have settled something, that you have felt enthusiastically what there is to abandon yourself to, that you can treat the others there are as those to whom the inhabitation of the world can now be left.

Emerson as Teacher

Merton M. Sealts, Jr.

"To every serious mind," Ralph Waldo Emerson liked to say, "Providence sends from time to time five or six or seven teachers" (*W* 10: 101).[1] Emerson was a graduate of Harvard College, in the class of 1821, but there was not a single Harvard professor on the private list of personal benefactors he drew up in 1836, when he was thirty-three (*JMN* 5: 160). And though Emerson was no professor himself, many other men and women of the nineteenth century, in all walks of life and with varying amounts of schooling, looked on him as their teacher and benefactor, known to them either through his published writings or by his appearance on local lecture platforms.

Considering Emerson in the role of teacher is not the customary approach to this "man without a handle," as the elder Henry James once addressed him.[2] Indeed, the problem of what to *call* Emerson has bothered critics and historians ever since his death in 1882. Matthew Arnold, when he came to lecture in America soon afterward, spoke of Emerson as one of the great "voices" heard in England during his youth and affirmed that "snatches of Emerson's strain" had continued to haunt his memory ever since. But though he warmly praised this "friend and aider of those who would live in the spirit" and singled out his *Essays* as "the most important work" written in English prose during the nineteenth century, Arnold found himself finally unable to categorize Emerson or to celebrate his achievement as that of either "a great poet," "a great writer," or even "a great philosophy-maker."[3]

Arnold's difficulty has persisted down to our own day: we too are uncertain how to classify Emerson, how to deal with his poetry, or even in what course or department to consider his *Essays*. As Arnold recognized, they are not exactly *philosophy*. Indeed, few professional philosophers later than William James and George Santayana have looked in a kindly way on Emerson, any more than professional historians of recent years have been hospitable to

From *Emerson Centenary Essays*, ed. Joel Myerson (Southern Illinois University Press, 1982). Reprinted by permission of Merton Sealts. A slightly compressed version of the essay appears in Sealts's *Emerson on the Scholar* (Columbia: University of Missouri Press, 1992).

[1] See also *JMN* 10: 300–301, and "Culture," *W* 6: 147.

[2] Henry James to Emerson, 3 Oct. 1843, in Ralph Barton Perry, *The Thought and Character of William James*, 2 vols. (Boston: Little, Brown, 1935). 1: 51.

[3] See Matthew Arnold, "Emerson," in *Discourses in America* (London: Macmillan, 1885), pp. 138–207.

Henry Adams. Like Teufelsdröckh in his friend Carlyle's *Sartor Resartus*, Emerson was a "Professor of Things in General"—*Allerley Wissenschaft*[4]— and was rightly suspicious of all compartmentalizing and departmentalizing. Indeed, he looked on specialization as necessary enough, but as a kind of necessary evil, or evil necessity. In an age of increasing specialization his American scholar should be "Man Thinking," speaking for Man to men—as a generalist rather than a specialist or narrow advocate; we might well say that the substance of the Scholar's discourse would be the substance of a liberal education. The Scholar as teacher, having access to what Emerson calls "this original unit, this fountain of power," is one who can help others to "possess" themselves—the phrase turns up again in Emerson and also in Arnold—by returning to the same fountain, the common source accessible to every one of us (*W* 1: 53).

Here is a clue not only to Arnold's response to Emerson but to Emerson's own admiration for Milton. "Better than any other," he said in an early lecture of 1835, Milton "discharged the office of every great man, namely, to raise the idea of Man"—capital *M*—"in the minds of his contemporaries and of posterity." Milton was thus a master teacher of true humanism, "foremost of all men . . . in the power *to inspire*" (*EL* 1: 148–49), and for Emerson the great business of books and teachers alike was "to inspire" rather than merely to instruct (*CW* 1: 56). "Truly speaking," he said at Harvard in 1838, "it is not instruction, but provocation, that I can receive from another soul" (*CW* 1: 80). The teacher may inspire or provoke; in the last analysis the student, responding actively and not passively, must finally *learn* for himself.

The occasion for Emerson's remark about "provocation" was a memorable one in his early career. He had been invited to address the graduating class at Harvard Divinity School, not by the reverend professors on the faculty but by some of the senior students themselves—young men who had been visiting Concord to talk theology with this sometime clergyman, a Harvard product who had resigned his own pulpit six years before. What Emerson said in his address at Cambridge was provocative enough to shock old-guard Unitarians, men who looked on his liberal ideas about preaching and teaching as "the latest form of infidelity";[5] it would be thirty years before he was again invited to speak at Harvard. Having in effect left the ministry, Emerson would have welcomed a professorship, as he freely admitted in his journal—if not at Harvard then perhaps in one of the "country colleges" like Dartmouth where he sometimes spoke; it would serve as a base of operations, he thought, and

---

[4]Thomas Carlyle, *Sartor Resartus: The Life and Opinions of Herr Teufelsdröckh*, ed. Charles Frederick Harrold (Garden City, N.Y.: Doubleday, Doran, 1937), p. 18.

[5]See Andrews Norton, "A Discourse on the Latest Form of Infidelity," an address delivered before a meeting of the alumni of the Harvard Divinity School on 19 July 1839 and subsequently printed as a pamphlet. The address is excerpted in *The Transcendentalists: An Anthology*, ed Perry Miller (Cambridge, Mass.: Harvard University Press, 1950), pp. 210–13, along with other documents in the controversy which Emerson's address of 1838 provoked.

challenge him with a stated task (*JMN* 10: 28).[6] But no such post was offered him, and in the absence of other opportunities he continued lecturing and writing, not to enrolled students in college classrooms but to a whole generation of general listeners and readers at home and abroad, inspiring and provoking an ever-widening audience as his reputation steadily grew. Like all teachers of power, moreover, he attracted a broad spectrum of students, not all of whom liked what they read and heard or stayed to finish the course.

In Cambridge and Concord, Emerson was able to teach directly—face to face. "What are you doing now?" he asked young Henry Thoreau of Concord in 1837. "Do you keep a journal?" Thoreau's response was prompt: "So I make my first entry to-day."[7] A Brooklyn newspaper editor, Walt Whitman, first knew Emerson indirectly, through his books: "I was simmering, simmering, simmering," said Whitman of the years before *Leaves of Grass*; "Emerson brought me to a boil."[8] But though Emerson heated up some students like Thoreau and Whitman, others who sampled his offerings were cooled off or turned off. Nathaniel Hawthorne, his neighbor in Concord, was never sympathetic to Emerson's teachings; he wrote with amusement of how the village was "infested" by the "variety of queer, strangely dressed, oddly behaved mortals" who pursued Emerson to his home.[9] Herman Melville, whose New York friends had warned him against Emerson's supposed obscurity, was pleasantly surprised on hearing Emerson lecture in Boston in 1849; "they told me that that night he was unusually plain," he explained. For years to come, both in private jottings and in published works, Melville alternately praised and damned "this Plato who talk thro' his nose."[10] Had Emerson "not been there both to stimulate and exasperate Herman Melville," Perry Miller once remarked, "*Moby-Dick* would have emerged as only another sea-story."[11] Miller no doubt exaggerated, but his basic point was well taken: Emerson could indeed both inspire and provoke—in every sense of both words. "*Emerson was their cow, but not all liked the milk*." So ran a caption in *Time* magazine some years ago under a panel of photographs: Hawthorne, Thoreau,

---

[6]"Why has never the poorest country college offered me a professorship of rhetoric? I think I could have taught an orator, though I am none" (*J* 9: 413). Moncure Daniel Conway, *Emerson at Home and Abroad* (Boston: James R. Osgood, 1882), p. 55, reports that Emerson once told him that when he graduated from Harvard "his ambition was to be a professor of rhetoric and elocution."

[7]*The Journal of Henry D. Thoreau*, ed. Bradford Torrey and Frances H. Allen, 14 vols. (Boston: Houghton Mifflin, 1906), 1: 19.

[8]Whitman, in conversation with John Townsend Trowbridge in 1860, in Trowbridge, *My Own Story* (Boston: Houghton, Mifflin, 1903), p. 367.

[9]Nathaniel Hawthorne, "The Old Manse," in *Mosses from an Old Manse* (Columbus: Ohio State University Press, 1974), p. 31.

[10]Melville to Evert Duyckinck, Boston, 3 Mar. 1849, in *The Letters of Herman Melville*, ed. Merrell R. Davis and William H. Gilman (New Haven, Conn.: Yale University Press, 1960), p. 79.

[11]Perry Miller, Introduction to *The Golden Age of American Literature* (New York: George Braziller, 1959), p. 12.

Whitman, and Melville, in that order, with Emerson gazing benignantly from one side.[12]

It was not only literary figures of the day who responded to Emerson. "His works, other men found, were in many respects diaries of their own which they had not kept," as Professor Lyon Richardson has finely said.[13] A good example is Rutherford B. Hayes, lawyer, soldier, congressman, thrice-elected governor of Ohio, and later president of the United States. As a young attorney in Cincinnati, Hayes helped to arrange for Emerson's first lectures there in 1850. Emerson remained his favorite author; in Hayes's judgment he had "the best mind of our time and race."[14] As Emerson continued distilling his lectures into published essays and his readers in distant places grew increasingly eager to see and hear him, like Hayes in Ohio, his field of operations as itinerant teacher inevitably expanded. By the 1850s he was in steady demand as a lecturer, not only along the eastern seaboard as far south as Baltimore but across the Atlantic to England and Scotland in 1847–48 and also beyond the Hudson into what was then "the West." The vogue of the popular lecturer and the growth of the lyceum movement in the United States during the second quarter of the nineteenth century reflected the prevalent desire for self-improvement and the widespread interest in adult education that accompanied westward expansion and growing national prosperity. By the 1860s Emerson was making annual western tours: to Ohio, Indiana, and Illinois; to Michigan and Wisconsin; and eventually across the Mississippi to Iowa and Minnesota. In 1868 James Russell Lowell called him "the most steadily attractive lecturer in America."[15]

Emerson traveled West by train, stage, carriage, and boat, often under the most trying conditions; during one cold winter he crossed the frozen Mississippi four times on foot. When he made his first trip to Ohio in 1850 for his engagement in Cincinnati, he was en route by Lake Erie steamer to Sandusky when the vessel caught fire off Cleveland, where it made port safely in time for local Emersonians to assemble for an unscheduled lecture he was persuaded to give.[16] The lecture in Cleveland was free; by the 1860s the going rate for a one-night stand in the larger western cities had risen to $50. Thus Emerson's contemporary Thomas Starr King, when asked what he lectured for, answered: "FAME—Fifty and My Expenses."[17] Emerson himself wrote of

---

[12]Review of F. O. Matthiessen, *American Renaissance: Art and Expression in the Age of Emerson and Whitman, Time,* 2 June 1941, p. 84.

[13]Lyon N. Richardson, "What Rutherford B. Hayes Liked in Emerson," *American Literature* 17 (Mar. 1945): 28.

[14]Letter of 5 Dec. 1889, quoted from *Diary and Letters of Rutherford B. Hayes,* ed. Charles Richard Williams, in Richardson, "What Hayes Liked in Emerson," p. 23.

[15]James Russell Lowell, "Emerson the Lecturer," in *My Study Windows* (Boston: James R. Osgood, 1871), p. 375.

[16]See David Mead, *Yankee Eloquence in the Middle West: The Ohio Lyceum 1850–1870* (East Lansing: Michigan State College Press, 1951), pp. 24–27.

[17]Carl Bode, *The American Lyceum: Town Meeting of the Mind* (New York: Oxford University Press, 1956), p. 201.

lecturing in the West as an annual wager: " 'I'll bet you fifty dollars a day that you will not leave your library, and wade and ride and run and suffer all manner of indignities and stand up for an hour each night reading in a hall'; and I answered, 'I'll bet I will.' I do it and win the $900" (*J* 10: 91–92).[18] Early in January of 1856, after a week of temperatures "varying from 20 to 30 degrees below zero," he observed that the climate and people of the West "are a new test for the wares of a man of letters. . . . At the lyceum, the stout Illinoian, after a short trial, walks out of the hall. The Committee tell you that the people want a hearty laugh, and [those] who give them that, are heard with joy. . . . These are the new conditions to which I must conform. . . . And Shakespeare, or Franklin, or Aesop coming to Illinois," would say, I must give my wisdom a comic form, instead of tragics or elegiacs" (*JMN* 14: 27–28). Emerson's words seem prophetic of Mark Twain, who in the late 1850s, as Samuel L. Clemens of Missouri, was learning to be a riverboat pilot on the Mississippi, his other vocation as lecturer and writer being still some years before him.

In the course of a long career Emerson filled nearly fifteen hundred lecture engagements in twenty-two states and Canada plus his lectures in England and Scotland. Some cities and towns brought him back repeatedly. He spoke on many subjects, from popular science, biography, and literature in the early 1830s to an address on Carlyle in 1881, the year before his death. During the 1850s, when he appeared most often, he was giving more than fifty lectures every winter; in the 1860s both his platform reputation and his fees reached their highest peak. Apart from local newspaper reviews, which varied widely in tone, some of the best testimony about what it was like to hear Emerson speak comes from younger contemporaries who attended his lectures repeatedly from their student days into middle age—men of letters such as Lowell, George William Curtis, and E. P. Whipple. With such younger listeners in the early years, if not with their elders or the authorities of Harvard, Emerson was immediately popular; for Lowell and his generation he became "our favorite teacher."[19] An older man once told Curtis that though *he* couldn't understand "Mr. Emerson," "my daughters do."[20] Emerson himself quickly recognized the difference in generations. He remembered a question his uncle Samuel Ripley had asked him years before, when as a boy of thirteen he had done his first actual teaching in his uncle's school: "How is it, Ralph, that all the boys dislike you & quarrel with you, whilst the grown people are fond of you?" "Now am I thirty six," Emerson reflected in the year after the Divinity School affair, "and the fact is reversed,—the old people suspect & dislike me, & the young love me" (*JMN* 7: 253).

<hr />

[18]See Eleanor Bryce Scott, "Emerson Wins the Nine Hundred Dollars," *American Literature* 17 (Mar. 1945): 78–85, which illustrates Emerson's western experiences with an account of his reception in Rock Island, Ill. on New Year's Day, 1856.

[19]Lowell, "Emerson the Lecturer," p. 375.

[20]George William Curtis, "Emerson Lecturing," *From the Easy Chair* (New York: Harpers, 1892), p. 22.

What the young people liked and understood in their teacher was less the explicit message than the spirit of the man who spoke it; as Lowell explained, "We do not go to hear what Emerson says so much as to hear Emerson."[21] Certainly they did not go for cheap popularization or sidewinding oratory, though both were common enough at a time when public speakers customarily performed with all stops out. Emerson never spoke extemporaneously or even from notes; he invariably read from a prepared manuscript, though he had a disconcerting habit of shuffling his pages about while he was talking. His delivery was simple and even conversational; when speaking he was "apt to hesitate in the course of a sentence," according to the senior Oliver Wendell Holmes, as though "picking his way through his vocabulary, to get at the best expression of his thought."[22] "There was no rhetoric, no gesture . . . no dramatic familarity and action," said Curtis, "but the manner was self-respectful and courteous to the audience, and the tone supremely just and sincere."[23]

Moncure Conway agreed: Emerson depended not on "tricks of any kind" but rather on "clearness of thought and simplicity of statement."[24] Henry James the elder emphasized his modesty and grace on the platform, recalling

> his deferential entrance upon the scene, his look of inquiry at the desk and the chair, his resolute rummaging among his embarrassed papers, the air of sudden recollection with which he would plunge into his pockets for what he must have known had never been put there, for his uncertainty and irresolution as he rose to speak, his deep, relieved inspiration as he got well from under the burning-glass of his auditors' eyes, and addressed himself at length to their docile ears instead. . . .
> And then when he looked over the heads of his audience into the dim mysterious distance, and his weird monotone began to reverberate in your bosom's depths, and his words flowed on, now with a river's volume, grand, majestic, free, and anon diminished themselves to the fitful cadence of a brook . . . and you saw the clear eye eloquent with nature's purity, and beheld the musing countenance turned within, as it were, and hearkening to the rumour of a far-off but on-coming world. . . .

It was all "intensely personal," James continued, and also "exquisitely characteristic" of Emerson the man.[25]

Audiences everywhere were particularly struck with Emerson's voice, which Holmes described as "never loud, never shrill, but singularly penetrating."[26] It had "a strange power," said E. P. Whipple, "which affected me more than any other voice I ever heard on the stage or on the platform."[27] But

[21]Lowell, "Emerson the Lecturer," p. 378.

[22]Oliver Wendell Holmes, *Ralph Waldo Emerson* (Boston: Houghton Mifflin, 1884), pp. 363–64.

[23]Curtis, "Emerson Lecturing," p. 26.

[24]Conway, *Emerson at Home and Abroad*, p. 55.

[25]Henry James, Sr., "Emerson," *Atlantic Monthly* 94 (Dec. 1904): 741 (written ca. 1868).

[26]Holmes, *Ralph Waldo Emerson*, p. 363. Holmes also remarks that "the music of his speech pleased those who found his thought too subtle for their dull wits to follow" (p. 376).

[27]Edwin Percy Whipple, "Some Recollections of Ralph Waldo Emerson," *Harper's Magazine* 65 (Sept. 1882): 580.

however entranced by Emerson's way of speaking, few of his auditors followed everything they had listened to or even agreed with what they thought he had said. Hawthorne's son Julian recalls leaving the lecture room in Concord one evening when he overheard "Prescott, the grocer, say to Jonas Hastings, the shoemaker, 'Did you get that about the Oversoul?' . . . Jonas . . . shook his head: 'No use wondering what he means; we know he's giving us the best there is.' "[28] At the other end of the spectrum there was downright hostility, particularly when Emerson ventured outside New England. In Wisconsin, for example, the *Kenosha Democrat* stigmatized him in 1860 as "an infidel—an abolitionist—a monarchist—all these, though he talk as musically as any dying swan."[29] Some unenthusiastic listeners, like the "stout Illinoian" Emerson himself mentioned, simply walked out of the hall. Those who stayed enjoyed Emerson's quiet humor, more characteristic of his lectures than of his published essays. They especially liked the illustrative anecdotes "that sparkled for a moment upon the surface of his talk," as Curtis remarked; "and some sat inspired with unknown resolves, soaring upon lofty hopes."[30] By the 1860s, when he had become something of an institution, Lowell felt that younger members of the audience were taking him for granted, failing to realize what they owed to him; their elders, Lowell said, recognized "how much the country's intellectual emancipation was due to the stimulus of his teaching and example."[31] Curtis, who was a successful lecturer himself, put the same idea somewhat differently. Emerson, he said, "was never exactly popular, but always gave a tone and flavor to the whole lyceum course . . . 'We can have him once in three or four seasons,' said the committees. But really they had him all the time without knowing it. He was the philosopher Proteus, and he spoke through all the more popular mouths. . . . They were . . . the middle-men between him and the public. They watered the nectar, and made it easy to drink."[32]

Like all teachers, especially those who teach other teachers, Emerson thus reached students even at second or third hand. "A teacher affects eternity," said Henry Adams; "he can never tell where his influence stops."[33] The thought is disturbing, since "when?" and "how?" and "by what channels?" and "to what effect?" are questions difficult to answer on any chart or evaluation, however well intentioned. Doubtless Emerson himself, who thought a discourse should have some edge to it, was not too troubled when the response of listeners and readers was not unanimously favorable, though the outburst occasioned by the Divinity School Address proved more than he had quite bargained for. Religious conservatives then and now have protested against his

[28]*The Memoirs of Julian Hawthorne*, ed. Edith Garrigues Hawthorne (New York: Macmillan, 1938), p. 99.
[29]Quoted in C. E. Shorer, "Emerson and the Wisconsin Lyceum," *American* 24 (Jan. 1953): 468.
[30]Curtis, "Emerson Lecturing," p. 22.
[31]Lowell, "Emerson the Lecturer," p. 382.
[32]Curtis, "Emerson Lecturing," pp. 23–24.
[33]Henry Adams, *The Education of Henry Adams* (Boston: Houghton Mifflin, 1961), p. 300.

liberal theology. When he lectured in Scotland in 1848 he was accused of being a pantheist.[34] At Columbus, Ohio, in 1867, a local Presbyterian minister preached against his appearance there, saying that "he had not expected to live to see the time when a Presbyterian pulpit would be disgraced by Ralph Waldo Emerson lecturing from it."[35] Among twentieth-century critics, Yvor Winters called Emerson and the transcendentalists "moral parasites upon a Christian doctrine which they were endeavoring to destroy,"[36] and Randall Stewart stigmatized him as "the arch-heretic of American literature."[37] On the other extreme, the obvious vestiges of clericalism in Emerson have always offended the secular-minded. D. H. Lawrence, for example, admired "Emerson's real courage," but disliked the limitations of his idealism. In Lawrence's words, "all those gorgeous inrushes of exaltation and spiritual energy which made Emerson a great man, now make us sick,"[38] and some contemporary readers agree.

There has been a similar difference of opinion about Emerson's political and social views, which have also offended the extreme left and the extreme right of two centuries. In the 1840s he inclined toward the principles of what he called "the movement party" (*W* 3: 263) rather than toward the conservatism of "the establishment" (*CW* 1: 190, 195), but he was never a partisan in the conventional sense. His increasing antipathy to slavery led him to support Free-Soil candidates and later to gravitate toward the new Republican party, though for a long time he resisted identification with the Abolitionist movement. But believing as he did that slavery was flatly wrong and seeing its evil increasingly compounded by abridgment of the right of free speech and coercion of Northern freemen as well as of Southern slaves, he ultimately found himself endorsing even John Brown's use of violence in retaliation. And so during the 1850s the peace-loving teacher became a militant activist, remaining so for the duration of the Civil War. If his moral activism seems inconsistent with his vocational role, it was not altogether out of character for a man who had insisted in his first published book that "The moral law lies at the centre of nature and radiates to the circumference" (*CW* 1: 26). To condone slavery was unnatural and immoral, a denial of human worth and dignity and freedom; he *must* stand up and be counted with the opposition. "I divide men as aspirants & desperants," he once told Holmes. "A scholar need not be cynical to feel that the vast multitude are almost on all fours; that the rich always vote after their fears; that cities churches colleges all go for the

---

34His lectures in Edinburgh occasioned a pamphlet entitled *Emerson's Orations to the Modern Athenians: or Pantheism* (*Life*, p. 338).

35Mead, *Yankee Eloquence in the Middle West*, p. 60.

36Yvor Winters, "The Significance of *The Bridge*, by Hart Crane," in *In Defense of Reason* (New York: Swallow Press and William Morrow, 1947), p. 587.

37Randall Stewart, *American Literature and Christian Doctrine* (Baton Rouge: Louisiana State University Press, 1958), p. 55.

38D. H. Lawrence, "Model Americans" [review of Stuart P. Sherman's *Americans*], *Dial* 74 (May 1923): 507.

quadruped interest, and it is against this coalition that the pathetically small minority of disengaged or thinking men stand for the ideal right, for man as he should be, & . . . for the right of every other as for his own" (*L* 5: 17).

However one may judge Emerson's reluctant foray into public affairs,[39] this prolonged engagement with moral issues at considerable cost to his own peace and prosperity illustrates what he liked to call "the scholar's courage" (*JMN* 10: 28), a form of his cardinal principle of self-reliance. In David Riesman's phrase, he was an *inner-directed* man, living from within. What he regarded as "the moral law of human nature" he had enunciated as early as 1833, when he was thirty: "A man contains all that is needful to his government within himself. He is made a law unto himself. All real good or evil that can befal him must be from himself. He only can do himself any good or any harm . . . The purpose of life seems to be to acquaint a man with himself. . . . The highest revelation is that God is in every man" (*JMN* 4: 84).

On this moral and religious basis Emerson deplored imitation of any model however fine and refused conformity to all wholly external patterns, rituals, creeds, sects, parties, precedents, curricula, or institutions of any kind, including churches, colleges, and governments. The law he followed, though wholly internal, was rigorous; "If any one imagines that this law is lax," as he said in "Self-Reliance," "let him keep its commandment one day" (*CW* 2: 42). When a man can look within and "read God directly," as "The American Scholar" has it, the hour is too precious for secondhand readings (*CW* 1: 57). On this same basis, looking back with a measure of detachment on the Divinity School controversy—that "storm in our washbowl," as he called it (*CEC* p. 196), he could write in 1840 that "In all my lectures I have taught one doctrine, namely, the infinitude of the private man. This, the people accept readily enough, and even with loud commendation, as long as I call the lecture, Art; or Politics; or Literature; or the Household; but the moment I call it Religion,—they are shocked, though it be only the application of the same truth which they receive everywhere else, to a new class of facts" (*JMN* 7: 342).

The "one doctrine" that Emerson specifies lay at the vital center of his teaching over a lifetime, whether the subject addressed was religion, morality, or teaching itself. His conception of "the private man" was essentially religious, idealistic, and optimistic. Where "desperants" such as his Puritan forebears and his less sanguine contemporaries stressed the finite limitations of humanity, as in the fiction of Hawthorne and Melville, his own abiding impulse, like that of Thoreau and Whitman, was to emphasize mankind's infinite potential, though the experience of his middle years brought him to an increasing realization of the limiting power of circumstance. By temperament Emerson was an idealist, an "aspirant." But as his journals reveal, he was

---

[39]I have discussed this subject in "The American Scholar and Public Issues: The Case of Emerson," *Ariel: A Review of International English Literature* 7 (July 1976): 109–21.

forever being reminded of that "yawning gulf" that stretches "between the ambition of man and his power of performance," and it is this disparity between desire and capacity that for him "makes the tragedy of all souls" (*W* 4: 183), a tragedy all too frequently compounded by distorted aims and wasted forces.

If the purpose of life, as Emerson thought, was "to acquaint a man with himself," the purpose of a teacher should be to foster one's full realization, in every sense, of his or her own worth and potential. This is the burden of the lectures, addresses, and essays in which Emerson touches in some way on learning and teaching: the Address on Education and "The American Scholar" of 1837, the Divinity School Address and "Literary Ethics" of 1838, the lecture on "Education" of 1840, and such essays of 1841 and 1844 as "Self-Reliance," "Spiritual Laws," "The Over-Soul," "Intellect," and "The Poet," this last with its Emersonian emphasis on the human need for self-expression—"It is in me, and shall out" (*W* 3: 40)—that not only brought Walt Whitman to a boil but also anticipated the teachings of John Dewey. Emerson's thinking about education, being of a piece with his general ideas, was essentially religious in character, though it has obvious secular implications and applications. To educate means *to draw out*; Emerson complained that "We do not believe in a power of Education. We do not think we can call out God in man and we do not try" (*EL* 3: 290). His own basic objective, to "call out God in man," was not inherently different from that of the builders of medieval universities or nineteenth-century church-related colleges. Like them, he believed that religion and learning spring from a common source. He delighted to celebrate that source, that "original unit" and "fountain of power," as he called it in "The American Scholar," common to all individuals and linking them both with "Man"—again, capital *M*—and also with nature.

Every human being, Emerson believed, stands "in need of expression," students and teachers included: "In love, in art, in avarice, in politics, in labor, in games, we study to utter our painful secret" (*W* 3: 5). It is no different in teaching, though what a teacher expresses, he felt, is less what he *knows* than what he *is*. For him there were two kinds of teachers: those who "speak *from within*," and therefore teach with firsthand knowledge and authority; and those who speak only "*from without*, as spectators merely," on the basis of secondhand evidence (*W* 2: 170). For him, only the former— Emerson's "true scholars"—deserve the name of teacher. Like Alfred North Whitehead in our own century, Emerson protested against dead knowledge— what Whitehead in *The Aims of Education* (1929) would call "inert ideas."[40]

---

[40]Emerson made his distinction concerning teachers as early as 1830, when in a sermon he commented on the "wide difference between the power of two teachers," one of whom speaks "*living* truth" while the other presents "dead truth, . . . passively taken . . . like a lump of indigestible matter in his animal system, separate and of no nourishment or use. It is, compared with the same truth quickened in another mind, like a fact in a child's lesson in geography, as it

"Life, authentic life, you must have," Emerson insisted, "or you can teach nothing" (*JMN* 7: 27).[41] If life and power are present within, they will manifest themselves outwardly, whether by our conscious intention or otherwise. "That which we are, we shall teach," he wrote, "not voluntarily but involuntarily. . . . Character teaches over our head" (*CW* 2: 169). "If a teacher have any opinion which he wishes to conceal, his pupils will become as fully indoctrinated into that as into any which he publishes" (*CW* 2: 85). Again: "The man may teach by doing, and not otherwise. If he can communicate himself he can teach, but not by words. He teaches who gives, and he learns who receives" (*CW* 2: 88).

Since for Emerson a student's self-realization meant self-reliance, he reminded himself of "the cardinal virtue of a teacher" exemplified by Socrates: "to protect the pupil from his own influence" (*JMN* 10: 471). Neither teachers nor parents, he cautioned, should try to make duplicates of themselves. " 'Get off that child!' he said in a lecture; 'One is enough.' "[42] His friend Moncure Conway, writing of Emerson's powerful stimulation of a variety of writers differing in both their aim and their style, rightly observed that "they who came to his fontless baptism were never made Emersonians."[43] His words would have pleased Emerson himself, who in his later years remarked in his journal, "I have been writing and speaking what were once called novelties, for twenty-five or thirty years, and have not now one disciple. Why? Not that what I said was not true; not that it has not found intelligent receivers; but because it did not go from any wish in me to bring men to me, but to themselves. I delight in driving them from me. . . . This is my boast that I have no school follower. I should account it a measure of the impurity of insight, if it did not create independence" (*J* 9: 188–89).

fulfillment—these were the "novelties" that Emerson taught as writer and lecturer, whatever his subjects and courses. The lesson was heard and repeated. "I would not have any one adopt *my* mode of living on any account," wrote one of his alumni, Henry Thoreau, in *Walden*. "I desire that there may be as many different persons in the world as possible; but I would have each one be very careful to find out and pursue *his own* way."[44] "Not I, not any one else can travel that road for you," Walt Whitman responded in *Leaves of*

lies unconnected and useless in his memory, compared with the same fact as it enters into the knowledge of the surveyor or the shipmaster" (*YES*, pp. 92–93). The parallel with Whitehead's "inert ideas" is striking.

41The teacher's "capital secret," Emerson liked to say, is "to convert life into truth" (*EL*, 2: 202; *CW* 1: 86). On the relation between life and truth, see also *JMN* 5: 324), and *CW* 1: 55.

42Conway, *Emerson at Home and Abroad*, p. 298; cf. "Education" (1840), *EL* 3: 295.

43Conway, *Emerson at Home and Abroad*, p. 297.

44Henry David Thoreau, *Walden*, ed. J. Lyndon Shanley (Princeton, N.J.: Princeton University Press, 1971), p. 71.

Grass, "You must travel it for yourself."[45] Even Melville chimed in, though with a note of warning, in *Moby-Dick*: "the only mode in which you can derive even a tolerable idea of [the whale's] living contour, is by going a whaling yourself; but by so doing, you run no small risk of being eternally stove and sunk by him."[46] So Emerson, by recurrent challenge and by cumulative example, provoked and inspired and *educated* his students—and in turn his students' students—to walk on their own feet, to work with their own hands, to speak their own minds, just as every great teacher invariably does. Indeed he is no teacher unless, like Emerson, he truly creates independence.

---

[45]Walt Whitman, "Song of Myself," lines 1210–11, in *Leaves of Grass: Comprehensive Reader's Edition,* ed. Harold W. Blodgett and Sculley Bradley (New York: New York University Press, 1965), p. 83. "The best part of Emersonianism," Whitman wrote later in an essay on "Emerson's Books, (The Shadows of Them.)," is that "it breeds the giant that destroys itself. Who wants to be any man's mere follower? lurks behind every page. No teacher ever taught, that has so provided for his pupil's setting up independently—no truer evolutionist." See Whitman, *Prose Works 1892,* ed. Floyd Stovall, 2 vols. (New York: New York University Press, 1964), 2:517–18.

[46]Herman Melville, *Moby-Dick,* ed. Harrison Hayford and Hershel Parker (New York: W. W. Norton, 1967), p. 228.

Chronology of Important Dates

1803	(May 25) Born at Boston, Massachusetts
1821	(August) Graduated from Harvard College
1826	(October 10) Approbated to preach as a Unitarian minister
1829	(March 11) Ordination at Second Church, Boston
	(September 30) Marriage to Ellen Tucker
1831	(February 8) Death of Ellen
1832	(October 28) Resignation from Second Church accepted
1832–3	(December–October) Travel in Europe
1834	(November) Moved to Concord
1835	(January–March) Lectures on *Biography*
	(September 14) Marriage to Lydia Jackson ("Lidian")
1835–6	(November–January) Lectures on *English Literature*
1836	(May 9) Death of brother Charles
	(September 9) *Nature* published
	(October 30) Birth of son Waldo
1836–7	(December–March) Lectures on *The Philosophy of History*
1837	(August 31) Oration on "The American Scholar" at Harvard
1837–8	(December–March) Lectures on *Human Culture*
1838	(April 23) Open letter to President Martin Van Buren protesting the Removal of the Cherokee Nation from Georgia (*W* 11: 87)
	(July 15) Address at Harvard Divinity School
1838–9	(December–February) Lectures on *Human Life*
1839	(February 24) Birth of daughter Ellen
1839–40	(December–February) Lectures on *The Present Age*
1840	(July 1) Publication of first number of *The Dial* (1840–44), leading Transcendentalist periodical, edited by Emerson starting 1842
1841	(March 20) *Essays, First Series* published
	(April) Brook Farm, Transcendentalist utopian community, opens in West Roxbury, Massachusetts (closes in 1847)
	(November 22) Birth of daughter Edith
1841–2	(December–January) Lectures on *The Times* (published, in part, 1849)

1842	(January 27) Death of Waldo
1844	(July 10) Birth of son Edward
	(August 1) Address at Concord on the anniversary of the emancipation of slaves in the British West Indies (*W* 11: 97)
	(October 19) *Essays, Second Series* published
1845	(July 4) Henry D. Thoreau begins his two-year, two-month residence at Walden Pond in Concord, on Emerson's land
1845–6	(December–January) Lectures on *Representative Men* (published 1850)
1846	(December 25) *Poems* published
1847–8	(October–July) Travel in England and France
1850	(July 19) Margaret Fuller drowns at Fire Island, New York, returning from Europe
	(September) Compromise of 1850 passed by Congress, driving Emerson toward abolitionist activism
1851	(March–April) Lectures on *The Conduct of Life* (published 1860)
	(May 3) Address at Concord protesting Fugitive Slave Law (*W* 11: 177)
1854	(March 7) Address at New York against Fugitive Slave Law (*W* 11: 215)
1856	(August 6) *English Traits* published
1860	(December 8) *Conduct of Life* published, Emerson's last major book
1862	(May 9) Address on "Thoreau" delivered at his funeral, then published (*W* 10: 449)
1867	(April 28) *May-Day and Other Pieces* published
	Writes "Historic Notes of Life and Letters in New England," affectionate-ironic reminiscences of Transcendentalist movement (*W* 10: 325)
1870	(March) *Society and Solitude* published, last book completed by Emerson without assistance
1872	(July 24) Burning of house
1872–3	(October–May) Travel in Europe and the Near East
1882	(April 27) Death at Concord

Suggestions for Further Reading

Emerson's Works

The long-standard edition of Emerson's writings is the so-called Centenary Edition: *The Complete Works of Ralph Waldo Emerson,* edited in 12 volumes by his son, Edward Waldo Emerson (Boston: Houghton, 1903–4). It will be largely superseded by *The Collected Works of Ralph Waldo Emerson,* a scholarly edition now being issued by Harvard University Press. Four of ten projected volumes (corresponding to volumes 1–4 of the Centenary Edition) have appeared as of 1992.

Of equal importance for understanding Emerson are his journals. The scholarly edition is *The Journals and Miscellaneous Notebooks of Ralph Waldo Emerson,* 16 volumes, ed. William H. Gilman et al. (Cambridge: Harvard University Press, 1960–82).

The best one-volume textbook edition of Emerson's writings, including essays, poems, and journal excerpts, is Stephen E. Whicher, ed., *Selections from Ralph Waldo Emerson* (Boston: Houghton, 1957). A much more comprehensive one-volume anthology of Emerson's prose writings is Joel Porte, ed., *Ralph Waldo Emerson: Essays and Lectures* (New York: Library of America, 1983). The best anthology of journal selections is Joel Porte, ed., *Emerson in His Journals* (Cambridge: Harvard University Press, 1982).

Advanced students of Emerson should also be aware of Emerson's *Letters,* 6 volumes, ed. Ralph L. Rusk (New York: Columbia University Press, 1939); volumes 7–8, ed. Eleanor Tilton (1990, 1991); and an additional volume of *Correspondence of Emerson and Carlyle* (1964), ed. Joseph Slater. Advanced students will also be interested in the four-volume *Complete Sermons of Ralph Waldo Emerson,* ed. Albert J. von Frank et al. (Columbia: University of Missouri Press, 1989–92); and the three-volume *Early Lectures of Ralph Waldo Emerson,* ed. Robert E. Spiller et al. (Cambridge: Harvard University Press, 1966–72), covering the period 1836–42. Finally, the University of Missouri Press has issued scholarly editions of Emerson's *Poetry Notebooks* (1986) as well as the first volume of a series of *Topical Notebooks* (1990).

Emerson Biography

Ralph Leslie Rusk's *The Life of Ralph Waldo Emerson* (New York: Scribners, 1949) is still the best comprehensive factual biography—readable, succinct, informative—although it has been supplemented and corrected at some points by Gay Wilson Allen, *Waldo Emerson* (New York: Viking, 1981). John McAleer's *Ralph Waldo Emerson: Days of Encounter* (Boston: Little, 1984) is less fully informed but sheds additional light on Emerson's relations with other people, both intimates and casual acquaintances.

The best intellectual biography, mapping and charting the growth of his leading ideas, is Stephen E. Whicher's *Freedom and Fate: The Inner Life of Ralph Waldo Emerson* (Philadelphia: University of Pennsylvania Press, 1953). A new intellectual biography by Robert D. Richardson, Jr., is forthcoming.

For psychological analysis of the young Emerson, the best source is Evelyn Barish, *Emerson: The Roots of Prophecy* (Princeton: Princeton University Press, 1989). For a discussion of Emerson's development in the context of nineteenth-century social history, see Mary Kupiec Cayton, *Emerson's Emergence* (Chapel Hill: University of North Carolina Press, 1989). For Emerson's transition from minister to man-of-letters, see *Apostle of Culture* (Philadelphia: University of Pennsylania Press, 1982), by David Robinson, whose bio-critical study of the later Emerson is forthcoming. For Emerson's involvement in contemporary political reform movements, see Len Gougeon, *Virtue's Hero* (Athens: University of Georgia Press, 1989). For a general interpretative biography along Whicherian lines, more distilled than Rusk and Allen but more documentary than Whicher, see Joel Porte, *Representative Man: Ralph Waldo Emerson in His Time* (New York: Oxford University Press, 1979).

Emerson the Writer

Still the most penetrating book-length discussion of Emerson as writer is Jonathan Bishop, *Emerson on the Soul* (Cambridge: Harvard University Press, 1964). Also excellent are David Porter, *Emerson and Literary Change* (Cambridge: Harvard University Press, 1979); Barbara Packer, *Emerson's Fall* (New York: Continuum, 1982), an intensive reading of selected major essays; and Julie Ellison, *Emerson's Romantic Style* (Princeton: Princeton University Press, 1984). For discussion of Emerson's poetry, see especially R. A. Yoder, *Emerson and the Orphic Poet in America* (Berkeley: University of California Press, 1978). On Emerson as journalizer, see Lawrence Rosenwald, *Emerson and the Art of the Diary* (New York: Oxford University Press, 1988).

For discussion of Emerson's writing and criticism in the broader context of the Transcendentalist Movement, see Lawrence Buell, *Literary Transcendentalism* (Ithaca: Cornell University Press, 1973). For Emerson's place in international Romanticism, see especially Leon Chai, *The Romantic Foundations of the American Renaissance* (Ithaca: Cornell University Press, 1987). For Emerson in relation to the culture of Victorian Britain, see especially George P. Landow, *Elegant Jeremiahs: The Sage from Carlyle to Mailer* (Ithaca:

Cornell University Press, 1986) and Philip Nicoloff, *Emerson on Race and History* (New York: Columbia University Press, 1981).

For further discussion of Emerson's place in and impact on the history of American writing, see especially Charles Feidelson, *Symbolism and American Literature* (Chicago: University of Chicago Press, 1953); Harold Bloom's essays on poetic succession from *Ringers in the Tower* (Chicago: University of Chicago Press, 1971) to *Agon* (New York: Oxford Univ. Press, 1982); Robert Richardson, *Myth and History in the American Renaissance* (Bloomington: Indiana University, 1978), Carolyn Porter, *Seeing and Being* (Middletown: Wesleyan University Press, 1981); and Richard Poirier, *The Renewal of Literature: Emersonian Reflections* (New York: Random House, 1987).

A unique casebook facilitating genetic study of a particular Emerson work is Merton M. Sealts, Jr., and Alfred R. Ferguson, eds., *Emerson's Nature: Origin, Growth, Meaning*, 2nd ed. (Carbondale and Edwardsville: Southern Illinois University Press, 1979), which prints an authoritative text, journal antecedents, and an excellent selection of critical essays.

Emerson the Thinker

For Emerson's social and political thought, see Gougeon, *Virtue's Hero*, Yehoshua Arieli, *Individualism and Nationalism in American Ideology* (Cambridge: Harvard University Press, 1964); Taylor Stoehr, *Nay-Saying in Concord* (Hamden: Archon, 1979); John Diggins, *The Lost Soul of American Politics* (New York: Basic, 1984); and Myra Jehlen, *American Incarnation* (Cambridge: Harvard University Press, 1986).

For Emerson in relation to Puritanism, see Sacvan Bercovitch, *The Puritan Origins of the American Self* (New Haven: Yale University Press, 1975) and *The American Jeremiad* (Madison: University of Wisconsin Press, 1978); and Mason Lowance, *The Language of Canaan* (Cambridge: Harvard University Press, 1980). For Emerson in relation to Unitarianism, see Buell, *Literary Transcendentalism*; Robinson, *Apostle of Culture*; and Wesley T. Mott, *"The Strains of Eloquence": Emerson and His Sermons* (University Park: Pennsylvania State University Press, 1989).

For Emerson as a philosopher, see especially David Van Leer, *Emerson's Epistemology* (Cambridge: Cambridge University Press, 1986) on Emerson as a post-Kantian philosopher; Cornel West, *The American Evasion of Philosophy* (Madison: University of Wisconsin Press, 1989) and Richard Poirier, *Poetry and Pragmatism* (Cambridge: Harvard University Press, 1992) on Emerson and the pragmatist tradition; and Stanley Cavell, *Conditions Handsome and Unhandsome* (Chicago: University of Chicago Press, 1990) on Emerson and modern continental philosophy.

For Emerson and issues of gender, see Erik Thurin, *Emerson as Priest of Pan* (Lawrence: University of Kansas Press, 1981); and David Leverenz,

Manhood and the American Renaissance (Ithaca: Cornell University Press, 1989).

Emerson Bibliography

For a full listing of Emerson criticism through the 1970s, see Robert Burkholder and Joel Myerson, eds., *Emerson: An Annotated Secondary Bibliography* (Pittsburgh: University of Pittsburgh Press, 1985). Its annotations can be supplemented and updated by recourse to the essay on "Emerson, Thoreau, and Transcendentalism" that has always constituted the initial chapter of *American Literary Scholarship* (Durham: Duke University Press, 1964 to present), an annual review currently edited by David Nordloh. For bibliographical essays appraising Emerson criticism from the 1960s through the mid-1980s, see Lawrence Buell, "The Emerson Industry in the 1980s: A Survey of Trends and Achievements," *ESQ* 30 (1984), 117–36; and Michael Lopez, "De-Transcendentalizing Emerson," *ESQ*, 34 (1988), 77–139.

For a fine short selection of modern Emerson commentary through 1960, see the predecessor to this volume, *Emerson: A Collection of Critical Essays*, ed. Milton R. Konvitz and Stephen E. Whicher (Englewood Cliffs, N.J.: Prentice-Hall, 1962); for a more compendious collection, judiciously chosen and ranging from Emerson's day to our own, see *Critical Essays on Ralph Waldo Emerson*, ed. Robert Burkholder and Joel Myerson (Boston: Hall, 1983).

Notes on Contributors

SACVAN BERCOVITCH is Professor of English and American Literature at Harvard University and author of *The Puritan Origins of the American Self, The American Jeremiad,* and other books and articles on premodern American literary culture.

JONATHAN BISHOP is Professor of English at Cornell University and author of *Emerson on the Soul* and other studies of literature and spirituality.

HAROLD BLOOM is Professor of Humanities at Yale University and author of *The Anxiety of Influence, Poetry and Repression, Ruin the Sacred Truths,* and numerous other studies of Anglo-American and biblical poetics.

LAWRENCE BUELL is Professor of English and American Literature at Harvard University and author of *Literary Transcendentalism* and *New England Literary Culture.*

STANLEY CAVELL is Professor of Philosophy at Harvard University and author of *The Senses of Walden, Conditions Handsome and Unhandsome: The Constitution of Emersonian Perfectionism,* and other studies reflecting upon the place of Emerson in American and modern philosophy.

MARY KUPIEC CAYTON is Associate Professor of American Studies at Miami University (Ohio) and author of *Emerson's Emergence: Self and Society in the Transformation of New England 1800–1845.*

JULIE ELLISON is Professor of English at the University of Michigan, Ann Arbor, and author of *Emerson's Romantic Style* and *Delicate Subjects: Romanticism, Gender, and the Ethics of Understanding.*

WILLIAM L. HEDGES is Professor of English at Goucher College and author of *Washington Irving: An American Study, 1802–1832* as well as shorter studies of early national literature.

GLEN M. JOHNSON is Associate Professor of English at the Catholic University of America and author of other critical articles on the composition of Emerson's essays.

PERRY MILLER was Professor of English and American Literature at Harvard University and author of the two-volume *The New England Mind* as well as *Errand into the Wilderness, Nature's Nation,* and other studies of American literary and religious culture.

RICHARD POIRIER is Professor of English at Rutgers University and author of *A World Elsewhere: The Place of Style in American Literature, The Renewal of Literature: Emersonian Reflections,* and other books and articles on American literary history and culture.

MERTON J. SEALTS is Emeritus Professor of English at the University of Wisconsin, Madison, and author of *Melville's Reading* and *Emerson on the Scholar*.

STEPHEN WHICHER was Profesor of English at Cornell University and author of *Freedom and Fate: An Inner Life of Ralph Waldo Emerson*, as well as co-editor of the predecessor to the present volume.